CONTAGIOUS OPTIMISM BOOK SERIES

10 HABITS OF
TRULY
OPTIMISTIC
PEOPLE

POWER YOUR LIFE WITH THE POSITIVE

DAVID MEZZAPELLE

FOREWORDS BY WILL GLENNON
AND JIM CATHCART

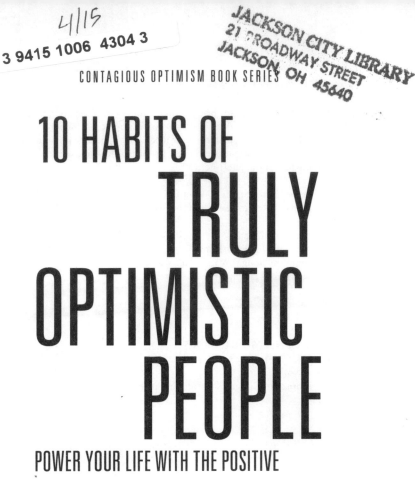

VIVA
EDITIONS

Published in the United States by Viva Editions, an imprint of Start Midnight, LLC, 375 Hudson Street, Twelfth Floor, New York, New York 10014.

Printed in the United States.
Cover design: Scott Idleman/Blink
Cover photograph: Dougal Waters/Getty Images
Text design: Frank Wiedemann

First Edition.
10 9 8 7 6 5 4 3 2 1

Trade paper ISBN: 978-1-63228-005-3
E-book ISBN: 978-1-63228-011-4

Library of Congress Cataloging-in-Publication Data is available.

To my family for putting up with my contagious optimism for all these years, and for being supportive of this project including the many hours, days, and weeks that kept us apart.

To our Contagious Optimism staff, coauthors, and fans for being the greatest anyone could ever ask for.

To our Contagious Optimism LIVE team for bringing all this to life on stage, radio, and television.

To our publisher, Viva Editions, for being psyched about this project and for their continued confidence in its growth.

TABLE OF CONTENTS

FOREWORD: AN ACT OF KINDNESS BY WILL GLENNON ix

FOREWORD: OPTIMISM IS VIRAL BY JIM CATHCART. xi

WELCOME BY DAVID MEZZAPELLE xiii

1 EMBRACE CHANGE. 1
   The Road Back Recipe • ROBERT HAMMONDS. 4
   The Power of Believing • ALISON NANCYE 7
   How Shaker Never Left Us • NORMAN WAIN. 10
   How to Address Your Biggest Fear • LIISA KYLE. 13
   The Fight for Sight • MELODY GOODSPEED 16
   Learning to Dance in the Rain • VANEETHA RENDALL 20
   Autism and Inner Strength • ANNE BENNETT-BREADY 23
   Good from the Bad • ERNEST FIELD 26
   The Fear Button • SALLY GATES 29
   The Rest of the Story • JANET BALES 32
   Angels Among Us • KARIE MILLSPAUGH 35

2 APPRECIATE THOSE AROUND YOU 39
   A Love Story • FRED MOORE 43
   The Magic List • HAYLEY FOSTER 46
   Our Brady Bunch • CHRISTINA CALLAHAN. 50
   Family Is Everything • CHARLES MARKMAN. 53
   Friendship Runs Deeper than Floodwaters. 56
   • CHRISTINE HENCHAR REED
   Father's Day Remembrance • MICHAEL CARLON 59
   How to Be Grateful for Your Spouse's Ex • CLAUDETTE CHENEVERT . . 61
   Francis • THOMAS COLLINS 63
   What Are You Really Forgiving? • SUSYN REEVE. 66

3 SAVOR EVERY MOMENT 71
   48 • SUZANNE MILLER. 74

Our Friend, "Mom" • COURTNEY SMITHEMAN 78

31,125 Days • PETER WALLIMANN 81

Last Night I Had a Dream • DR. COLLEEN GEORGES 85

To Hold Their Hands • FRED GILL 88

Coffee Cake • GEORGE HOGAN 90

My Very Own Miracle • EDITH BERGMAN.....................92

Deadlines Take On a New Meaning • JC SULLIVAN..............94

Hello, Nana, Can You See Me from Heaven? • COLLEEN MELISSA ...97

Love Trumps All • BECKY WOODBRIDGE.....................100

Tsunamis and Rainbows • SÓNIA TREJO.....................103

Being Held in Comfort • VANEETHA RENDALL 106

The Perfect Whistle • DIANE MAY 109

4 TAKE A LESSON FROM OUR YOUTH 113
Positive Pocket • REBECCA ZERBO 117

Prom Drive • ALLISON FRATTAROLI..........................120

Superheroes Do Exist • MELINDA PETROFF....................123

Get Your Head and Heart in the Game • JOHN HOOKS..........126

The Year the Goldbergers Had a Christmas Tree................128
• W.M. GOLDBERGER

My Youngest Teacher • DR. EMILE ALLEN.....................132

Pulling Out Bad Dreams • ARTHUR SCALZO....................135

OpporTuning • BARRY LINDSTROM..........................138

My Friend, Saint Nicholas • LEE SHILO 142

No Child Is Born Prejudiced • LEE LIVELY-GARCIA 145

Defining Adulthood in the Absence of Childhood 147
• KIMBERLEE M. HOOPER

5 BELIEVE IN YOURSELF AND THE VALUE YOU POSSESS 151
Biking Against All Odds • EMMANUEL OFOSU YEBOAH..........154

Darkness to Light • TERI CATLIN 158

You Never Know Where the Path May Take You...............162
• HENRY WISEMAN

The Case for Entrepreneurial Optimism • RICHARD MASTERSON ...164

The Journey, Not the Path • ERIC BENSON 167

The Power of Positive Feeling in the Workplace
• DR. DONALD E. GIBSON 170

Allowing the Way • NANCY KOENIG........................173

Be a Career Venturer • BHARATH GOPALAN....................176

Forging a New Path • MERRY NACHEMIN......................179

Courage from Optimism • DAVID MEZZAPELLE..................181

6   SERVICE THE ENGINE 185
Optimism Spans Generations • BARBARA WOODWORTH..........189

My Six Months with Florence Nightingale • ESTELLE BERK 193

The Healing Power of Opera • CYNTHIA MAKRIS................196

My Biggest Loser • PATRICK MCKAY...........................199

Courage Does Not Always Roar • JENNIFER CUTLER LOPEZ 201

Spinning • DAVID MEZZAPELLE 205

Eight Lessons Cancer Taught Me • JACKIE SAAD 207

Healing: You'll Never Walk Alone • MONSIGNOR ROBERT WEISS...209

Healing Is On Its Way • SOPHIE SKOVER 212

Lose Weight—Not Your Mind • LEE LIVELY-GARCIA..............214

My Fragility Is My Strength • SÓNIA TREJO 216

Medicine and Optimism: The Story of Art • BARBARA GELSTON ...219

Second Adolescence • BARBARA RADY KAZDAN 222

7   RECLAIM YOUR PERSONAL POWER......................225
The End of Resistance • SHANE J. REPMANN...................229

Second Chances • LEJUNUE BUGGIE-DENT 232

Help from a Cab Driver • ESTER NICHOLSON 236

A First Step in the Right Direction • GAY CARTIER 239

Are You in Love, or Love Addicted? • JED DIAMOND 241

Recovery • DEBORAH LITTLEJOHN...........................244

Yes, I Believe • JERRY KELLY................................247

My New Guiding Angel • LARRY GLENZ 249

Love Away Cigarettes • NANCY KOENIG......................253

The Gift of Clarity • JERRY KELLY 256

8   FIND YOURSELF IN SERVICE TO OTHERS 261
My Shining S.C.A.R.S. • KRYSTIAN LEONARD 264

Jerry Segal: Unbowed and Unbeaten • RICHARD J. ANTHONY, SR....267

Goodwill Has No Price • ROGER CANNON....................270

The Elevator Speech • JOEL HELLER 273

The Value in Shared Good Fortune • ALAN A. MALIZIA..........275

The Magic of Mentoring • NAVID NAZEMIAN 277

Why the Top Isn't Lonely • KIMBERLEE M. HOOPER 279

The Lightbulb Went Off • JC SULLIVAN 281

A Life Lesson from Tonga • STEVE UIBLE 284

Homeland Cambodia • NATALIE WEINRAUCH 287

9 STAY INSPIRED 291

Finding Strength • LANCE STRANAHAN 294

The Guru Appears • BHARATH GOPALAN 297

Revelation at 18,500 Feet • BECKY WOODBRIDGE 299

Life on Wheels • JORDAN LOWE 303

The Power of Sports • SALVATORE TRIFILIO .306

A Surprise Pearl of Wisdom • MARIAN HEATH AXLEY 309

What Does Your "Happy Fork" Look Like? • AMY SPENCER 312

It's Not about the Giraffe • SHARON DUNBAR 315

10 HAVE AN ATTITUDE OF GRATITUDE .319

Unexpected Gifts • PAUL LIPTON 323

An Ordinary Life • WILLIAM SWEET 326

Life's Pleasures and a Smile • ARNOLD SARROW 329

The Noise • KERRY FLYNN MOEYKENS 331

Finding the Good in the Bad • BECKY WOODBRIDGE 333

Mind the GAP! Gratitude—Accountability—Persistence 336
• SUSAN ROSS

Allowing Your Blessings to Overflow • DR. COLLEEN GEORGES 338

Live Life Out Loud • INEZ BRACY 340

Life Is What Happens When You're Busy Making Plans 343
• EILEEN KELLER

Grácias • HAROLD PAYNE 346

ABOUT DAVID MEZZAPELLE 351

ABOUT WILL GLENNON 351

ABOUT JIM CATHCART 352

MEET OUR COAUTHORS 353

ACKNOWLEDGMENTS 367

SHARE YOUR STORIES 368

FOREWORD: AN ACT OF KINDNESS

Years ago, I wrote *Random Acts of Kindness* with the belief that simple deeds can bring smiles to people's faces. My book reflects the Golden Rule that we all learned in elementary school: Treat others the way you want to be treated. I loved reading and publishing other people's stories of kindness—just as I now love reading this **Contagious Optimism** book series and its stories from the people who want to spread such a positive movement. I am proud to be part of a community that's making the world a happier place for the next generation. You, reader, have joined a wonderful community by picking up this book.

I consider this book an act of kindness. So many people are sharing their stories of loss and times of struggle in order to help others overcome their own experiences. The **Contagious Optimism** book series inspires others to find their way when they feel lost.

I recall an occasion of inspirational acts of kindness nearly two years ago when the world seemed to stop. Twenty-six children in Newtown, Connecticut, died in a school shooting. The light went out in so many people's lives and being happy seemed to be an impossible feat.

Instantly, people started to bring back that light. A "pay it forward" movement spread through word of mouth and social media. There was a "pay it forward" line outside a Starbucks drive-through. One photographer took free photos for families. Some left money beside vending machines to bring a smile to an unsuspecting customer. Though simple, these acts lifted hearts and inspired others to give back. People felt that they needed to do something, and that they did. I am most interested in the way these acts spread: by example.

Give this book to someone who feels stuck and needs an inspiration. Learn how people who have gone through the worst experiences overcame their obstacles. After you finish this book, think about what you will do to help spread optimism in the world.

Our acts of kindness can be small, but they can have great impact. In this **Contagious Optimism** book, *10 Habits of Truly Optimistic People*, the stories are small, but the messages are larger than life. I firmly believe that the more goodwill and happiness we spread, the better the world becomes. Enjoy this book and, above all, stay positive.

Will Glennon
San Francisco, California

FOREWORD: OPTIMISM IS VIRAL

The biggest goal you can have for an online posting is that it will go "viral." That's when it is so appealing that others spontaneously pass it along until it reaches far beyond your own capacity for promoting it. This is the same concept behind *10 Habits of Truly Optimistic People*. We want this to be so uplifting and enjoyable that you can't resist enthusiastically telling others about it.

I'm an optimist, a proud and bold optimist. I believe in the eternal possibilities for life to expand and improve. I'm convinced that anything can be better.

This book series is designed to spread that positive belief to the entire world. There is no need to settle for a life that can be tolerated when you can aspire to a life that can be celebrated. You and I can make this world better every single day through a myriad of small and large actions that will encourage others and improve circumstances.

Growing up, I never thought my life would matter much. It was my operating assumption that I'd serve my time, do some good, have some fun, and then be gone—forever. I expected to be a nice but unimportant person. One day all that changed. I heard a radio broadcast by Earl Nightingale that told me, "If you'll spend one extra hour each day studying your chosen field, you will become a national expert in that field in five years or less." I was stunned! What?! With just one extra hour a day? Even I could do that! That's the day my life changed direction. This can happen for you as well.

You can change the direction of your own life simply by

reading or hearing just one encouraging story a day about how someone else made this world a better place, or how they overcame a challenge or achieved a goal. Just one story a day and your life will change direction too.

You can also make a profound difference in your world starting now. Within one hour you can have a positive impact on someone or something. Look around you. There are things large and small that can be improved, and you are in a position to make them better. You may not be able to do it all or do it alone, but you can become the contagious force that starts the growth process. And as you grow and improve personally, you'll make an even bigger difference.

Because you are reading this book, you are already on the right path. Make that your new habit of choice: read something positive and uplifting every day. Even if it is just for a few minutes, do it every day without fail and you too will be "without fail." Sure, some things you try won't work as planned. But failure is not when things don't work; it's when you stop working! Gain a new positive mindset today and become a Contagious Optimist!

Jim Cathcart
Bestselling author, world-renowned speaker
Carlsbad, California

WELCOME

Welcome to *10 Habits of Truly Optimistic People*, the second volume in our **Contagious Optimism** book series. We are proud to continue our mission of bringing uplifting stories and insight to readers all over the world. No matter what may be happening in your life, it is encouraging to learn how other people have persevered and found their silver linings.

Real stories can be powerful. I learned this when I was young, during visits with my relatives. When I think back, I vividly remember visiting my grandmother in New York in the 1970s. I can still smell her cooking; I can still feel the comfort of her living room couch. However, what I remember most are the stories my relatives told. While I may have heard those stories a thousand times, I would give anything to hear them again today.

It was from those visits that I learned about the lasting impact of a person's stories, and it is why I made it my mission to capture real stories from real people around the globe. Stories connect us, and as the **Contagious Optimism** books strive to do, they can bring joy and spread optimism. I believe we all have the capacity to make optimism contagious just by sharing our life's adventures, our successes, and even our mistakes. Just look at it this way: Whether people are enduring good times or bad, just knowing that others have been in the same boat and have persevered is comforting. It spreads a message of hope.

The underlying theme of the **Contagious Optimism** book series is "positive forward thinking." Positive forward thinking means finding the silver lining in the difficulties of yesterday or today, and going forward with the confidence that tomorrow will be better. I believe that each of us has this ability, but sometimes we need to hear or read examples about the way other people have accomplished it. This series includes stories from people who have successfully found their own silver linings, even in difficult circumstances. Our books also include insight and guidance from a global team of professionals. These professionals include career coaches, life coaches, spiritual professionals, medical professionals, financial professionals, wellness experts, self-help experts, and many others.

I truly believe that reading stories of how others have persevered through their life's adventures will help you to discover positivity in your own life. These stories are proof that we can all find our silver linings.

We appreciate having you as a reader and welcome you as a potential coauthor in a future volume. Please see the "Share Your Stories" section at the end of this book to learn more.

Thank you for reading, and stay positive!

David Mezzapelle
Jupiter, Florida

CHAPTER ONE

EMBRACE CHANGE

*If you accept change and embrace what life offers,
it is more likely that you will be successful
when you come across the peaks and valleys of
    living.
If we don't evolve, we only stand still.*

Life frequently throws curveballs at us, some good and some not so good. It's how we handle those curveballs, learn from them, and move on that really matters. The curveballs themselves are temporary; they come and go. It's our reaction and our ability to persevere that reveals our true strength. We may not always have the strength we think we need, but we evolve, we learn, and we do ultimately find it. That's the beauty of every learning experience.

If we were Superman, we would not let anything stop us in our mission to protect what is important. Only one thing gets in Superman's way: kryptonite. How does Superman handle kryptonite? He avoids it. As a proponent of optimism for many years, I have always thought that I could write a screenplay for a new Superman. In my version, Superman finds a way to build immunity to kryptonite. This immunity would serve him well and give people around him the comfort that Superman is truly invincible. What is your kryptonite? Imagine your life without allowing your personal kryptonite to get in the way of your dreams.

This chapter focuses on embracing what life throws at us, including change. *Change* is a general term, but we look at it from the standpoint of life-changing and life-impacting events. Change, like curveballs, is inevitable in our lives. It is important that we accept change, learn from it, and evolve. By reading real stories and insight from all over the world, we learn how others have accepted change and moved on. We learn how they turned kryptonite into a stepping-stone that is no longer a threat.

David

Had I been rigid about my own ideas for a career path, I would have missed out on the incredible journey my life has taken. I am not only thankful for the many blessings in my life, but also for the flexibility that made me see that change is healthy, and something that should be embraced, not avoided.

—Molly Hoover, West Palm Beach, Florida

Hope requires us to believe in something bigger than ourselves. We should live our lives optimistically, striving to improve other people's situations more than our own. Optimism is hope manifested in our daily actions to make the world a better place for all to live in and enjoy. By being encouraging, honest, and hopeful, we can be the catalyst that positively embraces and transforms another person's attitude toward life.

—Mike Cuppett, Memphis, Tennessee

THE ROAD BACK RECIPE

ROBERT HAMMONDS

Don't go around saying the world owes you a living. The world owes you nothing. It was here first.

—Mark Twain

When the Financial Meltdown of 2008 hit, many hardworking people were negatively affected in ways not seen since the Great Depression. People had to reevaluate, reinvent, and reenergize their lives and work habits like never before while looking to create new ways to support their families.

I was no different. I was a mortgage broker and a pretty good one, but when I witnessed the devastation of a market that, overnight, ceased to exist, I knew I had to do something. I had three beautiful children and a wonderful wife who counted on me to provide for them, and it quickly became apparent that the old ways of making a living were gone.

While many of my contemporaries complained and pointed fingers at both Wall Street and the government, I decided that I could not bother getting caught up in such discussions. I had a family to support, and complaints and inactivity were not options. While I was frustrated and scared at times, I knew that the only true course for getting my career back started with me. I would have to clear out all the negative thoughts that were draining my energy and start adopting a positive mental attitude. The road back would have peaks and valleys; there was no question. However, I knew that I was no different from others who have had to deal with hardship, and that there had to be a silver lining.

I have always treated people well and have been fortunate to have built a diverse set of contacts over the years. I knew I would have to count on people to help me on my journey, so I used these potential advocates as my starting point. I adopted the attitude that I would not feel embarrassed or ashamed for something I had no control over, and I reached out to everyone I knew. Reaching out to my contacts and asking for help taught me my first lesson on the path back, which I will share with you: Continue to push yourself and hold yourself accountable for what happens next. Contacts help, but they have lives and challenges too. Therefore, let them know what you need and seek their advice and help, but know that your success is ultimately your own responsibility.

The second lesson on the path back? Look for ways to supplement your income. I taught classes at a local university, became an elected official of the town I live in, and delivered subpoenas. Additionally, I had another part-time job and continued to help my clients with mortgages. There is no shame in hard work, especially when the priority is your family. Today, I am grateful to have a steady job, and while it is not perfect, it has gotten me back to working full-time with benefits for my family, and I am thankful to have a consistent paycheck.

As I look back, I can say that I am most proud that I challenged myself to become better in all aspects of life, and with the markets showing some signs of improvement, I continue to look for the silver lining. So remember, the recipe to recovery starts with reaching out to people for help and knowing that action and a positive attitude are essential to getting back to where you need to be.

CONTAGIOUS REVIVAL

The world does not owe you a living. Reevaluate, reinvent, and reenergize yourself, and your growth will make the next phase of life even more rewarding.

THE POWER OF BELIEVING

ALISON NANCYE
When I was a little girl, I dreamt of finding my dad. The only problem was, no one knew where he was. My parents were only twenty years old and dating when my mom got pregnant, and they broke up before I was born. It was one of those things in life that just happens.

Growing up, I would often ask my mom what my dad looked like and what his personality traits were—I wanted to know who he was. I clung to the small pieces of information that she shared, and I would spend hours daydreaming that one day I might bump into my dad on the street and suddenly know he was "the one." But I was only a kid, and I didn't realize how unrealistic that was.

As I started to grow up, many people told me that it would be impossible to locate my father, and my dream of finding him began to diminish. By the time I entered my twenties, this dream was almost nonexistent. However, despite what people told me, a part of my heart always knew he was out there somewhere, and one day I'd be able to reach him. I made the choice to believe.

Although this belief stayed with me, I put it on the back burner until one day when I was thirty-three. I was doing a self-development workshop that was all about claiming your dreams and connecting with your true life path, and naturally, my dream of finding my dad came up. I realized that though I had suppressed it, it had never gone away. Rather than putting my power in the belief that I would find him, I had chosen to put power in my lack of faith. Once I discovered this, there was no turning back.

I became focused on my goal to find my father and restore that missing link. I was on a mission, determined to put my power back in the right place. After doing research and using all my resources, my resolve paid off: I found him. I discovered that my dad was living just twenty minutes away from my husband's family. After putting all the pieces together to ensure that he was my father, I decided to leave a message at his local bowling club. It was one of the happiest days of my life when he returned my call. I finally knew where my dad was, and, at thirty-three, I finally heard my dad's voice for the first time in my life.

Today I am forty-three and delighted to say that I still know my dad. He is very active in my life and is a big part of my family. Not only that, but as a result of finding him, my mom finally got her greatest wish: to marry a man she loves and have a child with that man—though it wasn't exactly in that order. It was at my wedding a year after finding my father that my parents reconnected after almost thirty-five years of lost contact. They reignited their love, got engaged a year later, and a year after that, they were married. To this day, my parents are still happily married to each other.

Finding my dad and witnessing how our renewed connection has influenced my life has been overwhelming. I finally have what I so desperately wanted as a child: a father. As a result of fulfilling this lifelong dream, I now work to encourage other people to go after their own dreams. I have also found the courage to go after more of my own. We only get one life, and much of our happiness and success come down to where we put our power. My advice to everyone is to put their power into believing.

CONTAGIOUS BELIEF

Even if you want something really bad, it can be easy to get discouraged—by others or by your self-doubt. But don't give up. Believe. There is so much power in just believing.

HOW SHAKER NEVER LEFT US

NORMAN WAIN

First I told my wife, Nina. She was shocked; tears flowed from her disbelieving eyes. "You really think it's best for us to move?" she asked.

I had been working with my two partners for several months on the possibility of moving from Cleveland, Ohio, to Westchester County, New York. I had the chance to leave the ranks of the wage earners and move on to an ownership position at a radio station—something I had been thinking about since I became a disk jockey. It meant that my partners and their families, and our own little group, would move to what we considered foreign land.

Nina was born in Cleveland. She attended Roxboro Elementary School and Heights High School. She had left Cleveland for a few years to study at the University of Michigan, but she returned to be with her family and friends. We had been married for ten years and we were very happy in our little home on Scottsdale Boulevard in Shaker Heights, a Cleveland suburb. Our three little girls, aged five, seven, and nine, had known no other home, and it was difficult deciding how we'd break the news.

Nina was elected by default to be the "quarterback" of the move. It wasn't pretty when we told the girls, even though Nina had every word and every moment planned out in advance. It would be an adventure, a trip of discovery, a bigger house, a chance to see Gramma Pearl more often, and a fun time for all. The kids weren't buying it. To their credit, they finally accepted the reality when we started the mundane tasks of packing and selling the house.

I actually thought we could pull off the move without too much grief. But then, all too quickly, like a thunderstorm that catches you by surprise, the reality hit us. We left the house behind, driving east to the end of our boulevard and turning right onto Warrensville Center Road. Then it happened—the unreal stillness in the car was broken by Cathy, our youngest daughter, who said simply, "Daddy, why do we have to go? Why can't we just stay here?" With that, three kids and two adults burst into tears. We cried for at least ten minutes.

Finally, when the tears subsided and I could see the road again, we continued toward the unknown land called Westchester County. The adjustment to new surroundings and new people was difficult. About a month after we made the move, the kids were restless at bedtime one night and refused to go to sleep, so Nina and I decided it was time for a family meeting. We did this from time to time to solve problems, and the kids liked it. At this meeting, we decided that the least we could do was buy them a dog as we had always promised. With assurances that we would look into it, we finally got everyone back to bed.

We rushed into action as soon as we knew they were asleep. Within two days, we were able to find a babysitter and race to the nearby shelter, and we eventually came home with an adorable dachshund puppy. We went to the kids' bedrooms, woke them up, and gathered them in the kitchen to welcome the newest member of our family. The girls were ecstatic. They took turns petting and feeding the puppy. All there was left to decide was his name. Suggestions came up but were rejected immediately. Finally our oldest daughter, Beth, solved the problem to everyone's deep satisfaction.

"Let's call him Shaker," she said. And that is what we did.

CONTAGIOUS CHANGE

New opportunities are full of the unknown, but are also full of possibilities. Embrace new beginnings, but don't forget your roots.

HOW TO ADDRESS YOUR BIGGEST FEAR

LIISA KYLE

What are you seriously afraid of? Stop for a moment and listen to your thoughts: Deep down, what is your biggest concern?

We all harbor fears at different levels. We might be anxious about the future or worried for the well-being of those we love. Sometimes we're worried about particular things we can't control, or frightened to speak in public, or panicked about meeting an important deadline.

These everyday fears usually mask something bigger, scarier, and more significant. Deep down, within each of us, is a fundamental fear: our worst nightmare—the thing that terrifies us to our core. Let's call it the "Big Fear." It could be the fear of being unloved, the fear of failure, the fear of being unworthy, or the fear of death.

The Big Fear affects us profoundly. It influences our actions, beliefs, and expectations. A lot of Big Fears are really overblown exaggerations of our worst-case scenarios. Let's take fear of failure for example. Deep down, it can feel like you aren't "good enough" and will never amount to anything. It can feel like you're wasting your life, or that you'll end up homeless, alone, and unloved. That's a Big Fear, and a heavy burden to carry around. It's difficult to be cheery with this fear in mind.

A few self-aware people already know the nature of their Big Fear, but most of us don't. Our minds want to protect us from pain and harm so we tend to bury our fundamental dread." Our brains find comically complex ways to prevent us from thinking about it. But until we know the true source of our fundamental fear, we can't address it or overcome it. We are blind to the very thing that affects our lives the most.

Although it takes courage to look inside ourselves and identify our Big Fear, the payoff of doing so is enormous. First, you will feel relief because you will no longer be tormented by this unknown entity. Recognizing your Big Fear means that you will be able to see how it affects you. You will be free to make different choices and to take different actions. You can better understand yourself, and, if you choose to, laugh at yourself (in a good way).

Often, when you find your Big Fear, you'll realize it's really not that bad, or that it's not applicable to your current life. It could be that, as a kid, you were fearful of failure, but now you realize that you are successful in many ways. This epiphany will allow you to let go of this Big Fear. It may have motivated you to achieve a lot earlier in life, but now you can release it because it is no longer necessary.

So let's identify your Big Fear. Clear your schedule. As fast as you can, answer the following:

As a child, I was afraid of _____
My parents were afraid that _____
As a teen, I was nervous about _____
As a young adult, I worried about _____
If I'm honest with myself, I'm really afraid that _____

You'll know when you hit upon your Big Fear. Your body will tell you. When you identify your Big Fear, you'll suddenly sit up straight, or gasp, or tingle. It may elicit tears, or anger, or a desire to bolt from the room. They don't call this reaction "fight or flight" for nothing.

Now, the first thing is to be proud for identifying what's really going on deep down. Be kind and gentle with yourself for taking this scary step in your personal development.

The next task is easier; it's time to address your Big Fear. Ask yourself: Is this Big Fear valid? What evidence is there to the contrary? Give yourself a reality check.

Next, take a moment to appreciate this fear. Yes, appreciate it. How has this fear helped you in life? What good has come from it?

Lastly, ask yourself how your Big Fear affects you today. What does it cost you to harbor this fear? What benefits would there be to releasing it? Is it time to release this fear? If it makes sense, let go of it.

CONTAGIOUS PRACTICE

Going forward, monitor your thoughts and actions. Should you find yourself feeling anxious or nervous or unreasonably fearful, see if you can detect the influence of your Big Fear. Pat yourself on the back for noticing. Bonus points if you can laugh about it. Understand what's going on and let it go. Release your Big Fear.

THE FIGHT FOR SIGHT

MELODY GOODSPEED
On a very ordinary day in 2003, I was driving to work, stuck in the usual 495 traffic. No worries, I thought, as I cranked up Dave Matthews, not caring what others thought as I broke out singing and car dancing. As I inched closer to work I went over lesson plans for my day as a teacher; I taught third-grade students with emotional disabilities, and I loved my job. Looking back, I wonder why that day in particular is so clear to me now. Maybe it was because during that ride to work, I realized everything in my life was almost perfect. I was twenty-six years old, I had an amazing job, and my coworkers had become close friends. I was working toward my master's degree in special education, and life to me was so sweet. It was a moment when I was able to reflect on what I had accomplished and take it in with a breath of gratitude.

However, several weeks later I started getting terrible headaches. I didn't think much about them at first, and attributed them to my busy schedule. When I went to the doctor, I was told my headaches were nothing more than cluster migraines, and I was sent on my way with steroids to calm the pain. But the pain never stopped, and it took several emergency room visits and tests before the true cause was discovered. I remember leaving an MRI fearing that the results were going to be bad, but I allowed myself to hope everything would be okay since the hospital released me.

Then, the phone call came.

I was told to come back to the hospital as quickly as possible. When I arrived, I waited in the ER with my parents for what seemed like years. The doctor came in and shut the door. He said something about a blood clot and pressure on my eyes, which would affect my sight. As I pulled myself out of the cloud of confusion, I looked around the room and saw teary-eyed faces of shock, pain, and hopelessness. At that moment, I thought about my drive to work a couple of weeks earlier, and I knew that my perfect world had changed.

As the nurses hooked me up to medicines to shrink the blood clot in my brain, I still allowed myself to hope. I went home after a couple of weeks, but a few days later I was so sick that I had to call 911. The next three weeks were the most painful time I had ever experienced. My vision was leaving me and there was nothing I could do to stop it. The pressure from the clot was too much for my body to take, and with each passing minute I could see the beauty of the world slipping away from me. Finally, one morning in June 2003, I awoke and it was gone. That is a day I will never forget.

I took a long time to heal, and I spent the next year sick and depressed. Eventually, the clot disappeared and other surgeries took away the physical pain, but the emotional pain and feelings of helplessness stayed with me. I felt as if I had lost everything, and I didn't know if I would be able to laugh or truly feel positive again.

However, after several months of being at rock bottom, I decided I had two choices: either give up or fight. I chose to fight harder than I ever had before, using my anger as fuel and my loved ones for support. I found myself going to rehab and learning to live as a person without sight. Each moment required so much effort and concentration, and though I had wonderful therapists, I moved through each day with no emotion.

While at the rehabilitation center, I used screen-reading

software that allows a person without sight to interact with the computer using speech. One day, I entered my computer class and was disappointed to find that I was the only student that day. This made me angry because I didn't want to be the center of attention during the lesson.

When my instructor, Charles, came over to greet me, he immediately said, "I can tell something is bugging you." I could hear the concern in his gentle voice, and I felt comforted and understood. Like me, Charles also had a disability: he was in a wheelchair, so he knew what struggle felt like.

As we started our lesson and I began slowly learning about spell check, I felt my frustration over my situation building. In the middle of the lesson, I suddenly exploded and broke out into uncontrollable sobs. I screamed, "I hate spell check! I hate being blind and I want to die right now!"

Charles went over and closed his classroom door, brought me a bowl of chocolate ice cream, and rubbed my back as I sobbed on his shoulder. He then told me the story of his accident over twenty years before when he lost the use of his legs. It was difficult for him, but he pushed on and kept finding purposes in life, such as becoming an instructor for the blind. Charles then shared that his daughter, Liza, had also lost her vision, and described how painful it was that he had not been able to prevent it for her. He asked if I'd like to talk to Liza. Once I pulled myself together, I was on the phone with a woman who sounded so free-spirited and happy. Charles and Liza showed me that I could overcome anything and find joy and purpose even in the worst situations. They helped place the first logs of hope and strength on my personal dam, and that was the first step in my walk with blindness.

Those three months of therapy were difficult, but I believe with all my heart that life never gives you more than you can handle. My teachers and loved ones helped remind me that life was not over—just different. Now, I feel extremely passionate about helping others through their trials in life. I want others to know that life is good, even if it hands them a bad situation. I had a hard road and I still do, but I have more blessings than hard times. I am a mother, wife, friend, family member, dog owner, coworker, and teacher, and I love life too much to let darkness fall over it.

CONTAGIOUS POSITIVITY

Loss is something we all have to endure in our lives at one point, but it is how we craft the situation that matters.

LEARNING TO DANCE
IN THE RAIN

VANEETHA RENDALL
"Why do you walk like that?"

That single question haunted me for years. Young children would boldly demand an answer as they pointed at me. Adults didn't dare voice the question, but looked puzzled as they watched me walk. As for me, I would ask myself that question daily as I struggled to understand why I had to be different from everyone else.

When I was in elementary school, none of my classmates were familiar with polio. With the vaccine's development in 1952, it became a disease that my friends only heard about from their parents. Even in India, where I was born in 1964, polio was almost eradicated, so the vaccine was no longer given to infants. However, at three months of age, I contracted the disease. Thinking I had typhoid, the inexperienced doctors gave me cortisone to lower my 105 degree fever, and within twenty-four hours, the virus had spread throughout my infantile body, leaving me virtually a quadriplegic.

With limited medical options, my family quickly left India and moved to London, where I had my first surgery at two years old. Shortly afterward, we moved to Canada and I went on to have twenty more surgeries, many at the Shriners Hospital, where I lived for months at a time throughout my childhood. Most of my operations were muscle transfers to help me walk, though I always had a pronounced limp—visible evidence of my handicap. The doctors recommended I try a special school for people with disabilities, but my parents were determined to keep me in regular public school so I could learn to survive in the real world.

While hospital life was lonely, it was less painful than the constant mocking I experienced in the real world. When I was seven years old, I was attacked by a group of boys on my way home from school. They threw stones at me and called me a "cripple." My self-image was so poor that I felt ashamed of my disability instead of feeling anger at the boys.

That was not an isolated incident: the bullying continued throughout elementary school. In fifth grade, one of my classmates tormented me daily by imitating my limp, laughing at my weak arms, and openly mocking me in front of everyone. One day, after humiliating me, she added, "You don't mind me doing that, do you? I mean it doesn't make you cry or anything? I just think it's funny, that's all." I fought back the tears and laughed instead. I wasn't going to let anyone see me cry.

I buried the hurt of that teasing to please others, yet it constantly whispered to me that I didn't count, that I didn't belong, and that I'd always be an outsider. However, at age sixteen, acceptance from an unlikely friend broke through that pain, convincing me that I was worthwhile for the first time. This high school friend was willing to look past my limp and get to know me. Undaunted by my handicap, she talked about it naturally, as if it were nothing to be ashamed of, which seemed to dismantle its power.

Before meeting her, I had never talked about my disability with anyone; I would immediately change the subject if anyone even broached it. By not addressing it, I somehow felt I didn't have to face it. In reality, I faced it every day, but I faced it alone, with my own assumptions of what others were thinking. My friend encouraged me to accept my scarred, misshapen body and see what it said to others: that I had suffered and overcome, that I had character and courage. Viewing myself through this new lens was liberating, and it changed everything.

Life has had its twists and turns since those long ago days of high school, and my struggles have not been limited to my physical disability. I have faced the death of a young son, a painful divorce, and a decline in my strength, each of which has brought its own sorrows. However, coming to terms with my handicap was the turning point for me, for it has enabled me to view all my circumstances through a lens of optimism and grace, and it has allowed me to find joy in unexpected places. For that, I am truly grateful.

CONTAGIOUS DANCE

We are resilient, we can overcome, and we will endure.

*Life isn't about waiting for the storm to pass—
it's about learning to dance in the rain.*

—Vivian Greene

AUTISM AND INNER STRENGTH

ANNE BENNETT-BREADY
When my son Nate was diagnosed with autism at the age of three, I was devastated. I was in shock for an extremely long time, and then decided that his disorder was my fault. I was not sure what to do because, back then, there weren't many resources available. Little was known about autism at the time, so I began to do research in order to help my son in any way possible. It was a journey that I was forced to travel, and it seemed as though there was no end in sight.

When I finally overcame the shock of learning that my son was autistic, I felt an urgency to begin some kind of treatment as though every minute mattered. However, when I began to gather information on treatment, the prospects were overwhelming! I had a long and confusing list that included every type of therapy, from drug therapy to dolphin therapy. Other types of treatment included auditory training, special diets, and specialized educational programs. I didn't know where to start.

I convinced myself I would find the end to this maze of treatments, and ensure that my son lived a happy, well-adjusted life. I knew that my faith, my inner strength, and the love I felt for my son would get me through, and my heart spent a lot of time convincing my mind that things would work out. Nate's salvation became my purpose in life. I let go of my own wants and needs, and dedicated myself to his recovery. However, though that was my choice, every choice has consequences.

I didn't think that ignoring my own needs for the sake of my son would result in long-term physical health problems as well as emotional distress, but I am still dealing with those issues today.

The stress I felt while caring for Nate was self-destructive and emotionally draining, but I couldn't stop putting all my effort into helping him. I was fortunate to have one of the best schools for autism located twenty miles from my home. This establishment was truly my life preserver. I learned that *autism* is not a bad word, but simply refers to a neurobiological brain disorder that affects communication and socialization. It did not result from anything I had done while I was pregnant or had done in my past.

In raising Nate, I learned that though I could not cure my son, I could gain some control over the situation. I began to take this control by reading and absorbing everything about autism, and by using this new knowledge as power. It was a great feeling to be in control and to focus on my son's abilities rather than his disability. His contributions to household chores, his passion to excel at school, and his unconditional love for others are just some of his amazing attributes.

I know my hard work and dedication has paid off, and for this I am grateful. It has been thirteen years since I learned that my son is autistic, and I feel as though I have lived a lifetime. However, I have made my peace with this "devastation," and I understand that I still have a long road to travel on my journey. Obstacles and setbacks still come up occasionally, but I will continue to educate myself and others about autism. I am lucky that I have inner strength, education, and a great deal of support from those around me. I have been blessed, and when I think of the past, I am grateful. If I hadn't gone through those difficult times, I would not be where I am today.

CONTAGIOUS PERSEVERANCE

Take a moment to reflect on some of the most stressful hurdles in your life.

1. *How have you handled these challenges, and how has dealing with the stress affected you—in both positive and negative ways?*
2. *What have you learned?*

By reflecting on the greatest difficulties you have encountered on your life journey, you will be better able to see just how strong you can be when the chips are down. Not only that, you may even find that your biggest challenges have been some of your most important teachers.

GOOD FROM THE BAD

ERNEST FIELD

Sixty years after having been exposed to SS cruelty and concentration camp starvation in the camps of Dachau and Buchenwald, I often wonder, has the experience affected the way those men and women who were prisoners with me look at life today? Is there any positive, lasting influence on a prisoner's character? I say yes. And like anything else, I believe it is possible to find something of value in even the worse experiences that a human can endure.

I'll never forget the day in May 1938 when I was forced to board a train with my brother and became a prisoner of the SS, which was an elite unit of the Nazi party that was founded by Adolf Hitler. Only two months before my incarceration, German units had entered Austria and taken over. Being Austrian Jews, my family had vaguely discussed the idea of leaving the country to ensure that we would be left alone, but there was no urgency in the discussions. In retrospect, we should have been more serious about emigrating because shortly thereafter, two police officers arrived at our home, looking for my brother and me.

As prisoners of the Nazi commandos, we were forced into a life of misery and cruelty that no one can imagine. If other prisoners disobeyed orders or tried to escape, we were held at gunpoint and forced to observe their punishments, which the SS felt should be an example to others. Not only that, if we attempted to look away, we could be subjected to these same unconscionable penalties. It was a nightmare, and those images remain burned into my brain, even today. In addition, we endured subpar working conditions, frostbite, infection, hypothermia, and starvation. Although we were eventually released and returned home to our families, I've always lived with those memories.

It was hard to move on from those experiences, but I have found that good can come out of even the most horrifying situations. For example, after leaving the concentration camp and returning home, I developed a tremendous respect and appreciation for freedom. That first breath of freedom after my harrowing year was surreal—I felt blessed. I was able to view life through a whole new lens, and when I look at life now, I see how beautiful it is, with all of its possibilities and opportunities. I always try to remind people how lucky they are to know this freedom, because not everybody is so fortunate. Even if someone hasn't gone through something like what I went through, I hope my story will teach them that they are one of the lucky ones.

I also came to realize that comforts in life are a relative thing. So many people are always yearning for more and feel unsatisfied with what they already have in their lives. People think they need the nicest house, the newest car, and the most up-to-date material things to be happy. But when I was serving time in the SS concentration camps, a simple slice of bread and a drink of water would have meant the world to the prisoners. Therefore, you should always find a way to appreciate the things you do have in life, such as a roof over your head, food to eat, and a loving family to come home to. Again, if you have even one of these things, you are one of the lucky ones.

Not only has my view on life and freedom shifted, but my character has also been affected. I have become less sensitive now that I know what true hardship and pain look like, and

I have acquired a healthy sense of fatalism. This belief that many things are predetermined, and therefore inevitable, helps me accept the things in life that are out of my control. My unwavering acceptance of all of life's highs and lows sometimes baffles those around me; it is hard for them to understand how I can be so at peace with everything that happens. For example, I've had to face several surgical operations in my life. My sons always ask me, "How can you be so nonchalant about it?" My response: Whatever is meant to be, will be.

I believe my days and nights in the hells of a concentration camp were surmountable based on my belief that we are all in G-d's hands.

CONTAGIOUS FAITH

There are times when the evils in this world present themselves in the worst ways. We might find ourselves helplessly defeated by life and its many woes. However, through faith, we will be able to overcome any difficulties that come our way.

THE FEAR BUTTON

SALLY GATES

The Fear Button—I never had it. I grew up being unafraid of living life on the edge and taking chances, and I'm sure that I got this attitude from my mother. My mother was a widow, but she was a strong woman, and she proved to me through her own example that I could do whatever I needed or wanted to do. She raised me to take care of myself, enjoy life, and to "go for it," and I did just that—she taught me well.

I was always told I had a "happy-go-lucky" personality, and people thought that I wasn't afraid of anything. They were right. When I graduated from college, I jumped right into life. I got married, moved 1,500 miles from home, started a career, had two children, and went back to school for a master's degree. However, life wasn't perfect, and without telling the story of my marriage, let me just say I got divorced.

And there it was: the Fear Button. I had spent so much time living a fearless life that I wasn't prepared when my marriage started to dissolve. Fear crept in. It was as though someone implanted a buzzer in my brain and I could not shut it off. The thought of divorcing my husband and supporting my kids by myself was scary, and I was overrun with fear of this new, impending life. But I remembered what my mother taught me, and I found the strength to do what was necessary.

After my divorce, my life went along most days as I imagine it does for any single mother. I never had enough time, and I always felt the need to do one more thing. All the day-to-day decisions and financial responsibilities were put on my shoulders, and somewhere along the line, I felt like I needed to control everything. I thought if I could control everything, nothing would go wrong. This was a pretty egotistical way of thinking, but it was driven by my fear. My worst moment came while I was driving all over South Florida for a job I did not enjoy. I remember having the fleeting thought that if I let go of the wheel of the car, I would crash into the ten-foot barrier wall, and I could end it all. No, I was not suicidal. I was just scared, and yearning for a little relief.

At the height of this stressful, fearful time in my life, my sister persuaded me to go to a religious retreat weekend called Cursillo, and at the retreat I shared my fears with a priest who told me two things. Number one: I needed to forgive my ex-husband so my children could be free to love their father as they needed. Number two: I had to let go of control. His words struck a chord with me, and though fear entered my life in various forms afterward, I always remembered his advice. By accepting that I couldn't control everything, I was able to come to terms with the fact that even though things might not go the way I'd like them to, I needed to just let life unfold or my fear would cripple me.

My extended family always tells me they are proud of me for being so strong. They admire my ability to "do it all," and to make tough, but good, decisions. They don't see fear in me at all. Now that I am approaching my retirement years, I look back and realize that I haven't been fearful for a long time. Although I sometimes hear the buzzer and feel the burn of fear charging through me, I am now able to push it aside and take positive action. I believe in myself, and I am optimistic that I can do it—whatever I want or need to do—just as my mother taught me.

CONTAGIOUS COURAGE

Everyone experiences some sort of fear in their lives, no matter how small or big. Often, the things that affect you negatively are out of your control. But you have the power to conquer your fears, and you can overcome these fears by believing in yourself.

THE REST OF THE STORY

JANET BALES

For those individuals who grew up with AM radio, the name Paul Harvey probably strikes a chord. He was a well-known radio personality who used the catchphrase "the rest of the story." Although that phrase never carried much weight for me as a young person, for some reason it was filed away in the archives of my memory.

As a child I was taught to obey without question, and I was told more than once to "do as I say, not as I do." However, I remember thinking at an early age how lovely it would be to have someone explain the whys of life to me—to give me "the rest of the story." There were many times I just wanted to know why we did certain things and didn't do others. But while I was consumed by that question, I didn't think I could ask it because I feared it would be perceived as a challenge to authority.

When I reached adulthood, these questions became less important. In fact, asking "why" as an adult was even more risky than when I was a child—someone might think I was stupid. I did not want to disappoint others or make any enemies, so I was always compliant. I did what I was told and expected the same from my children and others; I had lost the need to find out the answers. I favored feelings over factual data, and I learned a lot by observation. I became a pretty good reader of emotional situations, but in the process of "feeling my way" through life instead of asking questions, I missed a lot. I drew too many conclusions, many of which were wrong. Even when my conclusions were accurate, it took a great deal of effort and time to reach them, and this difficulty could have been avoided had I been brave enough to ask questions and seek information.

How many times have we wished others had made the effort to seek the rest of the story when they drew incorrect conclusions or quickly judged our actions? How many times have we been angered when others made blind assumptions about our friends or loved ones? Although we notice these judgments and often resent them, how many times have we ourselves rushed to judgment when seeing a situation we had no understanding of?

It's interesting that as we grow older, certain situations prompt us to review these types of judgments. For example, when I developed colon cancer, my doctor said, "When you are through with the treatments, you will never be the same." Unsurprisingly, I didn't ask "why." After the treatments were over, and my doctor and I talked about my future with a more favorable outlook, I broke my own rule and asked him why he had said I would never be the same. He replied, "After going through something like this, people either become more positive or negative. Your emotions and your reactions to things change."

I realized it was true. I told him how after going through treatment for cancer, I would see people who were moving slowly and wonder, why? I would wonder what was going on in their life, and whether or not they were sick. Now I find that I'm asking a lot more whys without apprehension or fear of judgment, and it's freeing. I don't care if I'm perceived as ignorant or foolish. We walk around flaunting a façade of perfection, and this only limits us. Once you take time to find out the rest of the story, it unlocks the door to a greater understanding in so many ways.

CONTAGIOUS CURIOSITY

Don't be afraid to ask questions. Instead, be curious and seek answers, and you will gain a better understanding of any situation you find yourself in.

ANGELS AMONG US

KARIE MILLSPAUGH
August 3, 2009: I will never forget that day for as long as I live.
It was 110 degrees in Las Vegas, and I was awaiting word that
our capital investors had deposited their first cash investment
into our start-up business that day. Jobs were scarce and creating a business seemed like the only solution. However, as I was
walking to my car, my sales director called and screamed that
the investors had backed out at the last minute.

As she told me the bad news, I felt an icy chill run through
my body. I literally had thirty dollars to my name, and I had
been waiting three months for that cash flow. "What do you
mean backed out?" I choked out, as my knees started to buck-
le. Desperate thoughts began to run through my mind: How
will I feed my five-year-old daughter? Who can help me? My
closest family member was over 2,000 miles away.

I felt helpless but determined, and I started to scramble in
my mind for a plan B. As the days went by, the domino effect
from not having an income eventually started to play out. I
received an eviction notice, my car registration expired, my
Internet and cable were turned off, and creditors started calling me every hour. My life started to get very dark. However,
in the midst of this darkness, I began to discover that angels
do exist.

One of those angels appeared in the form of a kind friend
who lent me $200 to buy groceries. Another angel was a sweet
doctor from NYC who had taken an interest in me for personal

reasons. Although I wrote the doctor, telling him my life was a mess and begging him to leave me alone, he replied anyway. He told me that God helps special people like me, and asked me which bills I needed to pay that month. Bless his soul, he sent me a check for that amount. The bank held his check for two weeks because I had zero funds and it looked suspicious, but his generosity was an enormous help.

Although I seemed to keep meeting angels, I was still in a very difficult situation. I would pass homeless people on the street and start to have a panic attack; I imagined myself joining them soon. I had never been in such a humbling situation before. My ex-husband and I had lived a very comfortable life during our twelve years of marriage. I wondered where we would live, how we would eat, and how we would get around.

Just as I was about to be evicted and locked out of my apartment, another angel entered my life. One of my friends was looking for a roommate, and told me that we could move into her spare bedroom. I was thankful to have a game plan, but it was heartbreaking to move all my things into storage, and I felt lost and empty as we moved into the tiny home with just our clothes and shoes.

My luck changed one day when I heard that a young entrepreneur was looking for someone to manage his North American tour of business coaching events, and I jumped at the job with a combination of fear and excitement. I sent my resume, and within a week he interviewed me. I will never forget the day he called and gave me the opportunity to join his team.

I knew in my heart that this was the right direction for me, but my loyalty to my start-up business started to play tricks with my mind. Even though I was in a terrible financial situation, I wasn't prepared to give up on it. As I sat in the parking lot after ending my call, trying to decide if I should abandon my start-up and take the opportunity, my phone rang again. I was informed that I was overdue on five car payments, and that my car was going to be repossessed. This was a sign. I didn't have time to feel guilty; I just needed to move forward and do the right thing. Sometimes we need a nudge, sometimes a hard shove, and I made the decision to join a dynamic business coaching team, which has changed my life, attitude, and mindset forever.

It was wonderful to receive my first paycheck as I started to slowly climb out of the pit I had created through my bad business choices. It wasn't until eight months later that my daughter and I were able to rent a home, but I learned that it is important to never give up. Angels are up there willing to lend you a hand. Let them help you, then be an angel in return for someone else.

CONTAGIOUS HOPE

Even when things seem hopeless, remember that there is always a light at the end of the tunnel. However, it is your job to work through difficult situations and find this light. As you work for solutions to some of your most daunting problems, remain open-minded, forgive yourself, and move forward from past mistakes, and humble yourself enough to reach out to friends and contacts who may be able to lend a helping hand. Accept that things may not always end up the way you initially envisioned them, but that the right mindset and hard work can help you get through anything.

LIFE IN EMOTION

A poem by Karen Lyons Kalmenson

Life is motion
Ever going.
Keep up
With this ocean
And you will
Be forever growing.
Whatever happens
Stay on the move.
Life flows softly
When you are
In the groove.

CHAPTER TWO

APPRECIATE THOSE AROUND YOU

Relationships have their ups and downs.
It's how we work together and respect each other
that controls the success of our long-term relation-
*   ships.*

Our love and our relationships are the only true
*   assets*
in our lives that have real lasting value.
Everything else is temporary.

And some relationships do end;
it doesn't necessarily mean
someone was at fault.

We often hear about ongoing issues that take place within a family. It can be an alcoholic uncle, an out-of-work parent, an argument between siblings—the list goes on and on. What I find interesting is the amount of energy that people exert steaming over trivial issues. What's worse is the amount of time relatives or friends spend apart from each other as a result of an issue such as this. I have seen this in my family and I am sure that many of you have seen it in yours.

I knew of two brothers from Chicago. They eventually got married and had families. For many years these two brothers were close. They lived near each other and, together with their families, moved out to the Chicago suburbs. Their children grew up together. In addition to their daily routines of being together at school and home, they spent many holidays and vacations together as well. Unfortunately, a petty argument over a minor issue led to animosity and complete disengagement. Now, years later, the families still do not speak. I find this to be a waste of energy and precious time.

Stories like this are important because they teach us a valuable lesson: not to "sweat the small stuff," as Richard Carlson has written. People should focus on the possible resolutions of an issue instead of letting it fester. Selecting the best resolution as early as possible is much better than allowing a trivial matter to morph into a massive lifetime disagreement.

Switching gears to relationships and marriage: Issues are always resolvable, no matter how angry the parties may be. Step back and take a bird's-eye view. This is necessary, not only for the two parties but also for those around them. When issues are beyond correction and all potential paths for improvement are exhausted, sometimes a breakup is the only resolution. Ending a relationship does not necessarily mean that either of the two parties, or both, are at fault. It takes two strong people to admit that something will not work. It is important to consider the rest of your life, and always take the path of the most optimal long-term solution.

What I have learned through experience is that nothing can trump the value of love and happiness. No amount of money and no amount of fame or success should deter people from following their bliss. I have seen myself dive headfirst into an abyss that nearly destroyed the most important relationship in my life. In addition, I lost valuable time that I can never get back. However, because of that mistake, I have become a better person, one who savors time and cherishes the moments that money can't buy.

The good news is that the divorce rate is decreasing in this country and has been for some time; according to several studies, it is at its lowest since 1970. This reflects two trends: People are working harder to stay together instead of simply bailing out; and the marriage rate has dropped among younger people. People are taking their time and not jumping into marriage too early. They are also considering the economics involved. This is important because economics is a frequent cause of conflict in a marriage.

The bottom line in all relationships is this: Do what you can to make it work. If you can't, move on. The goal should be compatibility, love, and harmony—not resentment and animosity.

David

We all experience our uphill battles, and we all need someone to help push us upward.

—Charles Markman, Oak Park, Illinois

If you want to relate with someone at the highest level, the most powerful relationship of all is the one you have with yourself. Love yourself, and when you do, you become an instrument of love because you come from a place of abundance.

—Ira Scott, Kings Park, New York

A LOVE STORY

FRED MOORE
When I was three years old, my parents got divorced and for reasons never explained to me, my mother received full custody of me. Shortly after, my mother remarried and we moved to Paris, where my stepfather became an executive of a French company. My stepfather was the only father I had known for most of my life, so it was a difficult time when he died fifteen years later on the eve of World War II. In the wake of his death, my mother and I returned to the United States. After losing my stepfather and leaving Europe, I must have felt like I was missing something, because I started to think about my biological father. He hadn't crossed my mind very much while I was growing up and living abroad, but once I returned to the States, I set my heart on finding him.

As my twenty-first birthday approached, my maternal grandmother asked me what I wanted for my important day. I surprised her when I told her that I really wanted to celebrate my birthday with my biological father. But there was a problem: I didn't know where he was. She said that she heard that he had married and that he was now a widower. But she wasn't sure, and my mother had no idea where he might be because she hadn't had any contact with him since the divorce. Since nobody seemed to know where he was, I gave up the idea of finding him.

We decided to celebrate my birthday at my grandmother's house with my mother and a few friends, and my grandmother asked me to come just after lunch to help her get things ready. I remember her opening the door of her tiny apartment, singing "Happy Birthday" as I walked inside. She then looked at me with a smile and added, "Here is your present." I was confused when she pointed to a man sitting on the living room couch until she said, "Fred Junior, please shake hands with Fred Senior."

I was shocked and speechless, but my father stood up and pulled me into a great bear hug. It was an amazing moment, and I was ecstatic to see him after all those years. We talked for an hour, and when he went to leave, I pleaded with him to stay for dinner. He stayed, but when my mother arrived later that afternoon, her reception wasn't so warm. She simply greeted my father with an icy "Hello." Somehow, we got through the evening!

About a month later, my father called and was rather insistent that I have dinner with him at a restaurant near my New York apartment. I agreed and I looked forward to catching up with him some more. But when I entered the restaurant and found my father, I was taken aback to see that my mother was sitting at the table with him. I thought I must have been dreaming. Before I could say a word, my father announced that they had been dating since my birthday party, and interrupted my shocked silence to add, "We've invited you here to ask for your blessing of our coming marriage."

It was a quiet yet beautiful church wedding, and I participated in the ceremony by giving my mother away to my father. Their rekindled connection was an amazing testament to how your heart can lead you down different paths in life. They lived together happily for twenty-five years until my mother's death. I've always considered their romance fate, and I've admired how they were able to grow, leave the past behind them, forgive each other, and fall in love all over again. Now, that is a true love story.

CONTAGIOUS REKINDLING

Once a fire burns out it can always be lit again. The same goes for romance. Time and distance can truly make the heart grow fonder, so don't rule out the possibility of falling in love again.

THE MAGIC LIST

HAYLEY FOSTER

I had taken our two small children and fled the house in fear for our safety more than once. After each event, John would transform back into the charming man I'd fallen in love with. He was always able to talk me back home.

This made me question my own perception. Was it me? I didn't know when something I'd say or do would set him off. Anxious and overwhelmed, I'd stay up late nights, alone, watching personal development programs, searching for ways to make sense of our situation. I'd cry and wonder, *How could this have happened to us?*

Completely distraught, I was barely able to get through the days. However, my best friend suggested a technique I hadn't used in years. "Make a list to define what you want," she said, "to see if John can be that."

I took out a notebook and considered what I wanted in my ideal lifelong companion. For weeks, I worked on that list. I liked being married and I desperately wanted stability and a positive male role model for my children. What more did I want?

Remarkably, The List grew to hundreds of very specific attributes. I wanted a self-assured, sober man who could iron better than I could. I wanted someone who would play outside with the kids, who was financially stable, and who could bring out the best in me. I looked at John. I looked at The List. After eleven years and two children together I wondered if he could be the one.

I was still asking myself that question when I flew from Fort Lauderdale to Dallas to attend a business conference a few weeks later. There, I met thousands of people from across the country who believed in the transformational power of personal development. While milling around and making contacts in the lobby of the hotel, no conscious thought of The List in mind, I was introduced to Steve as "our token rocket scientist" from California. We sat down along with our colleagues, chatting about the conference. Somehow, simultaneously, we simply stopped talking. When we locked eyes, it was neither romantic nor sexual; it was a profound connection. A hundred years of knowing in just one look. Someone asked a question, jarring us back to physical reality in the lobby. It was late, so the group disbanded to get some sleep. In a few days, the conference came to a close.

Returning home, I was back in the despair I'd temporarily left behind. One day soon after, I caught sight of my six-foot-three, 220-pound husband chasing our small son into his bedroom. Running behind them, I arrived just in time to see him pick Josh up by the shoulders and throw him across the room onto the bed in anger. I was dumbfounded. John had always made me feel responsible for his ugly outbursts, but surely, a six-year-old could not be the cause. The refrain from a Brian Tracy telecast rang in my ears: "You become what you hang around most."

If I stay here, I thought, I will be just like him.

In that instant, I knew what I had to do.

The decision was hard and the follow-through was harder, but The List gave me courage. Certain I could do better, I filed for divorce. Reviewing The List daily, I'd spend hours imagining what a solid partnership with the ideal man would be like. My thoughts soon turned to Steve, the man I had met in Dallas. He was thirty-seven, never married, had no kids, and was a Midwestern tractor mechanic who became a NASA engineer. Seems like a good candidate, I thought. Disregarding the fact that there was a whole country between us, I picked up the phone and called him.

When he answered the phone, I told him who I was and boldly said, "I'm getting divorced. How would you like to be the first in line?"

"No," he said. "First is a bad place to be." Steve had been around the block a time or two.

"How about first and last?" I asked.

"No, thanks," said Steve, hanging up.

Blatant rejection did not deter me. I picked up a pen and wrote, "I feel as if I know you, but I don't really. What I do know is that I like you very much. I really want to learn more about you. Will you let me?" I popped it in the mail.

A few days later, I called again. This time, Steve did not hang up. We got to know each other by speaking on the phone several nights a week. At one point he said, "I feel as if I'm being interviewed. Have you got a list or something?"

"Yes, as a matter of fact, I have," I said.

When he asked why, I responded, "When I get what I want, it's because I have been very specific. After all, as Mark Victor Hansen says, 'What you want wants you.'"

"I want to see that list," Steve said.

"I'll show you mine when you show me yours," I replied.

Steve resolved to put his mental list down on paper. Now we interviewed each other. Night after night, we shared our pasts and fantasized about our futures. Miraculously, Steve possessed many of the attributes on The List. Months into this long-distance romance, it occurred to us that we ought to get together in person. Before making the trip, we exchanged our Lists.

Six months later, we sat cuddling against a sand dune on a

Fort Lauderdale beach. Steve dug into his pocket, retrieving a many times folded piece of paper. He handed it to me. It read:

Hayley Foster, you are the love of my life. I want to spend the rest of my life with you. Will you marry me?

CONTAGIOUS EMPOWERMENT

If you are in a situation that makes you feel unappreciated or ignored, it is in your power to escape it. Be determined and be persistent to get what you want.

OUR BRADY BRUNCH

CHRISTINA CALLAHAN

Jim Harper

After college, Jim Harper set out to start his career, his family, and his life. Despite having a degree in genealogy, he took a job in sales for one of the largest oil companies in the world, which allowed him to support his new wife, Louise. However, after working in sales for a number of years, Jim eventually grew tired of the corporate life and decided to take advantage of a franchise opportunity in Columbus, Georgia. So he, Louise, and their first child made the move, and Jim opened his business in January 1959.

Jim's business was an immediate success, and his future was looking very bright. However, one day in October 1959, tragedy struck. At about 2:00 p.m. Jim told his wife, who was working as his office manager at the time, that he was going to meet with a client, and said goodbye. While he was at his client's house, news broke that there had been a fire at Jim's business and Louise had been rushed to the hospital. Louise was not doing well, and for days Jim would not leave her side. Unfortunately, on the twelfth day she passed away, leaving Jim to care for their two young children.

Months later, still devastated, Jim knew he had to find something to give him hope, so he decided to begin taking flight lessons at the municipal airport, six blocks away from his former business. Jim started going to the airport frequently and became friendly with his flight instructor, Jack. One day during a lesson, Jack invited him to a dinner party that he and his wife were having at their home. Jack mentioned that his widowed sister-in-law would be there and he wanted Jim to meet her. Deciding that he had nothing to lose, Jim agreed to go, and that is when Rachel Wilkerson entered his life.

Rachel Wilkerson

At the beginning of World War II, Rachel Wilkerson was offered a job at the Navy Flight School in Auburn, Alabama, where she met her future husband, Gary "Wood" King. The pair married in September 1945 and moved to Georgia, where Rachel's husband started a municipal airport.

In April 1946, Rachel gave birth to twin girls and decided to leave the airport to care for her children. One weekend that following year, her husband was booked to pilot a charter flight from Fort Benning to New York, and he invited Rachel to come along for a nice weekend away from the kids. Although Rachel agreed to go, she had a change of heart the morning of the trip and decided to stay home. That afternoon she received a phone call that would change her life forever. Wood's plane had encountered a violent thunderstorm and crashed, killing Wood and three other passengers. Rachel was left widowed with eight-month-old twin girls, and with two infants to support, she eventually made the decision to sell her late husband's airport to his two brothers.

Rachel began dating again but it seemed as though she was meeting all the wrong men. When her sister-in-law mentioned that she was having a dinner party at her home, and that a friend of her husband's would be there, Rachel was reluctant to be set up with him. But that weekend she decided to take a leap of faith.

At the dinner party, Jim and Rachel connected right away.

They had a lot in common and began to see each other more and more. Their feelings for each other grew deeper, and when Jim eventually proposed to Rachel, she accepted with one condition—Jim had to give up flying. He agreed, and in April 1961 the two were married.

Although Jim and Rachel have encountered heartbreak and tragedy in the course of their lives, they have also experienced immense joy. Jim and Rachel found love twice—two spouses and two happy marriages. They have been married for over fifty-one years.

CONTAGIOUS RISK

Never fail to take a leap of faith. Although life may throw difficulties your way, it is never too late to start over.

FAMILY IS EVERYTHING

CHARLES MARKMAN

It was a sunny afternoon. My family and I were having our customary, delicious Sunday dinner in the dining room. Dad and my sister Doris sat at the ends of the table, while Selma, Mom, and I filled in the gaps. The radio played in the background from the kitchen. A broadcaster gave us the play-by-play of a Chicago Bears–Chicago Cardinals football game. Then the announcement came:

The Japanese had bombed Pearl Harbor.

Although we knew that a war was going on in Europe and we heard of the growing tensions in the Pacific, that attack stunned us. All of a sudden, the war became more than just something we heard about on the radio. My friends enlisted or were drafted, and I immediately signed up to serve in Europe as well. The events that transpired during my two years of service will forever be in my memories. During this time, I lost many friends or saw them get hurt, and I could have been killed, too.

One time, a German hurled a grenade at me. I took cover behind a tree at the last minute and survived, though I found shrapnel embedded in my shoulder afterward. It is still there; I don't think it ever rusted. We never had enough time to celebrate our victories, and even then, we had to keep moving forward. From these stories alone, it might seem hard for anyone to be optimistic.

However, I was able to get through this traumatic time

with the help of people I loved. My family and I have always had a close bond, but we became closer during my two years of service. Throughout the war, getting packages from home was a big deal for us. Mail connected us to our other world—the one that existed apart from the constant fighting. Even though our V-mails and regular letters were censored—to avoid leaking any classified information—we all found other things to talk about. My folks sent me items that seemed ordinary to other people, but actually helped me a great deal. Everything I received from home helped me go forward.

I remember one instance in Italy in particular when we had been pulled from the line after a long spell in combat. We set up our camp in an olive grove where there were many olives hanging from the trees, but they were not yet ripe. Mail call came and I got a box from my folks. I opened it, with everyone looking over my shoulder, and found chocolate candy, some cookies, and a big can of ripe black olives from California. I think the candy and cookies were pretty much devoured by the other guys, but I got to enjoy a Markman family favorite: black olives.

Another time, my folks sent me a box of candles—because when I was a first sergeant, I often worked into the night, with little light. Other times, Dad would send me supplies so that I could draw cartoons for the Army's division newspapers. Mom saved the old letters I sent home and, because of that, I was able to put that part of my life into a story to share with others. I know that my folks watched out for me. All those gifts were simple gifts, but they reminded me of my destination: home. I could not wait to get back to having Sunday dinners at 601 South East Avenue.

When you have family, you have something to fight for. Knowing that I had family at home, thinking about me, enabled me to survive the war and all its challenges. When I talk about how much family matters, I am not only talking about wartime, but also about life in general. It was like having a whole company as backup when the enemy was pointing a rifle at me: my family was my support. We all experience our uphill battles, and we all need someone to help push us upward.

CONTAGIOUS CONNECTION

A family is not measured by size, or by bloodline or another common measurement. A family is a support system that is always there for you, unaffected by distance or time. The connection is solid. Show your appreciation by always being there for them as well.

FRIENDSHIP RUNS DEEPER
THAN FLOODWATERS

CHRISTINE HENCHAR REED

In the age of social media, many of us connect electronically with people across the country and globe more than with the people who live right in our neighborhoods. Nonetheless, in times of need, I have found that it was a special relationship with my next-door neighbors that mattered most.

My husband, Roland, and I first met our neighbors after we bought a two-story brick colonial with a lovely tree-lined backyard on a cul-de-sac. When we pulled up to our new house, we noticed a couple standing in the driveway next door and we introduced ourselves. They were welcoming and offered to lend any tools needed to help settle in. That initial conversation marked the beginning of an enduring friendship with Nynette and Rod.

We have been blessed to share many holiday celebrations with them, and we've gotten to know extended family members on both sides. We take care of each other's pets and homes when the other couple travels, and we even keep keys to each other's places for emergencies, to borrow things, or to be on call for servicemen when our schedules prevent us from being there. The four of us have spirited conversations about politics and infrequently agree on that topic, and our relationship reflects the values from our shared Christian faith. We have laughed together, prayed together, and supported each other through health crises.

One Saturday afternoon in May 2010, my husband and

I were anxiously anticipating the broadcast of the Kentucky Derby. The local TV stations kept on interrupting us with weather updates about heavy thunderstorms and possible flash flooding. We assumed that this storm would blow by, but as it rained, we noticed that some large puddles began to develop behind our home. Then Nynette called and told us to look out our back window. When I peered out back, I saw a river running through the main road of our neighborhood. I looked out the front window and saw that water was gushing out of the sewers, and in just twenty-five minutes, our yard was engulfed.

Our homes were badly damaged in Nashville's "1,000-year flood," which caused widespread damage to businesses and homes throughout the region. Nynette and Rod had just completed beautiful renovations of their kitchen and master bathroom, and we had two cars, which were just paid off, now saturated by floodwaters in our garage. Although we were aware that many other areas were also devastated, the experience was unbelievable. We moved out of our homes for the first half of the summer to complete all the repairs and rebuilding, thankful that we had the option to restore our residences. We rolled up our sleeves, began cleaning up, and rebuilt our homes and our lives one step at a time.

Throughout the repair process, we consulted with Nynette and Rod about contractors to hire for repairs. Together, we muddled through the paperwork and repairs in the months following the storm. The rebuilding process took almost a year, and it made a big difference to have neighbors who understood our situation.

I found that in the difficult time of crisis, the love in an already wonderful friendship exceeded the depth of any floodwaters. We also felt wrapped in love when many people from our community and local churches offered us food, helping hands, and loving arms. With our homes restored, we have returned to our happy life on the cul-de-sac with lots of good conversation, food, drinks, and laughter. Knowing that life is never free of adversity, we live in confidence that we can call upon each other when needed. Our friendship has proven that when you are friends with your neighbors, you can weather any storm.

CONTAGIOUS FRIENDSHIP

Never wait to build relationships with people, especially those who live close to you, such as your neighbors. Instead, make it a point to get to know people and to cultivate close relationships. That way, you will always have a support system, and you will not have to weather the storms of life alone.

FATHER'S DAY REMEMBRANCE

MICHAEL CARLON

What do an old pair of Nike sneakers, Paul Simon, *The Stamford Advocate*, and the State Theatre have in common? The answer is my father, Don Carlon. When I was growing up, my father taught me lessons of sacrifice, generosity, and frugality through the example he set for my siblings and me.

When I was young, my father had sneakers that were so old and worn that I remember being embarrassed by them. When I asked him why he did not get a new pair, he simply replied that it was because those old sneakers still fit. It is only now, as the father of six-year-old triplets, that I have come to see an additional reason why the old sneakers remained in his life for so long. He kept wearing old sneakers so that his children could have new ones. In this way, my father taught me about sacrifice.

My father is also a very generous person; he and my mother put all of us through college and some of us through graduate school, giving us the chance to have successful careers. In addition to being financially generous, my dad is also generous with his time. My twin brother, Jimmy, and I were paperboys for the local newspaper while in middle school, and we had a long route. Our route spanned many streets, and it was difficult to deliver the big Sunday papers in a timely manner on our bikes. So, on Sunday mornings, my dad would load us into his white Oldsmobile and drive us to deliver the papers. We would listen to Paul Simon's *Graceland* while doing so. To this day I listen to that album on a regular basis, and I think about my father taking the time to help us deliver those newspapers.

I smile when I think back and reflect on how frugal my father was. I remember the State Theatre as the place where you could see a fairly new movie for a fraction of the cost at other theatres. If there was a movie we wanted to see, my father waited for it to come to the State Theatre and we would see it, albeit later than most people in town. Prior to parking for the theater, we would visit the Food Bag convenience store to pick up soda and popcorn for the show. I could always count on him saying, "They rip you off at those concession stands; I remember when popcorn was a nickel." But the icing on the cake was my father trying to pass us off as children in order to get a lower ticket price—never mind the fact that my brother and I were both shaving on a regular basis.

As I look back on my childhood, I can't imagine growing up with anyone other than my father. Sure, he has his quirks—his creative swear word combinations and endless stories about the twenty jobs he had while putting himself through college. But I want to say something that I don't say nearly enough, and that is how much I love my father, and how grateful I am for all the things he taught me—and still teaches me every day.

CONTAGIOUS REFLECTION

Take the time to reflect on the lessons you learned from your parents, your siblings, or your friends. You might come to understand that their actions, which once seemed inconsequential, have had a positive impact on you.

HOW TO BE GRATEFUL FOR YOUR SPOUSE'S EX

CLAUDETTE CHENEVERT

I am a stepmother, and I know that I have not always been accepting of my husband's ex-wife and her presence in our lives. I was not only ungrateful, but I also hated her at times. Unconsciously, I blamed her for every unhappiness and every wrong that occurred in my relationship with my husband and his daughters. I constantly felt like an outsider, and I thought it was because of her—because she happened to be first in their relationship and affections, and I was second.

This all changed when I realized that I did in fact have a reason to be grateful for her—she gave birth to two daughters who are now an amazing part of my life. Instead of tightly hanging on to them and staying in her marriage because it was the "right thing to do," she walked away from a marriage that didn't serve her anymore. Her action gave me the opportunity to be a part of my husband's life and the lives of his daughters, making my life much richer.

My husband's previous wife also allows me to share the responsibility of parenting. When I tire of the demands of being a mom, I can be grateful that she is there, enabling me to take care of my own needs. By being able to have "me time" and time to spend as a couple, my husband and I feel better about ourselves, so we feel more capable of meeting our children's needs.

I give thanks that both my husband's ex and I have discovered the secret to making our stepfamily life work, though I cannot say it has been easy for either of us. There have been many occasions when there was no simple solution to the complexities of stepfamily life. When one of us was winning, the other was losing. However, we learned that the only way we can both win is when we work together to make the lives of our children better.

No matter where you are in your journey as a stepfamily, take a moment to give thanks. Be grateful for your spouse and the children who were welcomed into the world by your spouse's ex, and be grateful for being able to share parenting. Appreciate the ability to put the best interests of the children first in a relationship with someone who may never be your best friend. Be grateful for another day as a stepfamily.

CONTAGIOUS GRATITUDE

Stepfamilies put relationships on a whole new level. Often, relationships from the past and present must coexist. Rather than hold a grudge toward your spouse's ex, try to maintain a mutual understanding with him or her. Think of an arrangement that will have the best impact on your kids and your spouse.

FRANCIS

THOMAS COLLINS

"You! In the red shirt! I want a coffee that isn't cold." The demand came from an older patient who was known as the crazy "throwing" woman at the hospital where I volunteered. Glaring at me in her pink bathrobe, she thrust her cup of coffee into my hands. I noticed some nurses snickering at my misfortune.

I went up and down six flights of stairs to retrieve fresh coffee and, after giving it to her, had to listen to her reprimand me for taking so long. The nurses nearby continued to laugh, but something about this woman held my attention, and I barely heard them. Instead of walking away, I decided to listen to what she had to say, and when she realized this, she quickly ceased chastising me. She told me to grab a chair, and began talking to me as if I were an old friend. "My daughter wanted to be a police officer," she said. "Can you guess why? For the glory!" She clutched at her table vehemently. I was unaware that this conversation was the beginning of an important experience in my life.

Midway through her rant, she stopped and took a sip of her coffee. "Can you believe this? I bet they just heated the old one up!" She had evidently forgotten I was the one who had given it to her.

She continued, "Oh I lost my train of thought again. This happens quite often, I apologize." After laughing, she suddenly became somber and apologized for her behavior. "I'm sorry I'm like this. Most people can't stand it," she said. "My husband couldn't." I was surprised at her sudden change of character, but I let her know there was no problem.

We spoke about the past (mostly hers), the present, religion, the hospital, and her children. "If I'm boring, you don't feel obligated to loaf here. You can leave," she said, interrupting my thoughts.

"It's been an hour," I retorted. "If I was bored, I would have left by now."

All the while, I was thinking how sad it was that she was known as the crazy lady; after all, we are all imperfectly human. I saw genuine kindness in her, and her stories reminded me that she is someone's mother, someone's sister, and someone's daughter.

"Finally!" she said, after finishing another rant. "Finally there is someone in here who has taken the time to listen to me. This has been my first good conversation!" She asked me if I was going to be there tomorrow just as the nurse walked in.

"No, he's not," said the nurse before I could answer.

She looked away from the nurse; her eyes fell onto my name tag. "Well then, Thomas, it was nice talking to you. Have a good night. Go see your friends, go do other things, and leave this crazy old woman alone!" She said, laughing.

As the nurse was shooing me out the door, I asked the old woman for her name. She smiled and said, "Francis."

While volunteering in the hospital I discovered that Francis had a severe case of bipolar manic depression. While we were talking she would quickly switch from topics that made her happy to ones that made her solemn. My conversation with Francis influenced my life's philosophy—it made me think about who I am as a person. I had always had an interest in the way people think; this experience served to reassure me that I belonged in the mental health field.

"Be careful, she could run out and throw something at

you!" joked one of the nurses as I left Francis's room. Some of the nurses laughed along, but one surprised me and said, "No, she won't throw anything at him."

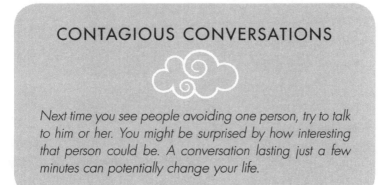

CONTAGIOUS CONVERSATIONS

Next time you see people avoiding one person, try to talk to him or her. You might be surprised by how interesting that person could be. A conversation lasting just a few minutes can potentially change your life.

WHAT ARE YOU REALLY FORGIVING?

SUSYN REEVE

One day, just before the holidays in 1985, I finally learned what it meant to forgive. Byll and I had been divorced for six years when I wrote to him asking for copies of home movies we had made during our marriage. My boyfriend was curious to get a glimpse of another time of my life, and I also wanted to see the movies of my dad, who had died eleven years earlier. Byll responded that he had considered my request but he did not want to send me the movies. I was shocked, particularly since some of the videos were of my dad, and Byll was the director of a hospice program!

I assumed he had decided not to send the videos to me because I had not included money to make copies of them. So I wrote to him, enclosed a check, and made sure to point out, with an attitude, that because he was a hospice director, he should understand that I wanted to see the videos of my dad.

Byll's next letter echoed the sentiments of the first: "I made movies before I met you and I've continued to make movies since we've been divorced and I will decide who gets to see my movies."

I thought, This guy has a problem!

Months passed. A friend invited me to a presentation on forgiveness at The Open Center in NYC. We listened to Robin Casarjian speak about the power of forgiveness. She led us through a guided visualization. I closed my eyes and concentrated on her words. She told us to "see a door on the right-hand side of the room." In a few moments, someone will walk through that door. Forgive that person." I imagined Byll walking through that door and going to stand directly in front of me.

My ego was ready to let go, to forgive with no strings attached. After six years of being divorced I was truly ready; I was happy personally and professionally, and I was eager to be free of any anger and resentment from the past. I said to Byll in my mind, *I forgive you for having affairs and for being unavailable during the time my father was dying.* Then I heard another voice, quieter this time, but concise and direct, as though it came straight from my heart: *I forgive you for loving me.*

I was stunned.

I knew this was the profound truth beneath all the obvious reasons I had been angry with him during our marriage. In order for me to have accepted his love, I had to first love myself, and I *didn't* love myself. I hadn't realized how deeply my feelings of "I'm not enough" were ingrained in me. When I was three years old my mother went into the hospital for surgery and I had to stay with my grandparents during that time. It was the first time I was away from my family by myself. My three-year-old self thought that something was wrong with me, that I had done something bad. I came to believe that I wasn't loved. This experience left me with very deep wounds.

Through the years of our marriage I had projected all my self-loathing onto Byll. The more he loved me, the more I projected. With this realization, I felt energized, lighthearted, and free. I knew that I had realized an important lesson.

Ten days later I was in New Hampshire, where Byll and I had once lived together. On New Year's Eve, walking through a giant supermarket, I felt Byll's presence; my intuition told me he was there. Sure enough, there he was! We said hello, and he asked, "Did you get the movies I sent to you about ten days ago?"

When I truly forgave Byll for loving me and ultimately forgave myself for believing that I was not worthy of love, the home movies that contained the memories of our life together were on their way to me.

When we finally let go of the hurt, the anger, the need to be right, and the need to make others wrong, we not only release ourselves from the bonds of resentment, but we also discover that the wonderful things in life find their way to us—and that love illuminates the path.

CONTAGIOUS FORGIVENESS

Take a moment to reflect and ask yourself if you are holding on to any past resentments or pain. If so, has holding on to these unhealthy feelings, memories, or thoughts helped you, or hurt you? Consider what you would gain by moving forward through forgiveness, rather than dwelling on past mistakes, anger, and injustices. If you have had trouble letting go of negative feelings, maybe now is the time to forgive another person, or even to forgive yourself. It is only through forgiveness and letting go that you can find real peace and happiness, and truly move on in your life.

FOREVER

A poem by
David Mezzapelle

*Forever... holding your
hand.*
*Forever... waking to your
beautiful face.*
*Forever... the feeling of love
and the warm radiance
of your glow.*
*Forever... the memory of
the day we met.*
*Forever... thinking about
you every second we're
apart.*
*Forever is how long I want
to be with you.*

CHAPTER THREE

SAVOR EVERY MOMENT

Life doesn't stop;
memories and spirits stay with us.
Value time with others and
appreciate mortality.

When we're young we tend to take for granted the time we spend with older relatives and family friends. I have vivid memories of events, holidays, and vacations when I was young. Back then, I thought those people and moments would last forever; it seemed as though I would age but they would not. I didn't anticipate that they would grow older and pass away. Now, as an adult, I recognize our mortality and value every moment.

I also value the path the deceased have paved for later generations. That path leaves a piece of them in all of our lives.

There is no question that death is a difficult thing for family and friends to endure. There are books, organizations, and support services that exist for the purpose of making it easier. Many of these services, such as hospice care, do a wonderful job comforting not only the patient, but also their loved ones.

When losing a loved one, I always find myself reflecting on their life and the imprint they left behind. Those reflections are important building blocks in my own life as well as the lives of other people this person has touched.

A big part of who we are comes from the learning experiences and legacies of those before us. Understanding and appreciating the imprints left behind by others is a powerful tool for adding wisdom and zeal to your own life.

David

Life is a gift for which there is no payback. There is no one on earth to thank, so give it your best shot, hold on to it tightly and lovingly.

—Ada Tarriff, Washington, DC

Signs of the people you have loved and lost exist if you pay attention and let them into your life. It is because of these signs that I have always known that my father, Jerry, is watching over me.

—Mary Kate McCormick, Andover, New Jersey

SUZANNE MILLER

When I was fifteen, my mom was diagnosed with pancreatic cancer that eventually spread to her liver. Three years later, I was by her bedside when she died. She was about a month shy of her forty-eighth birthday. It took me a while to go through the grieving process. I was a senior in high school; I had games to cheer for, colleges to apply to, and boys to have crushes on.

I don't think I really finished grieving until I met my husband, Rob—someone who was not familiar with my family, who wanted to know what this cancer experience was like, how it made me feel, and how it shaped the person I became. I vividly remember asking him if he was sure he wanted to marry me because my fear was I'd develop cancer, just like my mom.

Nearly twenty years later, Rob and I were married with two beautiful children, and we worked hard at successful careers. We had happiness, health, and faith. In October, a few days before our twentieth wedding anniversary, he was diagnosed with a brain tumor the size of a baseball. (Rob joked that the tumor was his anniversary gift to me.) I had been working at staying healthy to avoid what I thought was my fate. Now suddenly, at the age of forty-four, would cancer be his fate, just like my mom? While I had never wanted to give up hope that he would win this battle, there was always a fear that he would die young, just like my mom.

For three years, the love of my life endured multiple brain surgeries, four types of chemotherapy, and full-brain and spinal column radiation. His neurosurgeon told us we showed grace under fire. We certainly felt the fire, but we also felt the warmth from the love and support given to us by family, friends, neighbors, and coworkers. Finally Rob began to get stronger. He started to get his life back and he even set out looking for a job. To celebrate making it to the three-year mark we planned a vacation to Germany in September to visit his sister.

Then fear became reality after a routine MRI. The tumor was growing again. This was all too familiar. From that point on he declined and transformed rapidly, and he returned to the hospital where he stayed for ten long weeks until he came home under hospice care.

Cancer has haunted my life. I first watched my mom's positive attitude, strength of character, and deep faith in God give her hope throughout her journey. And then I watched her deteriorate and die before my eyes. I later watched how brave and determined Rob was to carry on. He never complained and had an attitude of gratitude. In fact his optimism was contagious and comforting, his faith unmovable. Together with my kids, we watched him deteriorate and die before our eyes. We were by his bedside when he died a week away from his forty-eighth birthday.

This warped, continual encounter with cancer does not end with my mom and my husband. While Rob was in the ICU for his final stay in the hospital, I was diagnosed with ovarian cancer. I went to the hospital for an emergency ventral hernia surgery and the biopsy returned showing serous carcinoma cells, indicative of ovarian cancer. When the doctor called to tell me the news, I told him that he was wrong, that my husband had cancer, not me, and I hung up. I collapsed. I thought I had escaped this fate, but cancer finally caught up to me. I was also forty-eight.

I had a hysterectomy while Rob remained in the hospital. It

was so hard not to share my bad news—my burden—with my best friend. But I wanted him to have peace and focus on getting home. It had only been two weeks into my eighteen-week-long chemotherapy treatments when Rob came home under hospice care. Our amazing group of friends traveled from all over the world to be there for us, to welcome him back home, and to care for him. Throughout both of our battles we received so much love and support: Lovely meals were delivered to our door, rides were provided for the kids, prayers never ended, and fundraising events were held to ease the financial burden while I was on short-term disability. It was humbling and heartwarming. Our kids experienced what it means to "love your neighbor," and it left a lasting imprint on our lives.

I finished my treatment alone, without Rob. I never told him I had cancer because I didn't want to upset him during his last weeks. Although I'm sure he was suspicious when I lost my hair, but perhaps he thought I shaved my head to show solidarity with him. The support we continued to receive from the community kept us strong. Now I ask myself: Is cancer really "haunting" me, or is it guiding me to do something big, to make a difference, to change my own fate or influence the fate of others? I've read that hardships are God's most favored gifts. So I anxiously wait to see what I can do as a result of these gifts, and I am excited to take the first steps as I begin my life after cancer.

CONTAGIOUS HOPE

Loss will make it hard for you to see optimism at first, but it also brings out the best in people, and exposes the humanity that everyone shares. Once you see this, you can gain strength and you can harness the power to support the next person who needs it.

OUR FRIEND, "MOM"

COURTNEY SMITHEMAN

I went to a funeral recently. It was not the unexpected or tragic kind where everyone asked, "Why?" This funeral was the kind we had anticipated every day since the dreaded word *tumor* was first spoken four years earlier.

It haunted me terribly that I had reached an age when my friends were starting to be taken away by Mother Nature, but I couldn't change the fact that my friend George was gone. I entered the church that day with apprehension in one hand and my husband holding my other. I was immediately greeted by George's daughter, who apologized for not calling me back right away after his passing. I understood; I had been overwhelmed with phone calls when people reached out after my own father's death. I gave her a big hug as the freshness of her hurt soul echoed in mine.

As the church service started and everyone turned their attention toward the pastor, I saw something that stopped me in my tracks. I stared in complete disbelief because the florist had made a colossal mistake: the huge floral arrangement on the altar read "MOM." Why didn't anyone notice before we all sat down? I couldn't believe I was the only one who saw it, but I noticed it too late because the pastor had already begun.

The pastor spoke of accepting God and Jesus Christ, and how our friend, George, had truly found God in the end. I believed him. It is in a man's nature to go looking for what he needs only when he truly needs it.

Through the hymns and readings, I found it nearly impossible to take my eyes off the flowers on the altar. I wondered if perhaps there was a woman's funeral before this one and they had accidentally left her flowers, but I forced my mind back to the prayers. The eulogy began. If it's possible to have a favorite part of a funeral, the eulogy is mine. The pastor announced that George's fishing group had some things they would like to say. Four men, spanning the later decades of life, rose from the front row. They wore nicely pressed suits and had a purposeful manner.

The first man spoke with a slow cadence, the kind that makes you lean in to listen. The other men, respectful and attentive, stood with their arms in front of them. The speaker explained that he and George were best friends. He missed his best friend, he said pointedly, with the face of a grandfather and the honesty of a child. With a long sigh, he took a moment to compose himself while the rest of us reached for a Kleenex.

The speaker told us that he and the men standing beside him, plus George, had started a State Farm fishing club thirty-five years ago that was still intact. He and the guys had gone on countless fishing trips and had many weekly lunches over the years. George was unfortunately afflicted with seasickness and would often stay behind to fish off the dock. Eventually, George would find his way back into the house and start cleaning up from the previous night's fun, and when the others returned, they would always find their rooms cleaned and the dishes done. The speaker revealed that they started calling George "Mother." He turned and pointed. The flowers on the altar were not a mistake; they were there to pay respects to their late best friend, "MOM."

The congregation burst into laughter. We laughed until we cried, as we had done with George many times before.

The slideshow of pictures and accompanying music revealed a beautiful, fulfilling life, a life we all hope our kids and grandkids get to enjoy. We relived the day George met the woman who would be his wife, smiled as we viewed pictures of their wedding, and were brought back to when George's three children were born. Even after George's children grew up, he always had a twinkle in his eye when he introduced his wife, Rosemary. My "first and last wife," he would say, and he was right: They were married for forty-four years. The pictures replayed all the happy moments in George's life, and reminded us why we had loved him. He was a good man, a good friend, and he could always make us laugh. In the end, that's all that mattered.

CONTAGIOUS LAUGHTER

A beautiful life is filled with laughter and friendship.

31,125 DAYS

PETER WALLIMANN
On January 15, 2009, I paused for an instant before entering the room of my old friend. I took a deep breath, pressed the handle, and entered on my tiptoes.

The room received me with a stillness and silence that I had become accustomed to during my weekly visits to the senior care home. My friend had been confined to his bed for months, unable to move and scarcely able to hear. Only his weak handshake and his bright blue eyes, which grew paler week by week, showed that there was still life in him.

When I first caught sight of my friend's corpse that Thursday, hands folded over his abdomen and mouth open wide, I was unable to hold back tears. The death of this man I had known for so many years touched me profoundly. Decades of friendship had, in a blink of an eye, passed into history. It was as if a part of me had gone with him.

After his death, I reflected on how the first few weeks of his stay at the senior care home had been a battle. In his eyes, it was impossible for anyone to do anything right. The food was either too cold or he had no appetite. The nurses came either too early or too late. The room was too hot when the sun was shining and too cold when the windows were opened. Yes, back then, the old man complained about everything, but I understood what he was going through and didn't argue.

Once my friend had come to terms with the fact that this

room was going to be his last, his criticisms became less frequent. Instead, we talked a lot about the past, about justice, about fate, and about missed opportunities. We also talked about good, beautiful, and funny things. There were days when he thanked me effusively, and there were days when he lashed out at me for things that had happened thirty years before.

The old man often liked to talk about a woman he had come to know after his divorce; the two of them had done a lot of things together. However, they had a falling out and he now regretted that they had lost touch. I suggested that I might try to trace this woman, and he eagerly agreed. I composed a message in his name that he signed, scarcely legibly, with a trembling hand. It was a letter of thanks, full of joyful memories. The last sentence read: "Dear H., if there is a 'life after,' and I believe firmly that there is, I hope we will see each other once more."

Two weeks later, my friend was thrilled to receive a letter from the woman's son. We learned that she lived in another senior care home, and that she was suffering from a severe heart condition; her time was almost at an end as well. Our letter had moved her to tears. She thanked us and echoed the hope that the two of them might meet again in the next world. A few weeks later, the fifteenth of January marked the end of the old man's life. A friend of his had been in prayer at his bedside and reported that he passed away peacefully.

After the body had been cremated and the ashes interred, I had a dream. I saw my late friend enveloped in a string of pearls, ascending in a spiral into the cosmos, leaving the shadows of this world behind. The contours of his body became fainter and fainter, and at the end, he was mere light. This light finally blended with the corona of the sun, and all at once many smaller lights sprang out of it. One orbited the moon, others danced with the planets, and others hurtled into the depths of the universe.

What a beautiful dream, I said to myself when I awoke. But when I opened my eyes I saw an angel-like being next to my bed. I recognized it immediately by its shining blue eyes. Wordlessly, it pointed to the ceiling above me, and as I looked up, pictures began to shuffle there.

First, I saw my friend as a cheerful boy growing up in idyllic rural surroundings. His greatest wish was to be a pilot, but he was thwarted by his strict father and was later forced to work for the family business. Despite all this, his desire to fly remained, and soon enough the young man was flying with the wind in his hair on a chrome 1950s motorbike.

The next picture showed him at roughly fifty years old. He had matured into a modest man who loved dancing and nature. He could name every one of the peaks of central Switzerland and speak about celestial constellations, planets, and the universe.

Then, I witnessed his wedding to a beautiful woman in white, who soon bore him a healthy son—his pride and joy! But the happiness was to last only briefly, and a few years later his wife left him, taking the child with her.

After his divorce, my friend threw himself into his work. He saved diligently for his son and sought solace in nature. He climbed several of Switzerland's highest peaks, and on cross-country skis he covered thousands of miles through snow-covered forests. Although he made great efforts, he never married again. Solitude and quiet became his truest companions until he was finally overtaken by cancer.

As these images on the ceiling faded, a voice spoke to me. It said, "I'm going back home now. Everything is fine."

I opened my eyes and answered, "Have a good journey, Dad."

My father died in his eighty-sixth year. He was 31,125 days old. Measured against eternity, this time span might look slight. But it was a rich, long, and fulfilling life.

CONTAGIOUS LIFE LESSONS

Experiencing the death of a close companion helps us understand the paradox of life: while we are alive, everything seems possible and infinite, while life is actually finite. Though life has an ending, nothing is stopping us from living without limits. Go on a journey, dream big, embrace joy, and live with no regrets. You can inspire someone else to do the same.

LAST NIGHT I HAD A DREAM

DR. COLLEEN GEORGES
Last night I had a dream.

I was walking through different rooms in an attic, each neatly organized and filled with various things I had collected. Each room represented a different stage of my life, and I felt a sense of peace and tranquility seeing everything put together so beautifully.

As I walked, I came across an undecorated part of the attic that had crumpled papers and small, broken items lying next to half-empty, disorganized storage bins. This bothered me at first, but then I yelled to my husband that we should get rid of the garbage and use the empty bins to store and organize other things.

Just then, I saw another area of the attic, far off in the distance, filled with things I wanted to get a closer look at. However, as I started walking toward it, I fell through some thin flooring. It wasn't a far drop and I fell softly onto some green grass. When I looked up, a person who appeared to be a construction worker was standing above me. He picked me up and told me, "It's okay, there's a solid path up there for you to walk on. Just stay on that path and you will get around fine." When I looked again, there it was, this paved concrete path in the attic. I immediately felt a sense of comfort and relief knowing I could walk around the attic safely.

This dream felt very timely to me. About a week before, someone very important to me passed away. Ricky and I met when we were sixteen, and he became my high school sweetheart and first love. Although we eventually stopped dating, we remained wonderful friends for over twenty-two years. When we both fell in love, married, and started families with different people, I was honored to call his wife my friend and watch our children play together. I envisioned Ricky and me growing old as friends and holding our grandchildren together—a life coming full circle. I now know that this vision will only live in my imagination.

With Ricky's passing, the optimist in me seemed to disappear. All I could ask was "Why?" I wondered how I was supposed to make sense of his death, and how his family—his mother, wife, and children—would possibly be okay. Anger and devastation over his loss mixed with a constant flood of beautiful memories. Ricky was a man who brought me great joy, smiles, and laughter, and his presence in my life had a profound impact on the person I have become. He made me into a better human being, and I struggled with the reality of his passing.

I didn't think I would be able to move past his death until the night I had that dream. When I woke and began to remember it, it seemed to contain all the wisdom and guidance my mind couldn't evoke while I was awake. The attic seemed to represent my mind and contained all these rooms filled with my memories, many of them beautiful and comforting. Although some of these memories were messy and unpleasant, I was able to discard them to make room for newer and better ones. And some areas contained questions and unknowns, which gave me a desire to examine them. But trying to ask questions we'll never have the answers to just leads us to fall down with despair. Yet, even when we fall down, it doesn't have to break us, and there are always people to help us get back up and guide us back to a path paved with memories of good times.

So who was the construction worker? Well, I believe it is no coincidence that you worked in construction, Ricky. I know it was you. And I know you will help all the people who love you. One day, I will tell your kids about the day I met you. I will tell them everything I remember, and when my son falls in love for the first time, I will tell him about my first love. I will make many more good memories with your wife, my friend, and continue to fill my heart and mind with beauty and joy. I will tell your mother that she created a person who brought so much goodness to so many people's lives, including my own.

Life is beautiful, and I intend to let the sunshine of your memory further brighten my path.

CONTAGIOUS REMEMBRANCE

When we lose people we care for, grieving is healthy and necessary to help us work through our feelings. However, it is also important to celebrate the happiness they gave us and to allow that joy to brighten our lives even after they are gone.

TO HOLD THEIR HANDS

FRED GILL

To hold the hands of the dying is to view life through the eyes of the living. By being confronted with the prospect of death, the living are granted the opportunity to review their own lives and make needed changes for the better.

I learned the importance of this lesson by volunteering at a hospital. This experience taught me about the need for human contact and how valuable a smile or a touch could be for someone who realizes the limits of existence.

My friend Susan had been admitted to the hospital because she suffered from bone cancer. Although her pain provided a daily reminder that life is difficult, her smile and conversation taught me to value my life, regardless of any external factors. The night before she died, we talked for more than an hour. Throughout that conversation I was reminded of the value of family and friends.

As humans we are defined by our actions and how those actions affect others. The material pursuits that are considered important lose their appeal when we are faced with the reality of our limited existence. Things we consider important are reevaluated when our life can be measured in hours. According to Susan, the Bible played a pivotal role in her acceptance of death.

Susan taught me to value priorities. Our limited existence cannot be measured by possessions, prestige, or power. These things do have importance, but do not define who we are.

Rather, we are defined by our qualities, and by the care and compassion we share with others. There is nothing wrong with working hard and wishing to succeed, but we should never stop valuing our priorities.

Volunteering in this capacity and spending time with patients like Susan really taught me the value of life, and showed me just how important it is to live life fully, generously, and honestly. I feel honored to have been able to hold Susan's hand at the end of her life, because it prompted me to really live my own.

CONTAGIOUS REFLECTION

Have you ever had to go through losing someone, or had any type of experience with death? If so, think about what that experience taught you about your own life. Did it prompt you to rethink your values or priorities? Did it motivate you to make any changes, set new goals, or reach out more often to friends and loved ones? Death is a very difficult reality to come to terms with, but it can also be a powerful teacher. Listen to its lessons, and make it a point to live your own life in a purposeful, meaningful way.

COFFEE CAKE

GEORGE HOGAN

When my grandmother was still alive, my friends would frequently visit her. They referred to her as "cool," and when I asked what they did during the visit, my friends would simply reply, "We had some coffee cake." I've replayed those conversations a number of times since my grandmother's death. I don't replay them because she made the best coffee cake on the East Coast, but because of what those conversations meant to me growing up.

It may seem odd to think that my seventeen-year-old friends used to visit my seventy-year-old grandmother, but she *was* cool. She was cool because a visit with her always left you feeling better than when you arrived; you would leave her house thinking that everything in life would work out. A visit with my grandmother always helped put things in perspective, no matter how complicated life seemed at the moment. She was a tiny, soft-spoken woman with a deep faith, a loving heart, and a wisdom that came from living through tough times. She was one of eleven children and raised her family during the Depression. She never had a great deal of money or fame, but she changed many lives.

When people visited my grandmother, they were always welcomed with a loving smile, a hug, and usually, a piece of coffee cake. She had a firm belief that everyone in the world was valuable and deserved respect and love. People could bring her any problem and she would listen closely, encourage quietly, and help them find the strength within themselves. Although she wouldn't give advice or try to solve the problem, she would recount some experience in her life that made you realize that you were capable of overcoming anything. With her, you could be yourself.

I'll never know what took place during my friends' visits to my grandmother's house. I never asked them what went on and I knew that if I ever asked my grandmother what happened she would answer, "We enjoyed some coffee cake." I've wanted to visit my grandmother on various occasions since her death. When life seems too overwhelming I often think of those visits, and I'll sit quietly and tell her my concerns. I can still hear a soft voice reminding me that with belief in myself, love in my heart, and a little faith, everything works out in the end. When life seems too much to bear, take a moment and enjoy some coffee cake, too.

CONTAGIOUS GRATITUDE

Even after the death of a loved one, you can still remember and use the lessons that they instilled in you. What are some of the most important lessons that your loved ones taught you? Does thinking back on these lessons help you keep the memory of your loved ones alive? Take a moment to feel grateful for what your family or friends have taught you. Each person is able to provide a unique perspective in your life, and you should cherish the advice they offer.

MY VERY OWN MIRACLE

EDITH BERGMAN

I believe in miracles. People who have known me for any length of time will shake their heads in doubt, because for the longest time I was a nonbeliever. However, a great life loss changed my mind and showed me that miracles do exist.

My husband, Albert, and I lived in a condo facing the Emerald Hills Country Club, and our apartment was separated from the ninth hole by only a small parking lot and chain-link fence. On Sundays, I would stand on my balcony and wave to my husband as he and his foursome approached the ninth hole. Albert always looked up and waved back. It didn't interfere with the progress of the game and it made me feel good to see him happy. He loved golf and he was really good at it, too. After his retirement, he played about four times a week. He tried to interest me in playing, but I could never work up enough enthusiasm for the sport. Although Albert's skills deteriorated in the last winter of his life, he never lost enthusiasm for the game he loved.

Our life together ended on June 26, 2000, and it was a very difficult blow for me. I found that though Albert was gone, I could not let him go. I didn't know how to live without him. When Albert's body was cremated, I knew exactly what I wanted to do with his ashes. When no one was on the course nearby, I walked to the chain link fence surrounding the golf course, and scattered the ashes on the green toward the ninth hole. I blew a kiss and whispered, "Goodbye, I love you."

About two months later, I was standing on my apartment balcony when something yellow caught my eye. Golf courses, as you may know, have well-manicured fairways, so I was shocked at what I saw when I looked toward the ninth hole. At the spot where I had scattered Albert's ashes, three tall, beautiful sunflowers stood waving at me in the breeze. Sunflowers were Albert's favorite flower, and no one had ever seen any growing on the course before. It was as if Albert was waving at me as he used to do when he played the sport he loved.

The sunflowers grew just that one time, but it was enough for me. They were my final, loving farewell from Albert.

CONTAGIOUS MIRACLES

Even beauty and miracles can be found in heartache and loss.

DEADLINES TAKE ON A NEW MEANING

JC SULLIVAN
In loving memory of Jan Scruggs

As I stuffed flip-flops emblazoned with pink flamingoes into a box for my dear friend Jan, I had no idea that she would never get to wear them. Her husband found pink flamingoes tacky, but they made the two of us crack up. Over time, I'd sent her plastic glasses, socks, T-shirts—anything with a pink flamingo motif, our private joke. I treasured our friendship, and I wasn't alone; everyone loved her.

Bubbly and blonde, Jan was a feisty, five-foot-four female who started a party merely by walking into a room, and the party rocked on until she left. She did it all, making it look so easy. Bursting with inexhaustible energy, Jan was our super-hero on Earth. Always the first to assist, she would spring into action while the rest of us balked on the sidelines, debating what to do. Having beaten ovarian cancer in her twenties, she worked tirelessly as a paralegal for clients whose breasts were damaged by implants gone awry, and her legal firm always won. It never occurred to us that there'd ever be an opponent strong enough to whip her and her incredible spirit, but that was before the call.

Jan, uncharacteristically professing to be "a tad tired," went to the doctor, who immediately checked her into the hospital. She was told she had leukemia, and that she had thirty days to live. But in typical Jan fashion, she was determined to beat it. We embraced her confidence, vowing to live each day.

We had many plans, but sadly, we didn't act on them. Life got in the way, and the vows and the promises were forgotten, temporarily shelved for a time in the future that would never quite arrive. Our goals were sent off to live in that perpetually sad land of "someday," "as soon as…" and "maybe next month."

"Don't worry, girlie," Jan had assured me. "I'll find a hot, single doctor for you. That's why I'm going in again," she said with a laugh. But when I told her I'd visit her at the MD Anderson Cancer Center, she said no.

"I don't want you to see me like this. When I get out, we'll get together."

That's when the severity of her insidious disease hit me.

I called Jan daily while she battled cancer again, and hoped for a second chance to live our dreams and fulfill our goals together. But life didn't allow us that second chance, and we all felt a collective grief when she lost her battle. Anguish took up permanent residence in me. I wondered what we could do to celebrate her memory. I wrote down the list of plans she and I had discussed and started attempting to do them, this time refusing to let "life" get in the way. For example, I made it a point to visit New Orleans. "Jan always loved that you were a nomad," her husband assured me.

On the day after Jan's passing, I sat with her husband and two of our other close friends, trying unsuccessfully to keep a conversation going. Jan's husband thanked us and gave us each a belonging of hers; I got a stuffed pink flamingo and choked up. What had been so important? Why hadn't we done more together? Jan used to say, "Live your dreams! Take trips. Hug your family." It was only after losing her that I realized the true importance of this advice.

"I always wanted to go to Argentina," I began, as I sat with my friends. As I said the words, a gust of wind swept through out of nowhere. Did that pink flamingo just wink at me? Jan was urging me on from the other side; leave it to her to do the unexpected.

Now I urge you to make two columns. In one, write what you dream of. In the other, write a deadline. Whenever I need guidance, I reflect, "What would Jan do?" because she encourages me. I make vows and deadlines, and I plow ahead in her honor. As I write down my plan, I sense a gaze. Glancing up, I catch my pink flamingo smiling at me.

CONTAGIOUS PROMISES

Don't make promises that you can't keep; it'll only lead to regrets. Instead, visualize the things you want to do or accomplish, and set a deadline to motivate yourself.

HELLO, NANA, CAN YOU SEE ME FROM HEAVEN?

COLLEEN MELISSA

> *Regrets are a waste of time, they're the past crippling you in the present.*
>
> —*From* Under the Tuscan Sun, *by Frances Mayes*

It's amazing how many memories come to the forefront of your mind just after someone you love passes away. Conversations long forgotten play like audio recordings in your head, vivid images of times spent together look as clear as yesterday when you close your eyes, and joyful emotions from years before fill your heart as if you are experiencing them for the first time.

In our busy lives, it is so easy to get caught up in just keeping up. There are jobs that need to get done, houses to be cleaned, errands to run, and then a new week of tasks begins. Particularly in our age of multitasking and pervasive technology, the time we spend using smartphones and social media often overshadows the time we spend with those we love. With everything we juggle and everything we have on our minds, we tend to find ourselves in a constant state of stress. When we are stressed, we can be less kind to and less appreciative of our loved ones. As a result, we may not dedicate enough time to keeping the memories of good times alive or making new ones. Yet when someone we love passes on, we remember. We recall the laughter, the parties, the vacations, and the silly moments, and we wish we could see them just once more and tell them we remember.

It is so important that we make it a priority to remember while we are together on this earth. When we are with our loved ones, we must allow ourselves to be fully present. When we are in the neighborhood, we must visit. When we have a quiet moment, we must make a phone call and at the end, say, "I love you." Then, when someone we love passes on, we can allow their passing to bring beauty rather than regret, and take comfort in knowing that we have another angel to watch over us and keep us calm during challenging times. We can know that they smile from above and celebrate our good times along with us.

Recently, my grandmother passed away, two days shy of her ninetieth birthday. While I will miss her and the smile she had every time my three-year-old son sang and danced for her, I feel blessed that the people who loved her most were with her when she made her way to heaven. My mother, father, and I saw her leave this earth peacefully. I feel honored to have been with her in that moment, but most importantly, I feel honored to have spent so many beautiful moments with her and my grandfather throughout my life. I so vividly remember the summer trips to the Poconos, the hotdogs from the local hotdog truck, singing songs in their kitchen, holidays at my parents' house, and evening visits to their home. I once told my son that Nana is way up in the sky in heaven and now she can see him sing and dance any time she wants to. So he played his toy drums, looked up in the air, and yelled at the top of his lungs, "Hello, Nana, can you see me from heaven? I'm playing my drums for you!"

I know you are smiling from heaven, Nana. Thank you for thirty-six years of beautiful memories.

CONTAGIOUS NOW

In today's fast-paced world, it's even more important to keep connected with your loved ones. Make fun and loving memories with the people you care about before it's time for them to move on to the next life. Cherish those memories and continue living life to the fullest.

LOVE TRUMPS ALL

BECKY WOODBRIDGE

Do you have a family member who drives you absolutely crazy? How are we supposed to get along with such people? My strategies have sometimes included ignoring them or dismissing them, but as I have found, this does not always work.

I grew up in a family with six children—five girls and one brother. We each had very different personalities, which made for loads of family drama. Mom, a sweet, petite lady standing just less than five feet tall, was the family mediator. Everyone loved this demure little lady, but I can assure you that when I was a teenager, she was larger than life, and commanded attention like the Incredible Hulk.

She had to. We were six little tyrants, in and out of diapers within a ten-year span. Some families deal with the terrible twos. We had the terrible threes, fours, and so on, until we were six teenagers going through puberty and dating. Now, we're six adults, still with very different personalities, not to mention families of our own. Needless to say, family drama has been enhanced exponentially.

One holiday season put us all to the test after our mother was diagnosed with Stage IV lung cancer. We went to Mom's house with the best intentions to be supportive and helpful, and prepared ourselves for what might be our last holiday season with her. We were determined to make the most of the season, but we processed the stress of her illness the only way we knew how—by taking it out on each other. Each of us thought we knew what was best for Mom, and dissenting opinions were dismissed as simply asinine. One morning, while swapping a few negative words with my sisters, I decided that enough was enough. I drew a line in the sand and said, "That's it, I'm done, and I will no longer talk to any of you."

Suddenly, my mother walked into the room; she had heard everything. She quietly came over and looked up at me with her peaceful, compassionate eyes and said, "Becky, of course you will speak to your sisters again, because you love them and that's what love is. Love is forgiveness and love trumps all."

Her words affected me physically; I knew she was right. I felt an immediate release of the tension in my shoulders, and my built-up anger and resentment washed away. I felt lighter.

I love my siblings, and I don't want to lose them. As she had when we were younger, my mom stood larger than life that day, not as the Hulk, but as a sweet, loving mother giving me a precious gift.

That Christmas, we gathered once more at my sister's house in Houston. As we sat around the dinner table, sharing stories and kidding with each other about our childhood, my sister Velinda asked if we could play a game. The game is one that she and her husband play, called "What I love about you is…"

To play, you pick someone in the room and say what you love about them. That person then tells someone else what they love about them, and so on. As we went around the table playing the game, you could feel the love grow in the room. It is so rewarding to tell others why you love them. And, needless to say, it's always good to hear such information about yourself. My father, a man of few words, picked me that day and said, "Becky, what I love about you is you know how to make people laugh." I never thought my father recognized that ability in me.

You may think you know why someone loves you, but that's not always the case. You might think that the reasons you have for loving someone are obvious, but sometimes they are not. Most of the time, we don't stop to ask ourselves why we love someone, or why he or she loves us. We should. Love between family members is not always awarded or expressed, but it should be given freely, because in the end, love trumps all.

CONTAGIOUS LOVE

Communicating with your family can be frustrating at times. You might feel unheard or unappreciated. But make sure to express your feelings to your loved ones— because a family becomes stronger when its members cherish each other.

TSUNAMIS AND RAINBOWS

SÓNIA TREJO

You cannot lose something that is part of your soul.

—Reverend Michael Bernard Beckwith

March 2, 2004, was a beautiful Southern California day as friends and family from across the globe gathered at our home to share stories, laughter, and tears. At 5:30 p.m., my husband, Anson, took his last breath as I held him in my arms. He was forty-six years old. In that moment, my world fell silent as I felt his life leave his body and soar right through my soul like a bolt of lightning. He had waited to say goodbye to those he loved, and he had waited for me to release him. "It's okay to go, my Angel. Until we meet again," I whispered, as our eyes met for the last time.

"I will be okay," I lied.

Neither my husband nor I had been particularly religious; one of us was a Jew and the other a Christian, grounded in the belief that God is universal regardless of the name assigned. We shared a deep spiritual connection and belief that this life as we know it does not end with "death" as many assert. Though I believed that death was only an extension of life's journey, and that it provided a sense of peace, I was not emotionally prepared to continue my journey alone.

I found myself staring in disbelief at the emaciated shell

that lay before me, which no longer contained his larger-than-life soul. His once athletic six-foot-two frame, ravaged by cancer, had become his prison. He's free now, I thought. I gently brushed my hand over his face one last time, closing his almond-shaped eyes before drawing a blanket over his lifeless body.

In that moment, the wind chimes that had been quiet all day came alive like a symphony. As the chimes sounded, the tsunami of tears and cries of anguish fell silent as everybody stood in awe of the magnificent sunset-lit sky, made more brilliant by the sudden appearance of a beautiful rainbow. The "bow" was more of a rainbow-colored cylindrical sphere shooting straight up through the sky before bending back to earth—how beautifully fitting. Anson had lived his life with such beautiful passion, and so it seemed, a beautiful farewell. I couldn't help but smile as I thought, he's already shaking things up on the other side.

The days that followed were packed, a blur of emotions, planning, paperwork, and phone calls. I was grateful for the diversion of being "on-task" during the day, and grateful for the friends and family who remained close and assisted with the memorial arrangements, occasionally sharing memories and stories that provided some much-needed levity.

I could feel Anson's presence everywhere, his voice and laughter always in my head. However, I dreaded the evenings, when I would inevitably have to lay my head down on my pillow. As I looked at the empty pillow next to mine, the excruciating reality of his absence was overwhelming. I felt a void without my best friend, lover, and soul mate to hold and comfort me. For fourteen years, even when we spanned the globe during business travels, his voice was the last I heard before closing my eyes to sleep and the first voice I awoke to in the morning.

Once everyone returned to their daily lives, the weeks and months that followed were filled with projects. I missed Anson's physical presence and I was lonely, but I never felt alone. Though he was physically gone, he was my constant companion. I found solace within my spiritual community and charity projects, which brought me out of the abyss of heartache into the light of love and gratitude. I began journaling my daily experiences and emailing them as letters to Anson. I sent him an email almost daily for nearly a year, always titled "Missing You." Some were heart-wrenching, and I would write until my eyes became blurred with tears. Some were philosophical and introspective, and some were angry.

God is a magnificent creator, but Anson was a magnificent and tenacious orchestrator, right down to the beautiful rainbow at the time of his passing. He was brilliant, funny, and unassuming. He was one of God's beautiful messengers, never realizing the impact he had on those he met. We were blessed with the desire to live, love, and cherish each day of our lives together as if it would be our last. We lived more fully in the fourteen years we shared than some do in a lifetime. My husband came into my life and changed it forever.

CONTAGIOUS LIVING

The greatest gifts live eternally in our hearts and souls.

BEING HELD IN COMFORT

VANEETHA RENDALL

Burying my precious two-month-old baby was devastating. Paul had been born with a heart problem, but he had survived the critical surgery at birth and was thriving. He came home from the hospital at three weeks old, and after a slow start, he began gaining weight. We were amazed at how healthy and beautiful he was, and with his winsome smile, easy disposition, and mop of curly dark hair, he delighted us all. Even the physician filling in for Paul's regular cardiologist was so confident about Paul's progress that he eliminated most of his heart medications, saying Paul didn't need them anymore.

At first, I was encouraged by the good news. But the doctor had made a foolish mistake, and two days later, Paul was dead. My son's death was completely unnecessary, and I struggled to accept what had happened. As I watched them lower his tiny casket into the ground, I said goodbye to the dreams and hopes I had had for his life, thinking that nothing good could ever come from such a pointless death.

And yet, it did. The good in my son's passing came from a song titled "Held." A dear friend of mine penned the song, and it opens with the story of Paul. The song begins with the words, "Two months is too little, they let him go. They had no sudden healing. To think that Providence would take a child from his mother while she prays is appalling." The chorus provides an explanation for this loss, answering, "This is what it means to be held, how it feels when the sacred is torn from your life, and you survive. This is what it is to be loved and to know that the promise was, when everything fell, we'd be held." For me, this song is about how God promises to hold us in our pain, and that is how I survived.

I knew the song was compelling, but its power hit home one rainy afternoon as I wondered if any good would come out of my suffering. It had been an impossible day and I was feeling sorry for myself. Partially drenched, I ducked into a bagel shop to grab a quick lunch. It wasn't busy, but the guy making my sandwich seemed so slow. I sighed impatiently, wishing that he would go a little faster. He was almost finished, when "Held" came on the radio. As I heard the familiar chords, I felt my irritation roll away. Thankful for the delay, I smiled and leaned against the counter to enjoy the moment, unhurried. Something healing had come out of my brokenness, and it was still healing me.

I was so lost in my thought that I didn't notice that the young man making my sandwich had stopped, and when I looked up, I saw he was crying. Our eyes met and he apologetically mumbled, "I'm sorry. Are you in a hurry? Do you mind if I stop for a minute and listen to this song? You see, my mom died a few months ago, and this song is the only thing that got me through. It has meant so much to my whole family."

Time stopped as this stranger and I shared the moment together. I stood in silence as he took in the song, mouthing the familiar words, as I recited them in my head. When the song was over, tears were streaming down my face as well. I knew that the song had touched thousands, but I'd never witnessed its impact firsthand. That day changed me; seeing purpose in my suffering was more redemptive than I imagined. I took consolation in the fact that a song birthed from my own struggle had offered comfort, encouragement, and hope to others who were inconsolable and hopeless. Though it couldn't take away my pain, it did take away its razor-sharp edge. Knowing that my loss had a greater purpose made it easier to endure. In that moment, I saw how joy and fulfillment could come out of anguish. That same transforming sense of purpose can arise from any loss.

In sharing about Paul and subsequent sorrows, I have found others desperate for words of hope and comfort. They want to talk about their pain and fear with someone who has suffered as they have, and it has been an honor to be part of their healing. I hear others asking the same questions I did: Will the aching ever stop? Will I ever laugh again? I now know the answers. God has carried me in my grief and comforted me through terrible trials, and because of this, I am able to offer hope to others who are suffering. And when I do, it is like rubbing balm on my own wounds. I get stronger. I gain courage. I feel joy again.

CONTAGIOUS COMFORT

We have all known some type of loss, but it's possible to find comfort and connection from our experiences. Know that you are not alone in your grief. Accept the comfort you receive and know just how much you can touch one person by giving comfort.

THE PERFECT WHISTLE

DIANE MAY

It's amazing what a little thing like a whistle can do and how long it can last—some eighty years in my case!

The whistle is a childhood memory of my father. I would normally be outside playing with my friends and he would whistle like a loud mockingbird to call me home for dinner every night.

Now, after all those years, a sweet memory remains of my dad and the sounds he created with his natural whistle. He's been gone over seventy years and I miss him every day. He died when I was eleven years old but I daydream about his whistle every day of my life. That sound, which replicates in my head over and over, is a packaged memory that pulls me through anything I have to deal with in life. Some days the dreams are so vivid, I can see his eyes. At times I know he's in heaven whistling four little words, "I love you, Diane," thus making it, for me, the perfect whistle.

The stirring memory of the whistle has lasted through most of my years; through my childhood, through my college antics, through my marriage, and through the birth of two wonderful children and two beautiful grandsons. I also ended up using the whistle in a children's story titled *The Perfect Whistle*, which I wrote about a mockingbird that mimics a famous melody it hears.

The mockingbird is named "Mockswell." Mockswell lives with a little girl in the Virginia countryside and was a gift from her grandmother. Mockswell was flying around Washington, DC one day and was pleasantly surprised when he heard the famous American march, "The Stars and Stripes Forever," written by John Philip Sousa in 1897. This magnificent march was being played by a big band with a piccolo player. Overcome with excitement, Mockswell landed on the shoulder of the piccolo player and just kept listening and repeating the song in his beautiful whistle. Once Mockswell was sure he knew the song by heart, he decided it was time to share this with the world. Mockswell said goodbye to the little girl and promised to return some day. He then flew all over the world to visit American soldiers and whistle "The Stars and Stripes Forever" to remind them of home.

It's amazing what a little thing like a whistle can do.

CONTAGIOUS MUSIC

A familiar song can be a time machine to a moment in the past. Music can trigger the most powerful memories. It has the power to evoke specific feelings and thoughts from a time and place that is long gone.

To My Beloved Mother

By Marilyn Salter

It's not the rich and famous who really change the
world
It's not the high and mighty who march with flags
unfurled
Not even mountain climbers who strive to reach
their peak
But those like you, dear mother,
Who only kindness speak.

With every thoughtful gesture,
With every helpful deed,
With every understanding glance,
You helped fulfill a need.

For goodness is contagious,
Can we ever guess its worth?
Multiplied a million times
It ripples around the earth.

Your laughter and your music
Brought joy to everyone you knew,
Our home became a haven
Where hopes and dreams were listened to.

With your husband by your side
For sixty-four wonderful years,
You shared your gifts of love
Through happiness and tears.

We all miss you, dear mother
But you have not really gone away,
For you still live within our hearts
And there you'll always stay.

CHAPTER FOUR

TAKE A LESSON FROM OUR YOUTH

A youthful view of optimism

Little League had a profound impact on me. My father traveled quite often when I was growing up, but he made sure his trips were as brief as possible. He always wanted to be home for major events like ball games and birthdays—even if it meant grabbing a last-minute flight from Japan, Australia, or some other distant country. One example was when my mother mentioned to him that our Little League team was in the play-offs. She didn't tell me he was coming because she wasn't sure he would make it back in time.

During one particular and crucial game, I stepped up to the plate with three men on base. I smacked the ball to deliver a triple and brought in three runs to ultimately win the game. To my surprise, my father came running down from the stands to give me a hug. I didn't even realize he was there. That was not only my first triple, but it happened to be the most critical play of the game. That moment resonates with me like no other. I thank my mother for the surprise and my father for flying fourteen hours to see the game. I hope one day I can bring that kind of joy to my son or daughter.

I feel fortunate to live in a time when we finally recognize that education is not only books and tests, but also experiences and memories that shape our mind and our future. What I read in a book may have taught me how to add, subtract, and multiply, but equally important is how much I learned from that Little League triple.

A lot of growth takes place during our younger years: academic growth, relationship growth, physical growth, and so on. This chapter focuses on the powerful experiences and the long-term effect of our younger years. Minor episodes seem to be major for the young. And major episodes and transitions are life-changing.

David

Some people you know are never children, or only briefly. Some have their childhoods much later in their lives.

—Marilyn Ducati, Goa, India

It is a life challenge when I have to pack my own food to go to birthday parties, friends' houses, and restaurants because I can't eat what everyone else is eating. But now I don't think about the food; I just have fun with whoever I'm with!

—Caitlin Aronson, Ridgefield, Connecticut

POSITIVE POCKET

REBECCA ZERBO

I was in sixth grade, waiting to go into the band room before school, when an eighth-grade girl came up to me and asked if she could see my band folder. As I started to give the folder to her, she suddenly grabbed it out of my hands, opened it up, and took out the music. After glancing at the music sheets, she started demanding to know how I had gotten them, and declared that I shouldn't have them because the music was too advanced for my level. I felt put on the spot, and became even more uncomfortable when she started tossing the music sheets to the other people in the room, asking everyone if they thought I should have that material. No one stopped her or said a word.

Once we were in class ready to begin practicing, the same girl came up to me again. To add insult to injury, she said, "You may think you're cool, but you're not," and continued to call me hurtful, rude names. I ran to the bathroom across the hall, where I knew no one would see me, and quietly cried in a bathroom stall. For the rest of the day, I felt upset because she called me ugly names, and embarrassed because others were around, watching. More important, I felt angry because no one stood up for me, including myself.

My anxiety about seeing the girl again distracted me, and I failed an important math test. I even avoided most of my friends for the rest of the day; I just wanted to go home. When I finally got home, my family tried to comfort me. They told me all sorts of positive things about myself in an attempt to counteract the experience of being bullied, but it didn't work.

I didn't feel any better later in the evening, but then I got an idea. I went on the computer and wrote down my favorite inspiring quotes, such as "I can do anything if I just put my mind to it," and I picked out a few pictures that made me feel good. I printed my card out, and the next day, whenever I felt anxious or self-conscious, I discretely pulled it out of my back pocket. Reading it was a reminder that I was self-confident and strong, and that I would be okay.

As I was leaving math class, the card fell out of my pocket, and my teacher saw it and asked what it was. Without thinking, I said, "It's my Positive Pocket, to keep good thoughts in my pocket wherever I go." When I showed my mom, she thought it was a brilliant idea, and my nana wanted some to give to her friends. I came up with more designs, more sayings, and more cards, and my mom would laminate them so that I could give them out to family and friends. I even created a website so that others would be able to get a card and create a Positive Pocket of their own.

One day, my math teacher surprised me and asked me to tell the class about Positive Pocket. I told my class about my experience being bullied, what I knew about bullying and self-confidence, and then explained my idea to them. My classmates were very interested, and wanted some cards—I wound up taking names and orders! Within a very short period of time, Positive Pockets were helping other young people that were enduring bullying and other similar issues. I felt that our mission had become a reality when I saw, firsthand, that our cards were helping others be strong and self-confident.

Word about my idea spread, and I was accepted into the Young Entrepreneurs Academy. I also won the national title for the Saunders Scholar Bright Ideas national competition, which was especially exciting because it enabled me to share my idea with people from everywhere. Now, I am often asked to speak to groups of people and tell my story.

The way I see it, Positive Pocket doesn't just inspire others. It inspires others to inspire others. Once you can gain self-confidence and feel comfortable with yourself, you can use that to help and motivate others.

CONTAGIOUS POSITIVITY

Bullying hurts, but it's possible to protect yourself and others from harm. Like Becca, create an idea that can help others who have experienced bullying, spread your ideas, and constantly inspire others to make the world a more accepting place. Remember: It's not what happens to you, it's what you do about it!

PROM DRIVE

ALLISON FRATTAROLI

On Easter Sunday this past year, I was looking at formal dresses online, trying to find one that I wanted to wear for my upcoming prom. However, as I clicked through the site, I was shocked to discover how expensive they are. I hoped that I'd be able to find one that was fairly reasonable, and thought about how upset I would feel if I saw a dress that I absolutely loved but couldn't afford.

However, as I scanned the dress selection, I realized that for many girls, that's exactly the case. I couldn't get this realization out of my head. I mentioned this to my parents, and we brainstormed about what I could do to make a difference. We wanted to find a way to give girls the chance to feel beautiful on their prom night without having to break the bank.

After a while, my parents and I came up with the idea of a "Prom Drive," and I instantly emailed Jennifer Kelley from Kids Helping Kids, which is a nonprofit organization that teaches kids the importance of altruism. I suggested that we start a drive to collect used prom dresses, shoes, and accessories. In a few days, one of my best friends and I planned, organized, and scheduled the whole drive to run at my school for about a week.

In the beginning of that week, I didn't know what to expect from the drive, and I told my dad that I would be happy if we received a dozen dresses. That would mean twelve girls who couldn't afford a dress would now have one, and I considered that a positive outcome. However, once people caught on to what we were doing, our success was incredible. By the end of the drive, my friend and I had received not only forty-eight dresses, but also sixteen pairs of shoes in all different styles and sizes. Having had only a few days to plan this event, we were overjoyed with our number of donations.

We were so proud of our success. However, it was disappointing to learn that because our prom drive had been organized so quickly and on such short notice, most girls already had dresses, or their proms had already passed. Although we were unable to give prom dresses to those who needed them right away, we were determined to see our plan through and make a difference.

As we considered what we could do with all the dresses we had collected, we came up with the idea to create a permanent store that would serve girls in need. We began looking into options, and a month or so later, we found out that the Yerwood Center, a community center in Stamford, Connecticut, was offering us a space to use for our cause. It was an amazing opportunity, and we decided that the store should not only be used for prom dresses, but also for clothes of all kinds. That way, girls could come and take the clothes that they needed without having to give a penny.

When we first saw the space, we immediately knew it needed work. It had white cinderblock walls, cement floors, and pipes sticking out of the floor, walls, and ceiling. We paired up with a designer to make the space look beautiful and worked for several weeks over the summer to design the space in the most cost-effective way. After months of renovations and hard work, our store, Handled With Care, was born.

We have already received hundreds of donations for our inventory, consisting of clothing for girls of all ages to wear and to feel confident and presentable for school, interviews, and formal events. This has been a long, hard process, but we have loved every second of it. It is so fulfilling to reflect on our journey and see how our original idea has grown. Although we originally planned to donate prom dresses and help girls feel good for one night, we are now able to donate all types of clothing and help girls feel good now and in the future. That is more than we could have ever asked for.

CONTAGIOUS IDEAS

A small idea can grow into a positive change. One girl's observation led her to take action and now a whole store with affordable clothing is available for girls. Even a small act of kindness can affect someone else in a big way.

SUPERHEROES DO EXIST

MELINDA PETROFF

Many kids dream of a superhero coming to their rescue. I don't ever remember having that particular dream, and I was never a superhero fan. But I am today! In fact, I was forty-seven years old before I found out what a superhero really was.

In May 2012, my great-nephew Gavin Morris was diagnosed with Stage IV neuroblastoma at the age of two. By the time of the diagnosis, the cancer had spread and caused Gavin a great deal of discomfort. Those first days in the hospital were difficult for a person of any age, but he faced it with tremendous courage. His family was amazed, and due to the way Gavin bravely faced his illness, the mantra "Be Gavin Strong" emerged. Through it all, Gavin had a steady resolve, and was constantly doing the "Strong Man" pose that he loved so much. He had a determination rivaling that of Olympic athletes.

As word spread about Gavin's diagnosis, it quickly became apparent that he and his family were not alone. Fundraisers popped up everywhere and people extended kind gestures to the family on a daily basis. Gavin's mother, Tosha, would update concerned family and friends on Facebook. Once she mentioned that Gavin smiled when he saw the Strong Man pose, so we thought if one makes him smile, we should give him 1,000 by the end of the month. Before we knew it, pictures of people doing the Strong Man pose started pouring in from all over our state, other states, and beyond.

We also could see what Gavin was doing for others. With

his endless smiles, unsurpassed courage, and remarkable spirit, Gavin had become an inspiration. Every day, messages poured in reading "Gavin is my hero" and "Gavin is my inspiration." One newly divorced mother, who was experiencing a difficult time, told us that every time she or her children felt despair they would say, "Be Gavin Strong." A man, who was diagnosed with cancer and refused treatment because he didn't want to face his illness, heard about Gavin and decided to fight. He felt if a little boy could be so brave, then he could too.

Children have resilience that is simply remarkable, and nothing, not even cancer, can take that from them. Joy can abound under difficult circumstances. I think there is a misconception that children afflicted with cancer languish in despair and that life stops. Life does not stop; in fact, every precious moment is highlighted.

Despite enduring chemotherapy, surgery, stem cell transplant, remission, and relapse—not to mention all the side effects, medications, and pain—Gavin is filled with enthusiasm for life. He cherishes all we take for granted, and every morning the first words out of his mouth are "Thank you, God, for another beautiful day." Days away from the hospital are spent on "adventures," as Gavin calls them, while days in the hospital are spent building sheet forts, blowing bubbles, and other activities that bring happiness to the day. Gavin does not think about the past or future; he lives in the moment. I think it is his endless enthusiasm and his beautiful ability to stay in the present that resonates with others so strongly. If we look back, many of us can remember cherishing special moments in life at some point, whether brief or long. Gavin awakens this ability in those he touches.

Yes, Gavin is my first real superhero and I am proud of that. With this story, I share the journey of Gavin and his family to show that we can recapture our enthusiasm for life. For Gavin and his family, cancer or no cancer, life is about living each day to the fullest. Cancer may try to take many things, but it will never take who Gavin is. He is and will always be Gavin, a superhero and part-time kid, and that is fine with him.

CONTAGIOUS ATTITUDE

Cancer and other illnesses may affect the body, but it is important to fight through and never allow them to affect the spirit. Like Gavin, live freely and embrace life. Cherish each moment, no matter what happens.

GET YOUR HEAD AND HEART IN THE GAME

JOHN HOOKS

I have participated in youth league sports for over twenty years. I have been a board member, coach, and team parent, and so I have seen how sports can positively affect those who participate. I believe our children's participation in any activity that fosters goal setting, teamwork, and determination will form habits to carry them through good times and bad.

However, just "showing up" does not bring a victory on or off the field, and it does not teach children how important it is to commit to something and try their hardest. To make the most out of sports and activities, and to be successful, participants need to first understand that it takes hard work, practice, perseverance, and heart.

In my opinion, having heart is the most important component to any type of success. In some religions, the heart represents the very core of our being, and it is used to describe one's will or spirit. Therefore, to have heart for a sport or activity means that you are giving it your all.

I once heard a story about a young boy who demonstrates how heart is all you need.

Brody was diagnosed at an early age with Blau syndrome, a rare genetic childhood inflammatory disease. Brody has spent more time in hospitals than most children his age spend on the playground. Because he suffers chronic pain and is susceptible to infection, he must wear a hospital mask when around other children and in public.

His love for the game of football, which can be dangerous and often entails contact, is one of the bright spots in his life. His mother sees his participation in playground pickup games with his friends as essential. She thinks his participation is so important because it proves that no matter the chronic pain and occasional injuries sustained during football, Brody always gets back into the game, eager to show that he will never give in.

Because of his spirit, he has recently appeared in a commercial with other children with inflammatory disease and some Philadelphia Eagles players, who, inspired by his big heart, want to help him "tackle" his disease by trying to find a cure.

Brody may never be the fastest, the strongest, or the most talented football player, but he continues to inspire his teammates. His determination proves that no physical or mental disability can hold them back if they show up, practice hard and long, give it their all, and commit their heart to success and improvement.

Next time, when you feel that success is out of reach, follow Brody's example and put all your heart into whatever you love doing. What have you got to lose?

CONTAGIOUS HEART

Hard work is definitely a key component to succeeding, but most important is the love for what you're doing.

THE YEAR THE GOLDBERGERS HAD A CHRISTMAS TREE

W. M. GOLDBERGER

What my son Jesse wanted more than anything in the world was a Christmas tree for Christmas. Many of our neighbors had Christmas trees, and so did most of his friends. But we had never had one, and despite his pleadings, we told him no. That was the Christmas of 1968: the year that our son Jesse was kidnapped.

My spine still tingles whenever I remember receiving that phone call from the police. I was in my office trying to get a few things finished before our Christmas break when the phone rang.

"Mr. Goldberger? This is a detective from the Bexley Police Department. You must come home now."

"Why? What's wrong?" My mind immediately raced to horrible scenarios, and I must have been shouting because others in the office were staring at me, motionless.

The voice on the phone was insistent, "You must come home immediately, sir. Your son was kidnapped."

I ignored my coworkers' questions as I ran out of the office, and I didn't bother with stop signs as I sped home, thinking only of my eight-year-old son. Once I arrived at my house, I saw a police cruiser with red lights flashing in our driveway; a panel truck from a local television station was already parked at the curb.

When I arrived, my wife, Marcia, was seated in the living room, shaking. She told me that she had been upstairs when she heard a car in our driveway, so she had looked out the window to see an old, beat-up looking car backing out onto the street. A man she had never seen before was driving, and Jesse was in the front passenger seat, being pushed down so as not to be seen. She wasn't sure, but there may have been someone in the backseat, and the car didn't stop, even as she screamed.

Our other three kids were huddled together in the family room at the back of the house, and my oldest son, Adam, said that Jesse had been with his friend from next door. He knew nothing more than that. It was very cold outside and they had been in the house all afternoon.

I went back to the living room to be with Marcia, feeling totally helpless. The television crew had lights shining on the front of the house, and I was feeling completely overwhelmed, when I noticed the father of the boy from next door coming up the porch steps. When I went outside to meet him, he told me that his son was also missing.

As we tried to make some sense out of what had happened, we heard shouts from the direction of the sidewalk where our neighbors had gathered. We were shocked when we turned to see two boys, my son and his son, getting off their bikes and walking toward us. Jesse was totally confused, and he looked at me and asked, "What's happening?" I grabbed him in relief, and as I picked him up, there was the bright flash as the news photographer took a picture, which ended up on the front page of the morning edition of the *Columbus Dispatch*.

Once the police and news crews were gone and the crowd had dispersed, we learned the details of their disappearance. After hearing Jesse's confession, we realized that had we been more astute, we might have solved the mystery without the police involvement. The first clue was that Jesse's sister's piggy bank had been broken into, and much of her change had been taken. Not only that, but there in front of the house, lying in the snow, was the second overlooked clue: a Christmas tree, illicitly bought and paid for.

Jesse had been determined to have a Christmas tree, so when he learned that trees were being sold at a vacant lot not too far from our house, he made a plan. Since he was more of a spender than a saver, his first problem was that he needed more money than he had. Hence, the bank robbery.

Next, Jesse knew that he needed help to bring the tree back, so he enlisted his friend from next door. However, that part of the caper wasn't too well-thought-out, and only after the purchase did they realize that the tree was far too big and heavy to carry by bike. Not wanting to lose the sale, the tree seller offered to help solve the dilemma. His helper would put the tree in the trunk of his car and drive it to our house. The boys would go with him to show him the way, and then he would drive them back to the lot to retrieve their bikes. Foolproof!

However, as with many crimes, despite careful planning, the unexpected can happen to trip up the criminal. In this case, it was the watchful eye of the criminal's mother who witnessed the "kidnapping." Her son wasn't being pushed down in the front seat of the getaway car; he had purposely bent over to avoid being seen.

Almost before we could properly rejoice in our family reunion, our neighbors began to bring us the many ornaments needed to properly decorate Jesse's tree. It was in 1968 that the Goldberger family celebrated Christmas with the tree Jesse always wanted.

CONTAGIOUS PUZZLES

Some details can be easily overlooked. When you get into a chaotic situation, or when your mind starts racing, don't assume the worst-case scenario. Remember that there can be many solutions or answers.

MY YOUNGEST TEACHER

DR. EMILE ALLEN, MD

Over the years, I've had a lot of teachers. Some were even world-renowned scholars. However, one of my greatest teachers wasn't a scholar at all. Actually, she never finished grade school; she was only eight years old, and she taught me one of the most valuable life lessons.

Her name was Mattie, and I met her in a hospital late one evening. Mattie didn't have a common childhood cold or strep throat—she was battling leukemia. When I first met Mattie, she was a frightened little girl wearing an animal-print scarf to cover her bald head, which was a result of her chemotherapy. She had been through so many painful medical procedures, and the chemotherapy had caused her blood counts to drop to dangerously low levels, leaving her vulnerable to various life-threatening infections and bleeding disorders.

Because of her vulnerability to infection, Mattie had to be sequestered in an isolation ward, and anyone who entered her room was required to wear masks, gowns, and gloves. This meant she was unable to feel skin-to-skin human touch, even from her parents. As she would watch TV and play with her dolls, Mattie's parents, Kelly and Mike, would sit just outside her room and talk to her through the glass wall. Can you imagine that?

Despite only knowing her for a few weeks, Mattie and I developed a very strong bond. Perhaps it was because I read to her from her favorite book, *Hope for the Flowers*, by Trina

Paulus. The story is about a caterpillar's life journey to become a butterfly, and hearing it seemed to give Mattie hope.

Despite the fact that Mattie had been through so many treatments, and despite her resilience, her leukemia didn't seem to be getting better. One day, the oncologist spoke to Mattie's parents about another round of chemotherapy. He said he would like to give her a lower dose in hopes it would be less toxic and perhaps provide their daughter with a little more time. When Kelly and Mike asked for my advice, I told them, "I don't think she could handle another round. But in reality it's not my decision or yours; it's Mattie's." Although she was only eight years old, I felt Mattie understood what was going on, and that she should be able to decide whether she wanted any more treatment.

To my surprise, Kelly and Mike agreed with me and immediately gowned up and entered Mattie's room. When they told her what the doctor had said, she responded, "Mommy, I don't need anymore medicine because it's time for me to turn into a butterfly. It's okay."

Our hearts dropped.

It was at that moment that Kelly and Mike became aware that Mattie's life plan was out of their control. However, they accepted the fact that though they were losing their daughter's physical body, they were not losing her soul. They decided to let go of the attachment of keeping her around as long as possible because they knew doing so was at the expense of Mattie, who was the one who would continue to suffer.

So Kelly and Mike honored their daughter's wishes, and soon she slipped into a coma. They both knew there was no further need for the sterile masks, gowns, and gloves, and for the first time in weeks, they were able to hold their daughter in their arms and feel her skin against theirs. When Mattie passed away a few days later, the sense of loss was overwhelming.

However, I was thankful that I had been a part of this brave little girl's life, and I was deeply moved that I had witnessed her metamorphosis into a butterfly. We were all changed.

If Mattie were standing in front of you today, she would be thirty-two years old. I imagine her saying to you, "Our identity is never constant; it is forever changing as we learn and grow from life struggles."

Mattie would tell you: "The quality of your life is not determined by the material items you have accumulated or by being 'right' in an argument with a loved one or coworker. Let go of those attachments and outcomes, because everything in life is on lease. We own nothing, including our physical bodies."

She would say: "It's up to you whether you want to remain a caterpillar or become a butterfly and live a life free of emotional turmoil. Just let go of what you are holding on to, and you will be able to fly."

Mattie was my youngest teacher. She taught me that nothing in life is constant and nothing lasts forever. We eventually have to learn to let go; if we release our attachments, we will be free.

CONTAGIOUS FREEDOM

When you have to decide to hold on or let go, your first instinct is to hold on tight; you don't want to lose someone or something beautiful. But you have to consider the other person's wants or needs. Sometimes it's best to let go.

PULLING OUT BAD DREAMS

ARTHUR SCALZO

In 2007, a friend and high-ranking official in the US Army contacted me. He asked if I would be interested in serving our country again by going to Iraq for a year and working as a criminal investigator embedded with the Army Infantry. I hadn't been involved in military operations since 1994, and at fifty-five, I thought my military career was behind me. I had come to think of myself as more of a family man until that phone call.

Although I felt privileged to have the opportunity to serve again, returning home from that second and final tour was one of the most joyous occasions in my life. I came home to a loving family, but I had changed. I was affected by this war more than I ever thought possible, and I needed time to adjust and to make sense of my life-altering experience.

However, I wasn't the only one who was emotionally affected by my deployment. My wife was physically ill and mentally exhausted while I was gone, and my five-year-old son, Nicholas, rarely slept through the night because of bad dreams. He described the dreams in great detail; they usually involved monsters. I became concerned, and wondered if this occurrence was due to my departure to Iraq.

I wanted to help him, so I came up with an idea that I hoped would solve the problem. One night, after a particularly difficult bedtime, I told Nicholas about a special ability that I possessed: I was able to obliterate nightmares before they even happened. I told Nicholas to be completely still while I took my right hand and guided it through his hair, making a buzzing sound, and stopped at a point on his scalp where I had located a bad dream. I advised him to hold his breath and pinch his nose while I dragged my finger to his ear, made a popping noise, and "pulled out" the bad dream. It appeared to be somewhat technical so Nicholas was convinced that it was working. He happily thanked me, and I gave him a kiss and said goodnight.

The following night, I tucked him in and he said, "Daddy, can you pull out my bad dreams again?" I repeated the process from the night before, again successfully pulling out several bad dreams. I then added an additional function that I called the "sonar phase." I lightly tapped my finger on his forehead with my ear pressed to his head. I explained that the sound of the tapping would travel through his head, thus locating "deeply buried bad dreams." This process delighted both of us.

This ritual continued every night for about a month. I tweaked the process to add the third and final step: sealing the top of his head to stop bad dreams from entering while he slept. During the first year I would usually pull out between five and nine bad dreams each night. Nicholas began sleeping through the night and functioning much better during the day. It has been more than five years since we began the "Bad Dream" ritual.

I often reflect upon what our ritual does for me and the effect it has on my life. It not only helped Nicholas, but it also helped me deal with my own bad dreams in ways that are hard to explain. Apparently, in pulling the "bad dreams" out of your children, you exorcise some of your own demons as well. I am thankful in so many ways to share these moments with my boy, away from all distractions that life brings.

To this day, Nicholas will yell out to me from his bed, "Daddy, you have to do my bad dreams." It would be nice if this lasted forever, but I know someday our routine will end. Pulling out Nicholas's bad dreams has become very important to me, as I know it has for him. Someday, when he is much older, I hope I can tell him how our ritual has helped me deal with my own troubling thoughts and made me a better dad.

CONTAGIOUS CONNECTIONS

Take time to be there for your family and friends. Helping others works like a boomerang—in the end, it always comes full circle.

OPPORTUNING

BARRY LINDSTROM

Years ago, back in middle school, we were running laps at the end of basketball practice. As we started our fifth lap, Coach walked out to center court dribbling the basketball, as he always did. He watched for the leaders to approach the end of lap five and then, without a moment's hesitation, he hurled the ball toward the basket behind him. The arc was perfect, and we were sure that this time he would make it in. But, as always, the shot careened off the backboard, and so our next five laps began.

During each practice when we ran the additional five laps, Coach would talk to us. He would tell us about things to watch for in the next game, or he would reflect on our well-played scrimmage. Often, Coach would share stories of former players who had gone on to become doctors, lawyers, or teachers. We would listen as we ran, and as the leaders approached the end of lap ten, Coach would joke about some of us looking too fresh and maybe needing another ten laps. Then, without a moment's hesitation, he would again hurl the ball over his head toward the basket behind him. We would all stop running to watch every time he threw this second midcourt shot because this time, despite the incredible odds, we knew the shot was going in. Coach would always holler, "Why are you guys stopping?" to which came the obligatory, unified response, "Because you never miss the same shot twice!" This question and answer routine was always followed by the swish of the lesson learned, as the basketball hit its mark and went through the net.

Much to my father's dismay, I stopped playing basketball after seventh grade, finding football more appealing than basketball, even though basketball was the sport that had made my dad a legend. However, I never forgot the wisdom of Coach Newsome and his unbelievable string of midcourt shots.

A few years later, I was playing in a championship football game. We had overcome two horrendous calls made by the clearly biased refs as well as a much more athletic team of adversaries. With less than two minutes to go, we were in the lead and the other team was eighty yards from the end zone with no timeouts. Forty years have not been able to wipe the memory of the next play from my psyche.

The other team lined up in the formation I had seen so many times on film and the chalkboard, and I drew an imaginary bead on the halfback who would surely get the ball. However, at the snap, I began to move in slow motion. I was perfectly positioned to intercept the lateral pass bound for the other player I was covering, but when it came, the ball seemed to pass right through me and end up in the hands of my opponent. I turned to tackle him, but my arms only cut through the empty air, and I missed him. I watched as each of my teammates tried to stop this opponent from reaching the goal line, but they were all as powerless as I was. As expected, the other team scored the touchdown, and within a matter of seconds, we had lost the lead. With ninety seconds to go in the game, we were given another chance to redeem ourselves. But in a defeat that I remember to this day, my best friend inexplicably dropped a perfectly thrown ball in the end zone as time ran out.

Our fans blamed my best friend for the loss and he took it very hard. But in the locker room after the game, I announced to the team that this loss was my fault, not his. If I had just made that interception or that tackle, we wouldn't have needed another touchdown. One by one, each of my teammates stepped forward and announced the mistakes that they had made throughout the contest. Soon, we were all feeling as miserable as our teammate who made the last mistake and dropped the pass that would have won us the game.

As we were all admitting the personal errors that we'd made, my old basketball coach, Coach Newsome, came in to console his good friends on the football staff. Remembering the lesson Coach Newsome had taught us, one of my football teammates shouted, "This ain't basketball, Coach. We don't get a second shot at this."

Coach turned and said, "Well, I'm certainly proud that after three and a half years of high school, Mr. Chomski knows that he hasn't been playing basketball." Some of us smiled, and Coach went on to teach us something that has resonated with me my entire life.

"Boys, I'm not going to stand here and tell you that losing a game like this shouldn't hurt, and I'm certainly not going to tell you that this wasn't a once-in-a-lifetime opportunity. It was. Now, I don't know why you weren't allowed to win here tonight, but I will tell you this. Just like the guys who are whooping it up over there in the other locker room, you're going to remember this game for the rest of your life. You'll remember what could have been if you had just made one different move. When your next once-in-a-lifetime opportunity comes along, and believe me, you'll all see a lot more of them, you will adjust and put yourself in a better position to emerge victorious. The important thing to remember is missing one shot does not make you a loser."

Just as in basketball, Coach Newsome taught us that just because your first shot doesn't go in, it doesn't mean that you'll miss your second one.

CONTAGIOUS WISDOM

Opportunities abound at the best and worst times, and you are not always able to take advantage of them and emerge victorious. However, missing a shot that you take in life only serves as a lesson, and it will make you stronger and more prepared when a second opportunity comes along. Just learn from your mistakes, aim again, and take a second shot.

MY FRIEND, SAINT NICHOLAS

LEE SHILO

I was twelve years old when my mother decided that I should have a dog. She had just separated from my abusive father and moved our family to a new town, and as a young boy, the transition was difficult for me. My only sibling was my sister, who was ten years older than me, and I felt isolated in my new home without my father in my life. I had other issues as well; I was hypoglycemic, so my blood sugar was often very low, and I also frequently wet the bed. It was a troubling time in my life. Concerned that I did not have any friends, my mom decided to get me a dog for Christmas.

We didn't have a car, so my mother asked a friend to make the hour-long drive to the Good Shepherd Animal Shelter with us. The shelter was an old, converted house run by nuns, and for a small donation we could adopt a pet. When we arrived, a pleasant nun wearing big rubber boots greeted us, and she was eager to show us around. After looking around at all the animals, we finally arrived at a cage with five dogs in it. All but one of the dogs came clamoring up, panting and barking, but the only dog that caught my eye was the small, short-haired fox terrier that was too little to make it past the other dogs. My mother had instructed me that the dog I chose had to be small, and I immediately wanted this one.

"What's that one's name?" I asked, pointing to the small dog in the back.

"His name is Saint Nicholas, oddly enough," the nun replied.

I thought the dog was perfect since it was the Christmas season, and I begged my mom to let me get him. The nun smiled as my mother relented and paid the small donation to the shelter. From there on out, I didn't go anywhere without Nicky. No one messed with me when he was around, and he was my friend throughout the difficult time after my parents' divorce. He protected me, and he was even allowed on my bed when it was time to go to sleep. When I lay down each night, Nicky would nuzzle under the blankets and keep my feet warm.

However, though Nicky comforted me when I felt alone in my new town, he didn't fix all of my problems, and my mother was getting increasingly concerned about my bed-wetting. It was an embarrassing issue for me, and she felt I was too old to be having that problem. My mom was desperate to find a way for me to control it, but being a nurse, she knew that forcing the issue wouldn't help. So, since there wasn't much she could do, she hoped that I would simply outgrow it.

One evening in May, just before my thirteenth birthday, my mother and sister were stripping the beds to do laundry. When my mother entered my room, she was horrified at what she saw. There was Saint Nicholas, standing on my bed, peeing on my mattress. My mother would have gotten rid of him after that if it was not for my incessant wailing to keep him, and my promise to take him out for regular bathroom breaks. Although that incident was the end of him sleeping on my bed with me, it wasn't all bad. Since my mother had caught Nicky in the act, she thought it had been him peeing on my bed all along. My dog had brought me back from the brink of loneliness during a difficult time, and inadvertently saved me from the shame of being a bed-wetter.

CONTAGIOUS FRIENDSHIP

Even when you feel lonely, remember that friendship often exists in unexpected places.

NO CHILD IS BORN PREJUDICED

LEE LIVELY-GARCIA

Have you ever known a child to be born prejudiced? You may have heard a child utter something prejudicial, but instances like these are no doubt due to the influence of an adult. This is how we end up hearing a child talk about a belief system that he has not had enough time in his life to understand. The child is just parroting the ideas adults have said.

Teaching our children to be prejudiced is not only an injustice to them, but also a reflection of how we are unable to rise above our experiences or lessons we learned from previous generations.

A situation that affected me tremendously happened when I was a day-care teacher. I was standing on the playground one day with a class of five-year-olds. One came up to me and told me that another child was not letting him play in one of the tunnels on the playground. I looked inside the tunnel and there was another child sitting there. I asked him why he was not letting his classmate play in the tunnel, and he looked at me very confused and said he had never tried to stop him from coming in the tunnel. So I asked the first child why he thought the other little boy wasn't letting him play. He proceeded to tell me that he couldn't go in the same tunnel with the little boy because he was white and the boy in the tunnel was black.

I honestly didn't know what to say. I had never experienced such prejudice in a child before and his matter-of-fact attitude about it was even more disturbing. He wasn't angry or mean about it; he was just parroting the opinions and beliefs that an adult had taught him. He thought it was "right" because someone he trusted told him so. I stood there thinking about the mistreatment of that innocent trust.

We all have experiences in our lives that shape and mold our opinions and beliefs, but is it right to pass on the negative experiences to our children? What we carry within ourselves happened to us, not them.

Children are born with completely clean slates, which is a gift that we should value and embrace. Experience the world through their eyes and give yourself the chance at a new perspective. We can send our children into a more positive future with this one simple and selfless act.

CONTAGIOUS INFLUENCE

Children are innocent and trust so easily. We should never abuse their trust by feeding them negative words and impressions. Doing so helps neither party. Instead, teach your children to be kind and open-minded; give them the opportunity to approach the world with an open, unbiased heart. In turn, you will come to feel better about yourself, and you will be someone your children can be truly proud of.

DEFINING ADULTHOOD IN THE ABSENCE OF CHILDHOOD

KIMBERLEE M. HOOPER

We begin our lives as helpless infants who rely on others to protect and provide for us. As we grow, we rely on what we have learned to guide us, and eventually become adults who look back on our childhood and teen years as tender reminders of our innocence, naïveté, and growth. We then use those memories and experiences to reflect on and shape the person we are today. But what if your childhood and teenage years did not exist? Would you be able to redesign your adulthood and reshape your future without any knowledge of your past?

When I was twenty-one years old, I became ill with a disease called encephalitis, an acute inflammation of the brain. I suffered a grand mal seizure and fell into a coma for several days, only to awaken with almost no memory of my past. I had no idea who I was, where I was going, or how I came to be. I was a stranger to myself. It would have been easy to give up and shut down, but I was not ready to take the easy way out. I felt that if I had worked so hard to get to that particular point in my life, it must have been for a good reason and I owed it to myself to continue on the best I knew how. I thought that if I did not know who I was, I would use what I had already set up for myself to redefine who I was going to be. My hope was that I had left enough of a path for myself to find a way back to what I was meant to do and who I was meant to be.

I spent a few years living in fear that if the encephalitis recurred, I would lose everything all over again. I would lose the new memories I made, the relationships I regained, the life I created from all the stories people shared to help me through, and I had nothing to fall back on because my childhood was already gone. Even today there are moments when the fear hits me rather hard and I worry that if the illness struck again, I would lose the memory of my husband, my daughter, and my baby on the way. But I've learned that all you can really do is embrace each day and be thankful for what you have at that moment. Create memories and cherish every second you have with loved ones. I may not have the memory of my childhood, but had I not lived it, my family would not have those memories to share with me, and I can honestly say that sharing memories can be as powerful as having them yourself.

Life can be trying but it can present you with situations that, if approached correctly, can act as opportunities that become the most defining moments in your life. Without those crucial memories, milestones, and firsts (first day of school, first best friend, first kiss, etc.), it can be difficult to understand how to create a life out of what seems like someone else's plans. However, past memories are not the only way to define who you will become in the future. Creating new memories and building from them can be as compelling as remembering old ones. There will always be opportunities to experience milestones and create memories. You can choose who you want to be, how you want to get there, and what will happen if your path is skewed along the way. Just remember that no matter how you get to where you are today, you are the one in the driver's seat and you can make a stop, a turn, or continue to move forward at any time. Your path is your own.

CONTAGIOUS CONTROL

Your past is not the only thing that defines you; your actions in forging your own future indicate who you are. You have the freedom to create an enjoyable future.

A Few Words for the Young

A poem by Karen Lyons Kalmenson

A few words for the young
Love with a heart
That is full and open
Never discard your dreams
And keep on hoping
Love with each cell
That keeps you alive
A life filled with love
Is the only way to thrive
Love with the gratitude
That we are blessed
Keep only positive attitudes
And discard the rest

CHAPTER FIVE

BELIEVE IN YOURSELF AND THE VALUE YOU POSSESS

You are not "a dime a dozen."
Life evolves for every one of us.

"I am not a dime a dozen!" This famous line spoken by Willy Loman in the Arthur Miller play *Death of a Salesman* was powerful when I was a teenager, and is just as powerful now that I'm an adult.

Evolving through our life, both personally and professionally, can be a positive thing. Many people want to advance through life, improve their financial position, and earn prestige and fame. But as time passes, and if things don't go exactly as planned, we tend to fall into that Willy Loman rut. We fear being a "cog in the wheel," especially when many around us seem to be advancing. As we age and watch others achieve more than us, the Willy Loman fear becomes even more apparent. No one wants to be referred to as "a dime a dozen." This fear has driven me to overachieve in many aspects of life at the cost of relationships and valuable time I will never get back. The countless nights, weekends, and years I have lost is something that I hope others will learn from as I share my stories, and the stories of others who have let "workaholism" prevent them from living a more balanced life.

When reading the biographies of successful people from the past 200 years, certain commonalities have always impressed me. First, many of them stayed positive and never lost sight of the goal; they persisted and persevered. Second, they surrounded themselves with talented people. Third, they never let competition or cynics distract them. Fourth, many lived a long life regardless of the healthcare conditions at the time.

You don't have to be the inventor of the automobile to exhibit similar traits and advance your professional life. You simply need to believe in yourself and your abilities, never lose sight of the goal, and remind yourself that happiness is tantamount to success.

David

> *My optimism and determination was positive and unassailable. I met most challenges head-on despite my disability. I grew up thinking positive, and believing in myself. I took pride in my abilities and was humble in defense of my shortcomings. I developed a surprising wit and sense of humor which has helped me cope with every obstacle I have faced.*
>
> —Linda Lattin, Saint Paul, Minnesota

> *My lack of experience and innate, high-strung personality made me that much more determined to succeed. In my eagerness, I attacked every assignment or chore with such intensity that inevitably I would mishandle or mess up on the first try. However, great news, the second attempt would usually go perfectly!*
>
> —Arnold Goldberg, Pompano Beach, Florida

BIKING AGAINST ALL ODDS

EMMANUEL OFOSU YEBOAH
Every story has a beginning, and my most important story started with a bike ride.

I was born in Ghana in 1977 with a missing right shinbone and a useless, dangling right foot. Since deformities are traditionally seen as curses in the deeply superstitious country of Ghana, my father abandoned my family in shame. I wasn't wanted by anyone other than my mother, Comfort, and friends and family even urged her to abandon or kill me.

Instead, my mother nurtured me and encouraged me to work hard and make something great of myself. And I strove to do just that. I took advantage of Ghana's free public education, and when I was too old for my mother to carry me the two miles each way to school, I would hop all the way on my one good leg. My schooling lasted until my mother fell ill, and at thirteen years old I dropped out in order to travel to Ghana's capital, Accra. Although most disabled people became street beggars, I wanted to work for my money, so I worked as a shoe shiner for just two dollars per day.

On Christmas Eve in 1997, my mother died, and her parting words became her last gift to me. She urged me to never let anybody put me down because of my disability, and those words stayed with me. They set me on a mission to prove that even disabled individuals could do great things. In order to show others that physically challenged people were not disabled in their minds, I decided I would bike 600 kilometers around Ghana to raise awareness for the struggle of the disabled. For my plan to work I needed to find a bike, so I wrote the first letter I'd ever written in my life to the Challenged Athletes Foundation (CAF), an organization in California that supports disabled athletes. The founder of the organization was so interested in the idea that he sent me a new mountain bike, biking gear, and $1,000.

With only my bike and my dream, I trained and sought support from my government for several months. After multiple attempts, I was finally able to arrange a meeting with Ghana's King Osagyefuo. That meeting not only made me the first disabled person to ever be granted entrance into the palace, but it also won me the King's support, and in 2001 I began my journey. Wearing a red shirt that read "The Pozo," slang for a disabled person, I rode almost 400 miles through Ghana with just one leg. Over the several months that it took me to complete my journey, I stopped to speak to disabled children, notable, high-ranking people, and church leaders. The media followed me on my journey, and my platform allowed me to speak out against the Ghanaian government's policy on the disabled.

After I completed my ride, the CAF invited me to participate in the 2002 Triathlon Challenge in California, and I completed the bike leg of the event in seven hours. While in California, doctors at the Loma Linda University Orthopedic and Rehabilitation Center examined me and declared me a good candidate for a prosthetic leg. They asked me if I would be willing to undergo an amputation to be fitted for the device, and I accepted the offer, recalling the athletes I had seen running and biking with prostheses at the CAF Triathlon. I hoped to one day be able to run, ride my bike with two legs, and even wear pants; just as some other disabled athletes were able to do.

In 2003, Loma Linda performed the operation free of

charge, and the staff at the hospital paid for my living expenses, as well as the expenses of my family back in Ghana. I will always be thankful for their kindness. The operation enabled me to wear pants and a pair of shoes for the first time in my life. Nearly two months after the operation, I again competed in the CAF Triathlon. The second time, I finished the fifty-six-mile bike course in four hours—three hours quicker than my initial attempt. Back home in Ghana, I proudly walked into my church on my own two feet for the first time in my life.

I have always tried to honor my mother's final wishes with my endeavors and success, and as a result, I have been humbled by the praise I have received for my achievements. In 2003, the CAF named me the Most Inspirational Athlete of the Year, and Nike presented me with $25,000 and the Casey Martin Award, given to honor an athlete who has overcome physical, mental, societal, or cultural challenges to excel in his or her sport. CAF generously matched that gift with another $25,000, and I used the money to create the Emmanuel Education Fund in Ghana. Through the fund, I have committed to putting fifteen disabled students through school each year and I have helped organize the distribution of hundreds of wheelchairs to disabled Ghanaians. I have made it my goal to ensure that disabled children have a chance for a good education, good medical care, and the opportunity to play sports, and my work has allowed me to prove that disabled Ghanaians should be proud of themselves. If they believe in themselves, there is no height they cannot reach.

CONTAGIOUS OVERCOMING ODDS

You can overcome any obstacle as long as you believe in yourself.

DARKNESS TO LIGHT

TERI CATLIN

This is my story of climbing out of the darkness.

I was born in Flint, Michigan, in 1968. I've never known my biological parents, but I do know that my mother was white and my father was black and part-Indian. I came out mixed, or as I like to say, "butterscotch," and after living in a foster home until I was almost two years old, I was adopted by two of the most brutally abusive people I have ever known. They beat, strangled, and burned me on a daily basis, and I remember sometimes, after abusing me, my adoptive father would look at me, smile, and ask me what I was crying about.

Throughout those years of abuse I began developing an interest in music, and that became my lifeline. At the age of five I began playing and making up songs on my adoptive mom's piano, and when I was seven, my adoptive parents had me take up the violin, which I soon grew to love. Playing was a safe escape, and I began practicing up to nine hours a day. I quickly became known as a child prodigy on the violin, and that classical training was the best gift my adoptive parents could have given me. My music was sacred; it was the one thing I wanted to protect.

When I turned fourteen, I realized that though my body could withstand the physical abuse, my mind no longer could. So, in order to keep my sanity, I ran away from home, doing anything to survive. I would play the piano and sing at hotels and restaurants for tips, which gave me just enough money to eat. However, I eventually fell in with the wrong crowd, and I started stealing in order to feed and clothe myself. I stole cars, broke into people's homes, robbed stores, and sold drugs.

I slept in abandoned buildings and on benches, and in the winter I'd sneak into unlocked cars or I'd crawl into big garbage bins to find warmth for the night. I saw people get shot and stabbed, and I would often have to fight to keep from being raped or beaten up. I eventually became addicted to drugs and alcohol, and there was no one to tell me that I shouldn't take six hits of acid at a time, or that mixing pills with a pint of liquor might kill me. I didn't care, anyway. I felt like an angry, wild animal, alone in the world, and I thought that overdosing would be a blessing. That was one of the darkest times in my life, but even then, I held on to my dream of one day using my music to free myself.

I eventually drifted from Michigan to Florida, and though I was still homeless, I decided to leave the stealing and fighting in Flint, and find a new way of surviving. During the day I would dip into bars and play pool for money, and one day, one of my new friends asked me if I wanted to stay with her because she had an extra bed. That act of kindness changed my life forever. With a roof over my head, I was able to get my first job at Sands Harbor Hotel. I saved up for four years, got my own place, and eventually bought my very first vehicle: a motorcycle. All the while, I looked for ways to use my music to create a life for myself.

Although I had improved my life, I continued to struggle with substance abuse. I'll never forget the moment when I caught myself on all fours, eating white lint balls off the carpet floor because I thought the lint was crack. I broke down crying, and I remember screaming at God, "You've given me this gift of music and I'm trying to use it!" I expected God to give me a sign, but it wasn't until a few months later that I realized that to use my gift, I first needed to save myself. So I made the decision to stop drinking and using drugs, and I have been completely sober since that day, with no interest or plans to look back.

Once I climbed out of the darkness, I was able to create light by following my passion: music. My music is everything to me. I have won many awards and contests, and I have shared the stage with many well-known people. It brings me the purest joy I've ever known. I have been blessed to share my story with thousands of people through music, and many have told me that my music has encouraged them to change their life in a positive way. I have accomplished so much on my own, but I know God has an even bigger plan for me. I owe it to the little girl who survived those horrific streets of Flint to be more successful.

Optimism pushed me forward, and it is my ultimate gift and contribution. All my music comes down to one thing: the experience of being alive, with all the joy and pain that goes with it. I feel that we are all going through a similar struggle, but we can get through it if we embrace our own light and share our experiences.

CONTAGIOUS PERSEVERANCE
WITH PASSION

You can find strength and salvation when you commit yourself to doing the things you love to do. Therefore, think about something that you have a passion for in your own life. What role has this passion played, how has it helped you, and what has it saved you from, if anything? Perhaps doing something you truly love has motivated you to keep going when you felt low, perhaps it has provided a positive distraction when you felt stuck, or perhaps it has just been a source of great joy and contentment in your life. Regardless, finding something you love and sticking with it is one of the most important things you can do for yourself. Therefore, find your passion, harness your talent, and allow it to strengthen you.

YOU NEVER KNOW WHERE
THE PATH MAY TAKE YOU

HENRY WISEMAN

We all fantasize during our youth about what we will be when we grow up. We think, I want to be a fireman, doctor, lawyer, or astronaut. Well, the truth is that the vast majority of us never go on to do the things we dreamed about. In fact, we rarely know what path to take and have no idea, once we choose it, where that path might lead us.

I grew up in a middle-class neighborhood in Baltimore, where I hung out on the street corner with seven other guys from the same socioeconomic background. None of us could have imagined that the small things we did, good or bad, would take us down such different paths. One of those guys went on to be the CEO of one of America's biggest corporations. Another has gone on to spend a lifetime fighting a drug addiction.

I have personally spent more than thirty-five years in the international transportation and supply chain logistics field. I can say I never thought about that field as a kid growing up, not even for a second. However, I essentially fell into my line of work because I got married during my last year in college, and I needed a part-time job. By chance, I went to work for a company that provided international transportation services. I had no intention of making that my chosen career path, but instead thought of myself as having a career in marketing based on the degree that I would earn upon graduation. However, once I actually graduated, I was offered the chance to work full-time instead of part-time, and in the height of a mini recession, accepting that job offer was practical. I did recognize that no matter what the job was, working hard and doing my best would lead to my own personal success.

Having finished my corporate career as a senior executive for one of the largest transportation companies in the world, I can say that is how it worked for me. Despite the fact that I had not envisioned myself in my particular line of work, I still gave it my all and worked hard, and that is how I found my success. The message here is simple: in today's world there are many career paths to choose from. The important point is that once you decide on a path, you have to apply yourself, and make it your objective to do the best you can in order to become successful in that job. This will lead to opportunities that will in turn lead to your overall success in life.

CONTAGIOUS PERFORMANCE

Give everything 110% and be the best at what you do. Don't worry when life is not what you envisioned. You never know where you will end up, but being a good, honest, hardworking person will certainly help you get there.

THE CASE FOR ENTREPRENEURIAL OPTIMISM

RICHARD MASTERSON

> *I'd rather be a failure at something I love than a success at something I hate.*
> —George Burns

I was the child of an alcoholic mother, I was only an average student, and I attended community college my freshman year. Reflecting on my youth, there was no indication that one day I would become a successful businessman, father, and philanthropist. However, I overcame my own setbacks and today I credit my success to the "four horsemen": hard work, integrity, passion, and optimism.

I have been an entrepreneur for over twenty-five years, accomplishing things I never thought possible. However, though I always worked hard, I never worked for the sake of money. Instead, I found the joy in work and eventually it led me to success. To date, I have made an internet company public, built a luxury hotel, operated a golf course, and became active in philanthropy. I am proud of what I have achieved, but none of this success would have been possible without optimism.

Optimism is not recognized on a balance sheet or income statement, but it is just as important as other assets. Although you are not likely to have more financial resources than all your competitors, and you may or may not have intellectual superiority, a "can do" attitude will fuel success. A positive attitude will not only keep you motivated, but it will inspire your staff to achieve more than they believe is possible.

In my early years, this positive attitude kept me going in my business pursuits, despite the fact that friends and family were not as supportive of my entrepreneurial decisions as I might have hoped. It was not because they did not love me. It was quite the contrary—they wanted me to avoid the pain of failure. But I remained determined, my optimism fueled by both my ambition and the fact that I really had nothing to lose. While many people may avoid choosing the entrepreneurial career path out of fear of rejection and disappointment, I was never one of those people.

If you have chosen the life of an entrepreneur, then you are in a select group of optimistic dreamers. Once you start your journey, the initial thrill of making the jump will likely fade and be replaced by numerous challenges and obstacles. However, most entrepreneurs I know had several failures on their way to success, and whether driven by ambition, optimism, or resilience, the most important thing they did was keep moving forward.

Although I recognize that it is not always easy to be optimistic, and though I often struggle with self-doubt and worry, I never let my worries get in the way of my vision. Even in moments of doubt, I remain enamored with an idea or an opportunity; I remain confident in my ability to surmount the risks, obstacles, and challenges.

As Dwight D. Eisenhower said, "Pessimism never won any battle." When I reflect on the highs and lows of my business career, I realize how true these words are. Even in my darkest moments, I used optimism to get me through, and that is how I came out a winner. Like an athlete who visualizes hitting a baseball or sinking a putt, I can visualize a future state where I have achieved an objective, no matter how ambitious it may seem at the time.

CONTAGIOUS DEDICATION

When it comes to finding success in life, your background doesn't matter. Instead, the passion, integrity, and hard work that you put into your job matters the most.

THE JOURNEY, NOT THE PATH

ERIC BENSON

I am frequently faced with students who are depressed, anxious, and, simply put, overwhelmed with the ongoing realities of adulthood. They often come from highly successful families and are therefore intimidated by a sense of responsibility to achieve greatness. When these students feel they are not ready to meet their perceived goal, or the goals their parents have for them, they often shut down and begin behaving in self-destructive ways. There are three common strategies I use with these students to help them change this negative way of thinking.

The first strategy happens early on in our academic relationship. I ask one simple question: If you knew you could succeed and knew there was absolutely no chance of failing, what would you like to do with your life? I am usually surprised by my students' answers; they provide some true insight into who they are. Once my students tell me what they would do if they knew failure wasn't an option, I tell them to go for it. I also explain that even if they don't achieve whatever lofty goal they have set for themselves, shooting high will surely take them on a journey greater than they have imagined.

The next conversation I frequently have with them is to say that they cannot control the future. I tell them that they cannot control the nature of the path or the obstacles that will come their way, and I give them a hypothetical situation to ponder. I say, suppose I told you to run through a forest that had no paths, unsure of the best way through. When you see a tree you avoid it, when you see a stream you cross it, and when you see an inviting meadow, you explore it. You do this all while traveling in the same general direction, and you know the path does not matter because you are creating it as you go. You also know that on some level even getting to the other side of the forest does not matter; it's the journey that's important. The only thing that matters is the pure joy of experiencing life in general. Enjoy the journey for what it is; no enjoyment can be gained by wishing the trees out of your way.

The last conversation I like to have with students concerns the Bhagavad Gita, a very famous Hindu text. In the story, two great armies are amassed for battle. Arjuna, the main character, is riding in a chariot driven by Lord Krishna, and he sees a great tragedy about to ensue because his family and friends are on both sides of the army. When Arjuna throws down his bow and openly refuses to fight, Krishna angrily calls him a coward and demands that he stand and fight. Arjuna is shocked by Krishna's response and does not understand why such a peaceful man, who has a reputation for nonviolence, is demanding that he fight.

Krishna goes on to explain that he reacted the way he did because Arjuna was allowing himself to be crippled by his fear of the future and the unknown outcome of the battle. Krishna insists that the outcome of the battle, and who lives and dies, is not Arjuna's responsibility; his only responsibility is to command his army and to do his part. The point is this: It's about playing your part, not about being tied to the outcome.

Of course, most of my students would be completely turned off if I started spouting scripture, so I often try to illustrate the idea differently. Imagine playing a game of chess. When you are playing chess, are you focused on the task of winning or worried you are going to lose? When you are truly enjoying the game, are you worried about either one? Most would say no. I suggest playing each move to the best of your ability and taking each situation as it comes. You may have some influence on the outcome, but you are not in ultimate control, and you share the outcome with your opponent. You are not alone in the experience; it is a dance and a game. It is a dialogue of mental, contemplative strategy, just like life. So just enjoy the game. It is not about winning; it is about the experience.

CONTAGIOUS EXPERIENCE

It's good to have goals, but achieving them or failing to achieve them is not as important as you may think. It is more important to learn from the journey and to continue to see life as a game from which you can gain knowledge—no matter whether you win or lose.

THE POWER OF POSITIVE FEELING IN THE WORKPLACE

DR. DONALD E. GIBSON

Smiling just feels good. It feels better to be in a positive mood than a negative one. Why, then, is being cheerful often considered suspect in business organizations? I've been told that the business environment is supposed to be "serious" and "rational," and if you want to be happy, do it on your own time—not here in the corporate world, where you should only focus on getting the job done.

I've found that many organizations support the idea that narrowing human feelings in the professional space is the best way to manage employees and foster job performance. However, according to recent scientific research, this widely accepted belief is wrong. Using evidence from a variety of fields, a recent meta-analysis of social psychological studies reveals that being in a positive mood and expressing positive feelings is actually critical to success in organizations and in life. This is because affirmative feelings can foster a person's desire to develop new goals and engage with them. Such feelings are also correlated with confidence, optimism, self-efficacy, likability, activity, energy, flexibility, and the ability to better cope with challenges and stress. Far from being a distraction from task performance, cheerful feelings may in fact motivate people, thus benefiting the workplace.

Let's drill down a bit on these research findings. Looking at job performance, the evidence shows that employees who are more cheerful also receive better evaluations from their supervisors, are better negotiators, are more likely to go above and beyond for the organization, and are more likely to make more money. The tendency for happier people to perform better on the job is especially true in the sales domain. Here, studies show how employees' upbeat moods can be "contagious," finding that happy salespeople tend to produce happier customers who tend to buy more of their product. In one study of shoe stores, employees' use of pleasant greetings, smiling, and eye contact with customers was related to the amount of time customers spent in the store and their willingness to come and shop there again.

However, positive feelings are not only related to sales performance. In the "serious" context of managerial decision making, researchers find that people who are in better moods are more likely to make good decisions. Happier people tend to ask for a greater amount of information before making their decisions, are more creative and flexible in the options they consider, and make more accurate decisions. One intriguing study found that doctors who were given a small gift of candy, which made them feel happy, provided faster, more flexible thinking in their diagnoses of hypothetical illnesses.

What about business leaders and their teams? Contrary to the idea that hard-nosed, cranky bosses are more effective at getting their employees to work harder, studies show that leaders do better by expressing happiness. When leaders are in a positive mood, team members tend to experience more positive moods themselves, exhibiting more coordination and expending less effort in getting the job done. Overall, studies are showing that a leader's positive mood is associated with stronger team performance.

These findings suggest that if leaders and managers want to foster creativity and higher performance in their work teams, they should encourage teams to work on their emotional sides as well as their technical sides. Some innovative corporate teams are finding that engaging in fun activities before addressing an important problem helps to foster inventiveness and creativity. Teams who have fun together, and who laugh more than they bicker, are more likely to adapt to changing situations and devise clever answers to critical organizational dilemmas.

That's the power of positive feeling: It helps us perform and lead better, make better decisions, and work in greater harmony with others.

CONTAGIOUS POSITIVITY

Put on that smile. Not only does it feel good, it will help you work better, too.

ALLOWING THE WAY

NANCY KOENIG

Three years after graduating from college, I decided I was going to become a writer for the National Hockey League. Most viewed this as a ridiculous pipe dream; fortunately, I did not. I found nothing preposterous about making the transition from waitressing to sports writing, even though I lacked a degree in journalism, did not have any powerful contacts in the industry, and was female. Looking back, I realize the odds against me were stacked up to the rafters.

As I sat next to my brother at Rangers games, I watched the media members in the press section in front of our seats. I pictured myself among them, smiling, with a press credential dangling from my neck. I had no understanding of the law of attraction back then, but I was a big daydreamer and I continued to hold this image on a regular basis.

My boyfriend of the era was a Bruins fan who created an incredible website. At the time, the Internet was just starting to become all the rage, and a start-up hockey site invited him to write for them. He declined but suggested they contact me. This website did not yet have a press credential to offer and they did not pay, but they took me on, someone who was greener than a summer leaf. I still get a good chuckle when I look at my earliest pieces, the first of which were written by hand since I didn't yet have a computer. Each week, I diligently sat down to scribble my opinions about all things Rangers, and my boyfriend typed my stories and emailed them to my editor. I had no idea at the time how kind this was—I was also a novice in the gratitude department.

There were two rules: we were not permitted to attend any events or speak with any players on behalf of the website. Never having been much of a rules girl, I broke both the same night. I attended a charity event and spoke to several players in attendance. The public relations representative from the Rangers overheard me chatting with one and called my bluff. "If you're writing a story about this, the guy you really want to talk to is Adam Graves." Ten minutes later, he directed me to him.

Graves was my favorite player, but I couldn't get myself any deeper into the mess I seemed to be creating, so I hid among the crowd on another level of this two-story gala. The PR guy found me. "What are you doing?" he asked, hands in the air. "Graves is waiting for you!" Knowing I could not escape again, I told him I'd be there in two minutes. Real reporters have recorders; I didn't even have a pen. I set off for my first NHL interview armed with the back of an event program and a crayon, the best writing instrument a Garden employee could produce.

Adam was his usual affable, gracious, incredible self; not only did he completely accept the crayon, but he also treated me as if I were from the *New York Times*. When I got home, I wrote a story about the event and sent it to my editor, along with an apology. "I understand if you don't want me to write for you anymore, but feel free to post the story anyway."

The following day, the story went up on the website—I didn't get fired. Then something even more miraculous happened: the Rangers gave the site its first press credential for me to attend games and have access to the players for interviews. Within a year, I was writing for NHL.com, the official website of the National Hockey League.

When it comes to our career, limiting beliefs can stand in the way of our dreams. We may believe opportunities are scarce, competition is high, and the type of career we want won't pay enough. We may struggle with limiting beliefs about ourselves, our abilities, or what we deserve. Monetarily, we may be absorbed in fear and scarcity thinking, which serve as barriers between us and our desires.

These fears and beliefs disguise themselves as realities, and grow stronger as we find evidence to back them up. By recognizing the ways we limit ourselves and looking for evidence of the contrary, we begin to create the professional lives we all deserve to lead. What shows up in our external world is merely a reflection of what is stored in our internal one. Exploring and upgrading our beliefs about professional possibilities and visualizing the results we want are crucial steps in allowing our desired careers to unfold.

CONTAGIOUS REBELLION

Don't let preconceptions and stereotypes stand in the way of your dreams. If you have the right drive and do whatever it takes to achieve your dreams, you can prove others—and yourself—wrong.

BE A CAREER VENTURER

BHARATH GOPALAN

I am a strong believer in the idea of "stay and play." I never fail to join my daughters in cheering on the "Minute to Win It" game show contestants on TV who choose to stay and play rather than dashing away with the cash. When we see people going beyond their normal limits and taking worthwhile risks, we get the urge to break out of our own comfort zones and to strive to be what we truly are capable of.

During the mid-nineties, I witnessed this firsthand. I worked in a banknote press in a sleepy little town in India and managed a crew of about thirty people in the finishing and packing section. Most people I worked with had no care or desire to stretch even an inch beyond their normal call of duty, but there was one person, Shant, who did. He was always striving to go above and beyond, and do things better. With the speed of a fielder in a cricket match, he would vault to attend to machine breakdowns; his enthusiasm was simply infectious. Though he was only an operator, he would call his crew for a chat in the evenings and set targets for the next day. He was raising the bar for his crew without any real authority bestowed upon him. Being his manager, I would often find myself embarrassed about my own leadership capabilities. Watching him gave me the desire to strive harder and be better.

Spotting his talent, the management thought Shant would be a better fit at the training center and moved him there. Highly enthused, he started conducting training sessions not only for workmen and staff, but also for officers. Some of the officers did not like this because they felt that hierarchy mattered more, and they threw Shant back to the machine operation section, where they believed he belonged.

Instead of working in a position that he knew was not right, Shant quit his job and ventured into a direct marketing business. Some of his previous colleagues doubted his caliber and made fun of his decision, and others predicted his doom in the coming days. However, his faith in himself proved stronger than the doubts of others. Today his business has flourished, so much so that I'm sure the very same people who didn't believe in him would not mind queuing up to join his growing business, abandoning their false sense of prestige. Shant made it a point to take a risk and go beyond what others thought he could do, and in doing so, he reached his full potential.

More often, it is "what we want to have" that holds more importance than what we want to actually *be* and *do* in life. When I meet up with young people who are looking for jobs, I invariably ask them, "What would you look for in your job?"

The usual reply would run along these lines: good starting pay, an impressive designation to flaunt, and of course, a big brand. While I do not undermine the importance of these tangible factors in making one's career decision, I urge them to pay heed to a more pertinent question: "What do you want to be doing in your job, day in and day out?" If we only let the pay and perks guide the decisions of our lives, or if we stay in a position just because it is safe, then we can't grumble about having a job that is essentially unappealing and unsatisfying to us. However, if we consider our passions and true talents, and then act on them, we can find real happiness and success.

Instead of looking at opportunities in terms of the material benefits, we should explore their scope to enable our self expression, which I would call an inside-out approach to career.

Here, you first try to find out who you are, what you stand for, what interests you innately, and what you are passionate about. When you have discovered yourself, you start doing what you are passionate about and then strive for excellence. Eventually, the opportunities show up to meet your talents, and in the process, you achieve what you have set out to conquer. If you ask me whether it is a sure shot to get what you want, I can only say it will take determination and hard work. However, working toward your goals will certainly lead to a sense of purpose and fulfillment in life, and a sense of achievement at the end of the day.

CONTAGIOUS RISK

Consider your passions and talents, and act on them.

FORGING A NEW PATH

MERRY NACHEMIN

For thirty years I worked as a social worker. The last twenty, I established and ran an outpatient mental health program for senior citizens through a small private agency. As time progressed, the state of the mental health field went awry, very much along the lines of the economy, but worse. The funding for my program was faltering and I knew it. I also knew it was time to shift gears. One day I was on the subway and saw an ad for the Image Consulting Program at the Fashion Institute of Technology. Although I had been fully engaged in the social work profession, I was always a fashion and makeup-oriented woman, so this program sounded appealing to me. I signed up and attended the first class on a Wednesday evening in June. It seems that following my intuition paid off, because on Thursday morning I got laid off from my job as a social worker.

When my boss called me into her office to tell me the news, she clearly expected me to have a meltdown. She had the chief of psychiatry there along with the head psychologist and our comptroller. She anticipated that I would be shaken, but when she informed me of my layoff, my mind immediately skipped ahead to an attorney and accountant I knew and how quickly I could get a new LLC up and running. After my boss told me the news, she said, "Merry, you don't even look upset!" I told her that I was simply in shock.

"I suppose you want to give me two weeks' notice?" I asked.

I was surprised when my boss informed me that she wanted me to continue working through the summer, and was even more surprised at my feelings of disappointment at that thought.

As the summer drew to a close, I finished my work for the agency, said goodbye to my clients and the staff, and never looked back. It took me no time at all to get situated in a new career, and now I am an image consultant and makeup artist, and I also do coaching for people who are transitioning in their careers. I have never been happier. Although I loved my job as a social worker, I am thankful that I followed my gut and my passion, and that I have been able to create a new life for myself doing something else that I love. Now that's embracing change and optimism with both hands!

CONTAGIOUS CHANGE

Change can happen unexpectedly, but that might not be a bad thing! A period of change can also mean a period of growth. So take this time to reflect on what you've wanted to change about yourself or your life. If you think that you would feel happier or more fulfilled by following a different path, then go for it. Only good things can come from staying positive and following your passion.

COURAGE FROM OPTIMISM

DAVID MEZZAPELLE

We have all heard the expression "Get up, dust yourself off, and move on." How easy is it to say that when fear isn't staring you in the face? For those who have endured life-changing adversity and traumatic experiences, getting up and simply moving on may be the last thing they are willing to do.

Our fears seem to stem from two distinct places. One of them is the unknown. Fears of the unknown are natural and innate, as if a resistance has formed and we can't seem to penetrate it. Our fears also come from past experiences. Whether we went through something scary ourselves, or we witnessed someone else go through a difficult situation, the experience stayed with us and left us with fear. Well, if you have ever known fear, I am happy to report that others have been in the same boat as you; you are not alone. And, for many, their perseverance ultimately led to surmounting those fears and establishing strong foundations of courage.

According to the Merriam-Webster dictionary, *courage* is defined as "the quality of mind or spirit that enables a person to face difficulty, danger, pain, etc., without fear." A synonym is *bravery*. This is a terrific definition because it tells us that we each have the ability to gather courage and bravery; as long as we can mentally and spiritually face difficult situations, then none of us are exempt from that ability.

Many people will tell you that courage can be found simply by facing your fears. This is true, but in my opinion, it's not true enough. I believe that courage can be found just like success—through effort, hard work, and optimism. Every success in life comes with some sort of effort and hard work, so if you work toward facing your fears and gaining courage, you will eventually get there. However, as the definition of *courage* states, it's not all about hard work; having a certain mental or spiritual quality is essential as well. That is where I believe optimism comes into play.

Optimism comes from seeing how others have overcome fears similar to our own, and realizing that if they can overcome their adversity, we can too. It comes from understanding that if we think positively and persevere, we too can emulate the successful outcomes of others. It makes the "fear monsters" shrink: we become the monsters with the ability to squash them.

Over the years I have had the privilege of working and communicating with people all over the globe who have surmounted their fears in the face of adversity. I have seen people find courage after a devastating breakup or divorce, after a financial setback, after a serious accident, or after the loss of a loved one. I have seen courage in people who were tired of hiding, tired of fearing the unknown, and tired of being in last place. These people are not gladiators, athletes, or titans. They are just ordinary people who, with a combination of hard work, mental determination, spiritual resolve, and optimism, found that they could overcome anything.

Watching and reading about others who have found courage in even the most difficult times strengthens us in multiple ways. Learning from another's example is how we find the resilience to form a mountain of our own courage, which can lead us down paths we never thought we could traverse.

CONTAGIOUS COURAGE

Don't hide behind your fears. Instead, study how others have summoned bravery and positivity, and then gone on to overcome obstacles. Learn from them, and move forward as the courageous soul I guarantee you already are.

Am I

A poem by Karen Lyons Kalmenson

Am I defined
By my career
Or by the love
Of those I
Hold so dear?
Do they define
Me by what I do
Or by my loving
Heart that
Beats so true?

CHAPTER SIX

SERVICE THE ENGINE

*Improve your health through moderation, not
necessarily elimination.
And stop worrying! It does not do a body good!
Healing is as much a process of the mind as it is of
the body.*

I started writing this chapter while my father was at a medical center in New York. He went in for surgery to eliminate a stenosis in his neck that was affecting his balance. Because my father is a very active and athletic person, this balance issue was becoming a major problem. Not only that, but the progression of the stenosis indicated that he would eventually be unable to stand and could potentially fall, causing more problems. Therefore, after careful consideration, along with the assurance from his doctors that the procedure and recovery would go smoothly, he decided to move forward with the surgery.

Unfortunately, three days after the surgery he developed several postoperative setbacks, including a major infection, that stymied his recovery. Thankfully, the team of specialists was confident that this would be resolved and he would resume his normal life. However, at that moment it was hard to imagine a solid recovery based on his condition. The delirium, infection, and inability to walk were unpleasant and unsettling. Despite his condition, my dad had a positive outlook and continued to persevere, and I continued to write with confidence in his recovery. In addition to the care of professionals we trusted, the optimism and prayers from myself, other family and friends were important factors in the favorable outcome that he ultimately experienced.

While I was in high school, my mother fought breast cancer. At the time, she didn't want the family to worry, so we didn't know too many of the details. We only knew that she was sick, but we were confident she would be fine. She lived a normal life and was determined to get this behind her. Fortunately, she beat the cancer after several surgeries and treatments. Today she is cancer free over thirty years.

Health and healing is a broad topic. Some of us view health and healing as a solely physical process, and we depend on others to treat our illnesses and make us whole again. However, despite our physical ailments and health issues, we have to have confidence and optimism to look past our current discomfort, just as my dad did. We have to have faith in positive results before we reach them, and know that recuperation is the right road to be on no matter how uncomfortable or unpleasant.

For others, health and healing is a form of mental endurance. People can hurt from sadness, depression, stress, and major life adjustments such as job loss, death, retirement, or divorce. As with our physical health, we have to follow the guidance of professionals, be confident in ourselves, and visualize the end result in order to properly heal. In both the physical and mental scenario, positive forward thinking is imperative.

Healing not only comes from medical and spiritual professionals—it also comes from within. No matter what difficulty you may be going through, it is important to believe that with proper care, perseverance, and optimism, you can recuperate. Make your health a priority, and your healing a mission, and you will find that you can get through almost anything.

David

Once we begin to realize the feedback loop between thought and inner and outer experience, we can begin to become a conscious participant in the dance of the cells and touch on what was thought of as being miraculous.

—Madalyn Suozzo, San Francisco, California

Stress is inevitable in today's fast-paced world. We cannot avoid or ignore it, but we can change our reaction to it.

—Kathi Casey, East Otis, Massachusetts

OPTIMISM SPANS GENERATIONS

BARBARA WOODWORTH
It was summer 1941. The air was hot and steamy—the kind of weather that called for swimming. It was this unbearable weather that prompted eleven-year-old Bill and three friends to bike five miles on rural roads to their favorite swimming pond.

True, there were warnings. The impending polio epidemic was rapidly reaching reality, and there were many cases of people getting the disease due to contact with infected water, but Bill and friends paid no heed. They were drawn to the somewhat murky waters by the thought of splashing, getting cool, and having fun. And fun they had in the cool water on that hot day. They promised to return the following Saturday.

That, however, was a promise Bill was not able to keep. It wasn't long before his body was wracked with pain and fever. His legs wouldn't work as they should, and his usual happy demeanor was dampened. His typically ready laughter and sense of humor was severely muted. After he was incorrectly diagnosed with Rocky Mountain spotted fever, Bill's worried parents called upon an old friend, a chiropractor, who came to the house. This time the diagnosis was correct—and devastating. Polio, an illness that was increasingly claiming the lives and limbs of more and more victims, many of them children, had taken hold of Bill's young body.

After days of near-scalding hot baths at home, Bill was admitted to Children's Hospital in Utica, New York—a facility that would be his home for the next year. "It was the Sister Kenny treatment of hot wool towels applied to my legs several times a day that I attribute to my healing," recounts Bill. "As painful as it was to feel the intense heat of those towels on my legs, I am certain that the treatment—and my optimistic belief that I would recover despite the pessimistic assertions of some doctors—enabled me to walk again."

In the hospital, in spite of continued pain, and in spite of witnessing polio claim the lives of two young patients he had gotten to know, Bill realized that it wasn't only his physical body that needed to heal; his emotional well-being was in peril as well. To combat the sadness caused by his unfortunate situation, Bill turned to optimism and humor, and completely let it take hold. "If my legs didn't work, I knew it was imperative to strengthen my hands so that they could take over, especially when it came to steering my wheelchair," he says. "I focused every thought on what I could do to make my hands and arms stronger and stronger. I also made certain that every experience I encountered, even if it didn't have a positive outcome, was meaningful and laced with optimism and enthusiasm. Optimism became my mantra. If an idea or action wasn't successful the first time, I felt sure that with increased effort and modification I could make it so."

From organizing and carrying out wheelchair races through the hospital hallways to playing tricks on nurses, Bill took charge. He encouraged the other children to smile, joke, and laugh as well. When Bill was finally able to return home and go back to school, he caught up on the sixth- and seventh-grade work he missed. He resumed his friendships, and though he was no longer able to run fast and play baseball as he once did, he was also able to slowly pick up old hobbies and activities.

After Bill finished middle school and graduated from high school, he climbed the highest mountain in New York State,

Mt. Marcy, with a forty-pound pack on his back, and volunteered for the Air Force during the Korean War. "During my physical I tried very hard to keep the doctors from noticing my flat feet and the muscle limitations in my legs," he recalls. Bill's efforts were rewarded, and for the next four years he honorably served his country in the United States Air Force. Assigned to the Strategic Air Command, he completed two tours of duty in Africa.

The military not only provided him the opportunity to grow, learn, and travel, it also allowed him to take advantage of the GI Bill and continue his education. After finishing his tours in the Air Force, Bill attended Oswego State College, where he met and married his wife, Barbara. Together, they completed their four-year undergraduate education in three years. That way, Bill was able to retain his $110 per month GI Bill stipend to cover the cost of his master's degree. Soon after, Bill became the father of three children, got a job as a teacher, and then optimistically set out to tackle another hurdle—a doctorate. He became a dearly loved professor for twenty-five years, but eventually post-polio syndrome and a bout with Guillain-Barre syndrome, also known as French polio, necessitated his early retirement.

Today, Bill's residual pain persists, and despite a failed triple bypass surgery, severe back problems, prostate cancer, and a physical inability to do all the things he would like, his optimism pushes him on. This unflinching optimism remains intact, fueled by his boyhood sense of humor. He frequently voiced these words to his undergraduate and graduate students: "Optimism and a sense of humor are as vital to life as bread and water." His three college-age grandchildren, young adults who will soon face life in a sometimes trying world, are now heeding these words as well. As Bill has demonstrated, any difficulty can be overcome with the right mindset.

CONTAGIOUS PERSEVERANCE

No matter what difficulties you may face in your life, it is important to remain optimistic, positive, and dedicated. This is because hard times do not define who you are. Rather, your mindset and willingness to persevere defines who you are, and by combating darkness with optimism and humor, you can ensure a full and happy life.

MY SIX MONTHS WITH FLORENCE NIGHTINGALE

ESTELLE BERK

Her name was Beatrice, and she was a Haitian beauty who captured my heart. Beatrice was a certified nursing assistant who had completed much schooling to become a registered nurse, and the home health agency sent her to me after I had taken a bad fall. She came to the emergency room to pick me up and drive me home, and at the time, after my accident, I can't say I was in any mood to make friends. But I had no idea how special she would become to me.

At first, both Beatrice and I were aloof around each other, each measuring the other. As an eighty-four-year-old woman, I did not see why I had to have any sort of relationship with my twenty-seven-year-old nurse beyond strictly business. Not only that, but I basically lost my independence when Beatrice entered my life. After my health began to decline, I had no choice but to give up my home and move into an assisted living community. Therefore, losing my independence and handing it to a younger woman felt like a defeat; I felt like I was losing a piece of myself.

However, the longer Beatrice stayed and cared for me after I left the hospital, the more I began to soften to her and the more I realized that I had been closed off for no reason. I came to see and appreciate Beatrice's best attribute: loving-kindness. Beatrice also had a great sense of humor, and a simple look from one to the other would often cause us to break out into a fit of laughter. Despite our age difference, Beatrice and I actually had much in common, and we were usually on the same page.

Beatrice took over many of my arduous tasks, and gave me a well-deserved rest. She showed me that she cared not only about my health, but also about me as a person, listening with rapt attention to every doctor's diagnosis. She was willing to do things for me that I was no longer able to do for myself, such as fix my car and drill a lock box into a cement wall, and that was only the beginning.

Beatrice spoiled me, and it was little wonder I came to love her. After Beatrice had been caring for me for some time, she informed me that she had completed an application to work at a local hospital in the evenings. Of course, this made me wonder what our future together would look like. Understanding how I might feel about the situation, Beatrice made it a point to let me know that though she would be working at the hospital at night, she would still take care of me during the days. I thought it wasn't humanly possible for her to work at the hospital from 11:00 p.m. to 7:00 a.m. and then arrive at my house at 9:00 a.m. to take care of me until 1:00 p.m.

As I had anticipated, once Beatrice's new schedule began, I could tell that the poor thing was exhausted, and the mother in me eventually came forth after I found her asleep at my kitchen table on several occasions. Although it was hard to accept, I knew that Beatrice's workload was becoming too much for her, and that she only stayed to take care of me to please me; she truly cared for me.

After getting to know and love Beatrice for six months, I came to the realization that I had to return the love and care she had given me. I had to let her go. It was difficult to say goodbye to Beatrice because she had become so much more than my nurse. However, I know that allowing my loving nurse to pursue her aspirations was the correct decision. I was overjoyed to learn recently that she is doing great at the hospital and has moved up the ladder. It comes as no surprise to me; I know she's a wonderful nurse.

I still think of Beatrice lovingly and often, and if I could say anything to her, I would thank her. At a time where I felt helpless and angry, she understood me, cared for me, and made me feel young again. She also taught me that the most valuable people in life can come to you unexpectedly, and she turned an unfortunate situation into a good one because I was given the opportunity to make such an important friend.

CONTAGIOUS OPEN MIND

Sometimes the most valuable people in your life come to you through the most unfortunate situations. It is important to be open to them because you never know what type of positive impact they can have on your life.

THE HEALING POWER
OF OPERA

CYNTHIA MAKRIS

I am a diva, and everything about me is a bit larger than life. However, it wasn't always that way. I grew up in a small town in Colorado, and as a teenager I went through a painfully shy period. Although there was nothing wrong with me on the surface, I felt isolated and insecure. No one, including me, would have guessed that I would find myself at home on the opera stages of the world.

I grew up in a good family, and though I was a smart girl with a pretty face, I always felt alone and unsure of myself. As a result, I dropped out of school and got married at a very young age. However, jumping into a disastrous relationship with another person didn't fix the relationship I had with myself, and by the time I was eighteen, I was divorced and the mother of a child with special needs. Finding myself alone again was difficult, but I realized that I needed to fight for myself or nobody would. I made the decision to go back to high school, which was one of the best things I could have done. I not only got my diploma, but I also got a scholarship to study music. That's when my life took off.

I was twenty when I heard my first opera aria in a student recital. The girl on stage started to sing "Pace, pace, mio Dio," from *La forza del destino* ("God, give me peace," from *The Force of Destiny*). Her performance moved me so much that before I knew it, I was crying; I had never felt more alive. In that moment, I knew what I was meant to do with my life.

From that point on, I committed myself to music, and I found people who believed in me. A wonderful teacher convinced me to go to Europe to audition, and it was there that I found the life I had been looking for. I sang my heart out for a living.

Opera enabled me to discover passions within myself that I never would have imagined were there, and it also gave me the chance to live and work all over the world. Most importantly, it gave me permission to crack open the shell protecting my deepest feelings. There was such freedom in exposing who I really was. Opera not only allowed me to sing, but it also allowed me to play different roles on stage. By being able to portray certain characters in my performances, I found I had the capacity to love and to hate; I was a victim, I was noble, I was despicable, and, most of all, I was me. I discovered that there was nothing wrong with me. Playing imperfect characters helped me come to terms with the fact that I was imperfect, and I realized that the feelings I didn't want to own and accept actually made me a richer human being.

Throughout my many years of singing, I found that the more vulnerable I could make myself to my audience, the more empowered they could become to experience their own vulnerability. This became my mission. I wanted to open up to other people so that they could experience the openness, humanness, and greatness within themselves. Opera lets us live big because the moments in opera are big. These moments represent and depict the key moments in a life: the greatest sadness, the greatest joy, the greatest love, and the greatest tragedy.

It is a beautiful thing to be able to experience these moments and feelings through opera, especially since we so often live on the surface of life. Our lives have become compartmentalized and somehow very small. By contrast, the characters in opera are huge. They show great strength, deep love, aching desperation, limitless joy, and overwhelming anger. They are archetypes that represent facets of ourselves that live under our surfaces and exert great power over us. If we can bring these pieces of ourselves to the surface, then they will no longer terrify us. Opera allows us to experience the conflict we have within, and to start to accept it and even celebrate it. For me, I found that it was through opera that I became more compassionate with myself, and then became capable of feeling compassion for others. That is how opera helped me heal.

I would like to leave you with a story. A famous Indian dancer was very troubled by his outbursts of rage, so he asked his guru if the guru could remove his anger. The great teacher said, "Yes, I can do that, but you will also lose your ability to dance." This story teaches us that we are the sum of all of our parts. They help make us glorious and unique. Therefore learn to accept and love yourself through whatever means necessary. It is through opera that I have come to truly love myself. How do you want to experience your own magnificence?

CONTAGIOUS LOVE

We all have flaws that make us unique. Don't focus too much on what you consider to be your bad parts. You just have to find an outlet through which you can express yourself, and which allows you to embrace exactly who you are.

MY BIGGEST LOSER

PATRICK MCKAY

Several years ago, a nineteen-year-old girl who was just over five feet tall came to me weighing 364 pounds. I remember her being very depressed and self-conscious, and her negative self-image was largely the result of the way others treated her due to her size. Her classmates not only made fun of her because of her weight, but it held her back in many areas of her life. Instead of participating in extracurricular activities, she was a homebody. She was never invited to parties in high school, and when it came time to go to prom, she went alone. Not having a date really upset her, and though friends and family tried to set her up with somebody, she refused to let someone take her to the prom "out of pity."

High school was a difficult time for her, and it wasn't until she graduated that she chose to do something about her health. When her doctor insisted that she start an exercise program and healthy diet before things got even further out of control, she decided that she was going to make a commitment to change her life. She wanted to look better in order to feel more accepted, but more importantly, she wanted to feel good about herself. So she decided to use her negative past experiences as motivation, and once we started talking, I saw someone who was extremely determined to make the necessary changes in her life.

To start her on her journey to a healthier life, we made adjustments to her diet and food portions, and we began with basic weight training and low-impact cardio exercise. After the first of year of training, she had lost seventy-eight pounds, and she was physically, mentally, and spiritually stronger than she'd been in a long time. It wasn't always easy and there were speed bumps along the way, but she continued to push herself and would not accept failure as an option.

By the end of her second year of watching what she ate and working out regularly, she had lost another ninety-four pounds. She was not only seeing amazing results from all her hard work, but she had also become a huge inspiration to many people in our gym, as well as to her family and friends who had sometimes doubted her. It's now four years later and she has reached her goal of 140 pounds—a total weight loss of 224 pounds. Although there were many times when she wanted to quit, her incredible perseverance won out.

All you need to do is look at her results to see that doing something consistently and keeping a positive attitude really works. This whole experience has now motivated her to become certified as a spin teacher and boot camp instructor. More importantly, she has learned to love herself. I sometimes like to think that I inspired her to reach this great achievement. But she was the one who inspired me never to quit, no matter what life throws my way. There are always going to be people who say you can't do something or point out why you won't succeed, so it takes a strong, optimistic person to push forward when things aren't going your way.

CONTAGIOUS HEALTH

Losing weight is not an easy thing, but if you are committed and have a great support team, you can achieve whatever goal you set for yourself.

COURAGE DOES NOT ALWAYS ROAR

JENNIFER CUTLER LOPEZ

When we take a moment to look around us, we discover courage in everyday life. Courage isn't reserved only for the heroes we see on the six o'clock news. At times it is subtler, perhaps found in a person's decision to persevere despite difficult, life-changing circumstances. Mary Anne Radmacher was right when she wrote, "Courage does not always roar. Sometimes courage is the quiet voice at the end of the day saying, 'I will try again tomorrow.'" Courage can be found in everyday people such as BethAnn Telford, who hung those words on her wall after her first brain surgery and walked by them each morning before leaving her house to seize another day.

When BethAnn was thirty-five, she received a call from her doctor who informed her that a recent MRI uncovered a frontal-lobe brain tumor behind her left eye. After traveling the country consulting neurosurgeons, one finally agreed to operate. When BethAnn woke from surgery, she learned that the tumor could not be completely removed because its tail was snaking around a major blood vessel to her brain. The prognosis: two to three years to live, and though she may walk again, she would most likely never run.

BethAnn made two courageous choices that day: to ignore the prognosis, and to fight the cancer. That was nine years ago. Although she was unable to walk immediately after her first brain surgery, BethAnn's first act of courage was picking up a piece of paper and a pen as she lay in a hospital bed and writing a bucket list. The goals she set for herself included mending past relationships, buying her dad a new car, raising money for brain cancer research, and completing the Kona Ironman World Championship.

She started on these goals right away, and four months after her first surgery, she entered a 5K race. BethAnn walked for the first half of the race, but when she saw her dad cheering for her from the sidelines, she began to run, and she didn't stop until she crossed the finish line. She continued to train tirelessly in preparation for the other physical goals on her bucket list. Boston Marathon: check. Marine Corps Marathon: check. Lake Placid Triathlon: check. Even in the wake of all this success, she didn't forget her toughest goal: the Kona Ironman World Championship, a world-class triathlon.

For seven years BethAnn entered the Kona lottery, but her time wasn't fast enough to qualify for the Kona Ironman, and for seven years she was rejected. However, she was determined despite the odds, and she didn't give up. One day, her training partner discovered Kona Inspired, a new program that gave seven slots for the Ironman World Championship to people with inspirational stories. BethAnn's friends worked with her to create a video outlining her courage and determination to live her motto, "Never, never, never give up." The Be Inspired finalists were narrowed down from hundreds of entries until one day BethAnn received a call at work from a friend.

"Miss Beth," her friend said, "You're in."

In preparation for the Ironman World Championship, BethAnn's day began at 3:00 a.m. with running, biking, and swimming before going to work at 8:00 a.m. Finally, the day arrived when BethAnn stepped onto the start line at Kona, eight years after she wrote her bucket list in a hospital bed. Over seventeen hours, she swam 2.4 miles, biked 112 miles, and ran 26.2 miles. With no sight in her left eye due to her brain tumor, she followed the swimmer in front of her, kicking when he kicked, ingesting so much seawater that she was sick as she began to bike. The pacemakers inserted into her lower back for her failing bladder rubbed against her skin, and she self-catheterized for the entire race. But she never stopped, running for the people who couldn't run for themselves. As she ran through the finish line, she carried a large white flag over her head, the word "Hope" written along the top. Below that were hundreds of names. They were the names of children who had died from cancer, names of children fighting cancer, and the names of the children she had taken under her wing.

These children, young people with steadfast positive attitudes and energetic personalities, inspire BethAnn. After placing a checkmark next to Kona World Championship on her bucket list—her final goal—BethAnn continues to tirelessly raise awareness for people affected by brain cancer. With the word "hope" tattooed on each wrist, BethAnn has raised more than $450,000 for brain cancer research, run more than thirty marathons, spoken at dozens of sports events, and received awards for her positive and courageous spirit. She has been featured in a Discovery Channel documentary and has earned the title of World Champion Ironman—all to raise awareness and money for the National Brain Tumor Society and Accelerate Brain Cancer Cure.

BethAnn's journey over the past nine years is a testimony to how courage can change a person's life. It takes courage to consciously switch the way we view life events—to transform a world of struggle to one of opportunity, and to turn a death sentence into a new lease on life. As BethAnn says, "Since this happened to me, my life has changed for the better. I'm a much more giving person now."

BethAnn's courage roars back at brain cancer some days. On other days, such as when she was learning to walk, or when her strength wanes, or the weeks when she is unable to exercise after another surgery, she tells herself, "I will try again tomorrow."

CONTAGIOUS COURAGE

Everybody encounters obstacles in their life, but it is how they face their obstacles and move forward that determines their success. For BethAnn, facing her health obstacle and fighting back with courage meant creating a bucket list and pushing forward to complete personal goals. If you had to create a bucket list right now, what would be on it, and how would you go about completing your goals? Now, imagine if you were facing health issues or the prospect of death: which goals would you choose as most important and worth fighting for? Our time isn't guaranteed, and we don't have forever to do what we need or want to do. Therefore, make it a point to move forward with purpose, complete your goals, and check things off your list, and you will feel even more fulfilled.

SPINNING

DAVID MEZZAPELLE
When I look at life, I believe we spin as the earth does. We spin through our daily routines and we spin through our lives. Think about the pattern of work, family, and commitments that most people are involved in. When you multiply it out, billions of people are, in fact, participating in a rotational pattern—with no end in sight.

This is not a bad thing, and I'm not suggesting we stop. Our routines and commitments shape us and give us meaning. They enrich our lives. However, just as our routines are important in helping us define who we are to some degree, it is equally important to take breaks. Our ability to jump off the spinning wheel of life is necessary and critical to our human function. Those breaks allow us to interact with others and ourselves in a different, healthy way. They allow us to wind down from the constant spinning, truly appreciate what we see and hear daily, and more importantly, give us strength and endurance to take on our normal routines.

For me, throughout my personal and professional life, I have always taken on projects that were step-intensive. This book series is a perfect example. In addition to building the foundation, creating and managing teams, tracking content, and adhering to strict quality control, among other tasks, I have been on an infinite loop in terms of the promotion necessary to spread the **Contagious Optimism** movement. Now, even though the project is an absolute labor of love, I would easily burn out if I didn't take a step back once in a while to recharge. Unfortunately, I learned this the hard way. I lost an entire decade of life, my thirties, being a workaholic. Building my company became my focus while, at the same time, hobbies, family, and relationships all but vanished. Had I forced myself to have a better work/life balance, I probably would have excelled the same, possibly more, instead of wasting all those valuable years.

People who don't take breaks often lose their ability to perform at work and they often lose their ability to interact with family and friends in an enjoyable way. They tend to push people away and destroy relationships. The expression "stop and smell the roses" is more profound than many realize. Don't let yourself get in a rut. Open your eyes and enjoy what's around you as often as possible.

CONTAGIOUS REPOSE

Constantly being on the move can cause you to burn out. There's always a limit to what you can handle, so it helps to remove yourself from the routine when feasible.

EIGHT LESSONS CANCER TAUGHT ME

JACKIE SAAD

1. **You can stop being selfless without being selfish.**
   It's okay to put yourself on the list of things that are important. Sometimes it is about you, and that's okay.

2. **Everything doesn't require a gold medal effort.**
   During the Christmas season that I was ill, I did half the decorating and simplified my preparations everywhere I could. No one noticed.

3. **It's okay to ask for help.**
   People really want to help but often don't know how. Just tell them what you need and let them feel good about their efforts.

4. **Everyone reacts in their own way.**
   You will be sorely disappointed if you expect even the people closest to you to behave in the way you think they should. Unfortunately, there will be those who can't cope, even if they love you and have the best of intentions. People may say stupid things or avoid you altogether. Take a deep breath; they are doing the best they can.

5. **You don't have to prove how brave you are by toughing out the pain.**
   There are drugs to help with pain management, and taking them isn't a sign of weakness. If you need them, take them. You don't have to be brave all the time.

6. **Reporting side effects isn't whining.**

   It is okay to tell the doctor if bad or uncomfortable things are happening to your body as a result of treatment. It is highly unlikely you will tell her something she hasn't heard before. She can't help alleviate side effects if she doesn't know you're having them.

7. **Small pleasures are life's treasures.**

   Treatment side effects like nausea and "chemo brain," a mental fogginess that can affect memory and concentration, can impede your ability to enjoy some of the small pleasures you once took for granted, like savoring a cup of coffee or doing the Sudoku puzzle in the morning paper. While sometimes hard to accept, those losses aren't permanent and you will appreciate things in a whole new way when you recover. In the meantime, there are many small pleasures still to be enjoyed, like a beautiful sunset, an old movie, or the sound of a laughing baby.

8. **Hair is highly overrated.**

   You can do a lot with those thirty minutes you normally spend each morning fussing with your hair.

CONTAGIOUS UPSIDE

Looking at the bright side of even our toughest life episodes can help to make the experience less difficult, and also help others who may be enduring similar events in their lives.

HEALING: YOU'LL NEVER WALK ALONE

MONSIGNOR ROBERT WEISS

December 14, 2012, was a day like no other. It was a day when the event that took place in our town was unimaginable. We are a quiet place where people choose to live because it is a safe harbor from so much of the noise and distraction of the world. It is a place where you can raise a family, and where strong values abide. Sandy Hook is, we thought, a place where children are protected.

However, that day challenged everything that we thought we knew about our hometown. Initially, we heard that there had been a random shooting in the Sandy Hook community. But we could never have guessed what really happened, and the call to come to Sandy Hook Elementary School was unexpected. Twenty-six people were going about their day in a loving and caring school environment when they were violated in the worst possible way. Twenty children and six dedicated educators had their spark of life extinguished forever.

When I arrived, I stood at the entrance doors of the school; I still hear the sound of broken glass under my feet in my sleepless nights. I knew I had been called to something for which no one is ever prepared, and I prayed and wondered what I could do. All the seminary information and academic degrees did not provide a manual for this, and all I could do was put myself and everyone else in the hands of God.

So I stood in the bays of the firehouse as roll was called. First responders grappled with what they had just experienced, and the valiant teachers, the real heroes in my eyes, stood in disbelief. As students' names were read out, startled children were lovingly guided home by their parents. However, the parents of the children who did not respond "Present" were escorted to a private room to wait and to hope. It was humanity at its worst and at its best. It was pain, suffering, fear, hope, love, and every possible emotion and human feeling wrapped into one. We all waited together until the final word came, and one by one, the families left, holding on to one another more tightly than ever before. It was time to pray, to ask the hard questions of life, and to accept incredible new challenges. We were all changed forever, and all we could wonder was, where do we go from here?

I left, only to walk into the rush of the media looking for stories and for answers. It was overwhelming. No one knew the whole story and certainly no one had any answers, so I went to church to prepare a service, wondering what the Lord would put on my heart to say to a stunned and broken community. I accompanied the state police to the homes of families to verify the harsh reality they were praying never happened. As I arrived back at church from the home visits, I saw two carloads of college students enter the church. They occupied the first pew, on their knees, crying and praying. Seeing the outpouring of love and prayers from those young students showed how deeply this tragedy had touched everyone's life.

After the church service, there was nothing left to do but go home. I struggled with what had happened, and I needed something to lift my spirits. At 3:30 a.m. on Saturday, I turned on the television, hoping that one of the traditional Christmas movies would be playing. I was surprised to see the musical *Carousel* was on, just at the time they were singing "You'll Never Walk Alone." That was the message I needed, the encouragement for which I was praying. I knew who was walking with me and I knew I would never be alone.

Faith remains strong, and that aspect of people's lives has been a tremendous source of healing and encouragement. As a community, we are doing our best to support each other, from support groups to religious education for both children and adults. The pain, sadness, and questioning are still part of us but we have never turned away from the reality that this was an evil action, not the hand of God. Light overcame the darkness, and we are trying to stay in that light. This event will always be part of who we are but it will not defeat us or destroy all that we are about. We are walking this journey together! We have tried to maintain as much normalcy as we can in our parish. That does not mean forgetting what happened, but it means encouraging the healing to be able to move forward. For some, that is impossible right now, but with God's grace and our faith, that day will come.

You are never alone, even in the worst possible circumstances. And so, the story continues and the healing is beginning to happen in our community, but only because we are not alone in anything in life. Our God is always there, and because of this, light will overcome the darkness.

CONTAGIOUS FAITH

Good conquers evil, even when life seems to be at its worst.

HEALING IS ON ITS WAY

S O P H I E   S K O V E R

I was a college student-athlete, girlfriend, and socially dynamic young woman who lived every moment to the fullest. In high school, I was seventy-five pounds overweight, but by my freshman year in college I had lost fifty pounds by changing my diet and exercising. I still wanted to lose more weight, but the demands of college life became so overwhelming that I turned to food in an abusive and unhealthy way.

External struggles triggered turmoil on the inside, and I had no clue how to handle these inner battles. I found myself obsessively overeating every time I felt stressed, but then the guilt of eating became so unbearable that purging became a form of relief from the shame. In addition to my food problems, I used recreational drugs and drank alcohol in excess. I didn't understand the negative effects this would have on my life, and what I did know I chose to ignore.

In 2001, I experienced what I like to call a "divine inspiration" while at home from school for Easter weekend. My mom, dad, and I went to church, where the sermon was about "new beginnings." It really resonated with me. As I sat on the porch later that afternoon with my mom, reflecting on the sermon, all of a sudden I felt the urge to confess that I had been throwing up my food, doing drugs, and getting drunk. Coming clean felt like a weight was lifted off my shoulders. My mom was upset and worried by my revelation, and she asked me to make a commitment to stop purging, drinking, or doing any drugs for the rest of the semester. I agreed.

I didn't realize how crucial that decision was until a week after returning to school, when one of my closest friends was killed in a car accident. The shock of her death devastated me. I knew if I hadn't confessed my disorder, and if I hadn't made the commitment to my mom to improve my lifestyle, I would have been in that car with her. That incident was a pivotal point. That fall I started going to church and began educating myself on eating disorders. I discovered that I needed to work on my body, my mind, and my spirit to become healthy once again.

I know now that the imbalanced thoughts and feelings that have hurt me in the past have taught me great life lessons. Through my long journey of healing, I recognized that peaceful living had never been a part of my awareness. However, once I had this insight, I was able to look at each day's challenges in a different way.

Today, I practice healthy living and I honor my life with gratitude, balance, and focus.

CONTAGIOUS HEALING

Healing is on its way to you. Recognizing and confronting your trials will ultimately lead you to discover ways to live life to the fullest.

LOSE WEIGHT—NOT YOUR MIND

LEE LIVELY-GARCIA

Trying to lose weight can be one of the most stressful and unrewarding ordeals—unless, of course, you find something that actually works. If you are like me and have tried virtually every diet with little or no permanent success, then you will understand what I mean.

I have struggled with my weight my entire life, leading me to believe that I have become an expert in the field of unsuccessful weight loss. When you try continually to lose weight and get no visible, lasting results, it is discouraging and maddening. We have to eat to stay alive, so it is not possible to just quit eating, and eating nothing but lettuce all day is no way to live either. So what is the answer?

Part of the answer is to never give up. The most important thing is that we care about our overall health, and that we become more accepting and forgiving of ourselves at the same time. It is not a bad thing to want to be successful at whatever we choose to accomplish, but it is not a good idea to measure our personal success, failures, or self-worth solely by the outcome. The courage to try in the first place is what counts.

We tend to measure ourselves by the outward appearance of others, such as celebrities, athletes, or models. As a lifetime member of the "Fat Chicks' Club," it took me a long time to find the strength to stop comparing myself to others and beating myself up over all the things I wished I could be. Once I learned how to do this, I was able to love myself more. For everything I thought I was not, I found something in me that was far more significant. How can we model ourselves after anyone when each of us is one of a kind?

The next time you feel "less than," "not as good as," or "not as thin as," stop and think about everything that is substantial and significant about you. Look at yourself in the mirror and tell yourself what is special about you when no one else does. There is only one you, and there will never be anyone exactly like you: this makes you precious.

Keep your goals in sight and don't ever give up. But keep yourself in sight, too. It is important to work hard to accomplish a goal, but self-love and self-acceptance are crucial if you ever want to find true acceptance.

CONTAGIOUS SELF-LOVE

Comparing your appearance to another person's appearance does not help your mindset. Instead, think about your own qualities, and be grateful for the ones that only you can possess—they make you special!

MY FRAGILITY IS MY STRENGTH

SÓNIA TREJO

Only those who will risk going too far can possibly find how far one can go.

—TS Eliot

When I was diagnosed with multiple sclerosis, several neurologists told me that "statistically," I would be in a wheelchair within ten years. Not only that, but because one of my symptoms was optic neuritis, there was a probability of permanent loss of vision. That was in June 1995, two months before my wedding. I was thirty-eight years old, and I had never heard of MS. This was long before any celebrities publicly acknowledged their battles with this "silent" disease.

At the time, I was a successful fashion designer—athletic, healthy, and just weeks away from marrying the love of my life. It should have been a happy time, but all I could think of were the words *wheelchair* and *blind*. Shocked, angry, and terrified, I felt the those words assaulting my very existence. As feelings of despair began to overshadow all my hopes and dreams, a small voice from within my soul kept saying, "Not so."

Although I am not a religious person, I have been a student of philosophy since the age of thirteen. A strong spiritual foundation and the gift of intuition have guided me through many trials and tribulations in my life's journey. I trusted that small voice within; it was the strength within my fragility.

The following day, armed with the love and support of my fiancé, Anson, I researched everything I could find related to MS. It was mind-boggling, but the more I read, the more I wanted and needed to know. Knowledge opened the window to possibilities, and the fear that had rendered me hopeless began to subside. I found that MS manifests itself differently in everybody, and every relapse can be entirely unique. I realized that if MS was to be my companion for the rest of my life, I needed to be a hundred percent committed to being proactive in my self-care.

A day later, I spoke to a fourth neurologist and requested MRIs of my brain and spine prior to our appointment. I am a visual person, so as the doctor began to explain the MRI report, I asked him to show me a comparison of my brain and a healthy brain. He did so, pointing out my several lesions and explaining that what I was told previously by other doctors was not necessarily so. We discussed how proper nutrition, plenty of rest, and reduced stress factors were beneficial in minimizing the progression of MS.

Living with a degenerative disease for which there is currently no cure has changed my life in many ways. In my quest to defy the statistics, I have explored many treatments, both alternative and traditional, and used a combination of both. More importantly, I have learned to embrace the challenges, take nothing for granted, and live life fully in gratitude. Since my initial diagnosis, I have developed thirty-one lesions in my brain, the result of several stressful, unavoidable events in my life. To the surprise of my medical community, my status remains, for the past six years, happily unchanged.

Fast-forward sixteen years after my diagnosis. Instead of being confined to a wheelchair, my closest relationship with two wheels and a seat is my bicycle. I have journeyed more than 4,000 miles, raising funds for various causes, including my yearly 160-mile Bike MS ride. It is my way of paying it forward in honor of my family, friends, clients, and those I meet along the way whose courage, love, and indomitable spirit continue to inspire me.

On this journey I have learned that statistics are meaningful on paper but not necessarily in reality, and that doctors are human too: sometimes they make mistakes. I have also come to learn that knowledge trumps fear, that it is important to believe in the possibilities of the impossible, and that your best advocate is always yourself. Most importantly, I've come to embrace the fact that my fragility is my strength, and that the small voice within is only as small as I allow it to be.

CONTAGIOUS TRIUMPH

It is possible for you to be physically weak but still mentally strong. When encountering health obstacles, you must believe that nothing can defeat you. This belief will allow you to move forward with strength and purpose.

MEDICINE AND OPTIMISM: THE STORY OF ART

BARBARA GELSTON

My husband, Art, had been having stomach issues and bouts of bleeding that led him to a gastroenterologist for a colonoscopy. Unfortunately, the results were what no one ever wants to hear: he had a cancerous mass that had to be removed immediately. During Art's surgical ordeal I waited outside with my family, and reality began to set in. Then tears came.

The surgeon came out a few hours later and said that after he had removed nine inches of colon and fifteen lymph nodes, the tumor appeared to be contained. Everything appeared normal, and thankfully, the doctors were optimistic about the outcome. However, even though the prognosis was good, Art went to another oncologist for a second opinion. The oncologist told us he was concerned because the tumor had gone through the colon a fraction of an inch, so there was a risk the cancer had spread. The odds of the cancer not returning were eighty percent with chemotherapy, so we scheduled the chemo, concerned but reassured that the odds were still good.

After about six months of chemo, we received an unexpected update. The oncologist told us that Art's colon cancer marker was higher than he would like, so he ordered a CT scan. All the fears of the last six months erupted, and I began to cry. Art was tense but in control, and he reached over and held my hand. When the results of the CT scan arrived, we saw that Art had a growth at the surgical site and there were changes in the liver. We were told that Art's prognosis was poor—there were multiple cancer spots in the liver, the spleen, and also possibly in his back. When Art asked how long he had, the doctor replied, "Eighteen to twenty-four months, though chemo might extend that a few years—but I'm not sure what the quality of your life will be like."

When we got home, Art and I sat on the porch looking out on our new pool. We held each other, and we both cried. It broke my heart when Art told me he felt he had let me down. He thought it may have been something he had done that had caused the cancer, and now we weren't going to enjoy the life we had envisioned after retirement. I tried to assure him that cancer happens; it could have easily been me. He wanted me to promise that we wouldn't do anything differently than if he were well. He didn't want his illness to change his way of life.

Despite feeling angry, anxious, and depressed, we wanted to live normally but we couldn't seem to get away from the dark cloud of cancer. We tried additional chemo, hoping Art's cancer would go into remission, but with each additional treatment, Art developed more problems; the test results were confusing. With all the test results and opinions of several specialists, it had become an emotional roller coaster that veered between whether or not Art still had cancer.

Our oncologist eventually decided to perform a biopsy on the sites in question, and we discovered that the lesions on the liver were actually scar tissue, Art's spleen looked fine, and the growth at the surgical site was benign. I will always remember the surgeon's first words when he delivered the report: "It's all good news."

As difficult as the ordeal was, we underwent many changes along the way. Art and I now cherish each day. I've learned not to worry about the little things, to make more time for people, and to enjoy life. Art and I have also witnessed how kind people can be. Our family is a good example; they went through this with us every step of the way. We realize that it is so important to offer comfort to others when they are having a difficult time. We often think of the other patients we have gotten to know, admiring the courage and strength they have shown in fighting this disease. We wish they could all have outcomes like ours.

As for Art and me, we have grown closer, if that is possible. I admire Art so much for the way he handled his illness. He was always optimistic and upbeat, and he rarely complained. We seemed to draw strength from each other, but, honestly, I was more often on the receiving side. We know how precious life is.

CONTAGIOUS TENACITY

Cancer can hurt both the body and the spirit. But even though certain moments seem grim, you must remember your friends and family, who are there with you every step of the way. Have hope, but be realistic. Give in, but never, ever give up.

SECOND ADOLESCENCE

BARBARA RADY KAZDAN

I had put my career on hold to raise my children, and as a stay-at-home mom, the irony of motherhood was not lost on me. I knew that I'd have to accept that fact that I would need to raise my children and then simply let them go, and maybe that's why I had mixed feelings when they left home to make their way in the world. I was happy for them, but sorry for myself. I had invested so much, maybe even too much, of myself in them, and their departure left a gaping hole in my life.

Over a ten-year period, I went through three painful partings until the so-called nest was bare. I wondered if the mothering stage of my life was over, but I discovered that the "empty nest syndrome" describes a significant change. It signifies a shift from parents providing a safe physical and emotional space for a child to a grown-up moving out of that space and into the world. I wasn't done mothering; I was simply doing it remotely, on an "as needed" basis.

From a distance I engaged in my children's discoveries, stumbles, and successes, and our relationships continued via visits and frequent conversations. True, there was much that didn't come up in conversation, as each of us had thoughts and experiences we forgot to mention or chose not to share. However, we were still present in each other's lives. It took a while, but that became our new normal.

I became so used to this new normal that I didn't foresee that the nest would fill up and empty again. On more than one occasion all my children came home at once, only to leave again in birth order. The first time they all flew from their homes to mine to celebrate a festive occasion, the house was almost as full as my heart. Then the eldest left, followed by the next oldest, and then the youngest. I watched them leave, one by one, until the house was quiet again. Each time the nest filled up and emptied, the parting became a little easier.

The resulting heartache, like the brief reunion and subsequent return to our separate lives, hit and dissipated quickly. I was the only one who thought this was a condensed version of the empty nest syndrome. Years later, all my children came home again for their father's funeral, and this time they stayed longer, then left one by one, once again in birth order. But I had gotten it by then; the empty nest syndrome no longer applied.

Once my children left, I entered a second adolescence of sorts, and I began to fill the hole my children's parting left in my life. As my kids grew and entered new phases in their lives, so did I. Through a mix of engaging in new activities and meeting new people, I began discovering what I wanted to be when I grew up. I knew that the loss I felt is what all parents experience when their children leave home to establish independent lives. Now my adult children and I lead separate but connected lives. They can and do come home from time to time; surprisingly, I can and do let them go again.

CONTAGIOUS CATCH-AND-RELEASE

We tend to hold on to certain things only to discover that we eventually need to let them go. It might be difficult at first to say goodbye to what we've held on to for so long, but it is a necessary part of life that gets easier with time.

RE: TIRED

A poem by Karen Lyons Kalmenson

We reach an age
When we are not
Considered young
But we are vital
And way far from done.
So we take this time,
Throw in wisdom acquired
From a lifetime,
And we start to live even more
As we are never
Truly retired.

RECLAIM YOUR PERSONAL POWER

No matter what life holds, you are not alone.
There are people who have been through it
and together you can surmount the obstacles.

Addiction and, in some cases, dependency are concepts that conjure up images of suffering, hopelessness, and desperation. Playing a word-association game, most people would list matches with negative connotations. Few would select correspondences such as "opportunity," except for those who have experienced the countless gifts that can come from recovery.

It is said that the deeper one traverses through the darkness, the brighter one can then experience the light. Someone in the depths of addiction can embark upon limitless healing if awakened just enough to want it more than he or she fears it. The recovery process is like a special road that leads to unexpected treasures. This road isn't shown on any maps, and many people who have not experienced addiction or other significant challenges will never find it.

People who have never had an addiction may never be exposed to the education in healing and self-care that can come from recovery, or to the support and accountability necessary to execute lasting changes. They may just continually go through the motions of life, reacting to circumstances, unaware of the role they play in the creation and perpetuation of those circumstances. The treasures of true happiness, health, and success can be found in recovery, with each day sober providing another opportunity to discover them.

Addiction comes in a variety of forms and levels of severity, but in all forms it has the ability to debilitate one's life. Whether someone is struggling with an addiction to drugs, alcohol, shopping, or social media, the connection to one's true self and higher power is blocked and seemingly absent.

This perception of separation feels painfully real even

though it's an illusion. Like an exotic plant displaced in a cold climate, someone in the grasp of addiction simply cannot flourish. However, once the proper conditions for healing are in place and one develops the courage to face and release the pain and fear that surface when removed from the addictive process, blooming is inevitable.

Through the years, I have worked with clients in a variety of settings, starting with counseling at a halfway house for women who were mostly coming from situations of homelessness, domestic violence, or prison. Since becoming certified as a life coach, I have worked with clients privately, doing one-on-one coaching, crisis work, case management, and more, sometimes even living with clients as they acclimate to sober lives. I also do sober transporting/escorting, which involves taking clients to treatment centers around the globe. This frequently includes accompanying them to high-risk potential relapse events and even on vacations. Regardless of the environment, the common denominators have always stood out more than the differences. Low self-esteem and low self-worth are the norm.

Whether my services are sought out or initially forced upon a client by a loved one or the legal system, my starting point is always the same. If I can convince a client that recovery will bring gifts beyond the boundaries of imagination, then that client has a chance, even if their initial motivation is low and external. Once motivation turns to inspiration, anything is possible. The clients who are willing to change are capable of great miracles.

The following stories have been written by those who dwelled in the darkness of their own, or a loved one's, addiction before unearthing the treasures of recovery. Allow their stories of hope and inspiration to guide you to your own inner light, where serenity, happiness, and countless other gifts await.

Nancy Koenig

If you are in the early stages of recovery, listen more and think less. Keep it simple by addressing today instead of attacking the future. Allow yourself to look at the past but do not stare at it, otherwise it will continue to consume you.

—David Briskham, Plettenberg Bay, South Africa

I have come to understand that by allowing my monsters to overcome me, and by obsessing on negativity and all the things I can't control, I am inadvertently overshadowing all the other positive, beautiful things in my life. Therefore, I have made a conscious choice to recognize when I am letting the monsters in, and to combat them with positivity.

—Joan Ashplant, Jupiter, Florida

As we soon learn when we walk through the doors, addiction is a family illness and we need recovery too! As our attitudes and behaviors start to change, a new person starts emerging—we soon start to regain our peace of mind, well-being, and serenity.

—WISE, Orange County, California

THE END OF RESISTANCE

SHANE J. REPMANN

This is it. I'm out of options, I thought.

I was three weeks into my thirty days of inpatient drug and alcohol rehabilitation, when I was strongly recommended by a panel of doctors and counselors to continue rehab at their three-month extended care facility. My alcoholism and dependency on prescription drugs had finally brought me to a crossroads, and I needed to get better.

Although I knew in my heart that I needed more treatment, I vehemently said no when I was presented with the choice to continue my stay in rehab. Panicked, I decided to call my family for support, hoping that they would contest the facility's recommendation. However, unknown to me, the rehab facility had already contacted my immediate family, and all three of them agreed that I needed more time to heal.

I spoke to my father first, and since he already knew about the endorsement for extended care, he was prepared to present me with an ultimatum if I were to refuse more treatment. The call ended abruptly with great anger on both ends. I then called my mother. Apparently, she was instructed to follow the same script as my father, and another call ended angrily. They both promised a complete and permanent cutoff of communication if I were to reject extended care.

I was devastated. I realized I could either agree to my family's terms, or I'd be on my own. I didn't want to lose my relationship with my family, but I wouldn't allow myself to think that I needed more treatment.

I will have to start my life over, alone, I thought. I was only six months shy of my thirtieth birthday. I didn't have a significant other, and many of my friendships had been destroyed by addiction. What was more, I would have been unemployed because my brother was my boss. Without my family, I would have nothing, I thought.

However, instead of taking the blame for my addiction and my situation, all I felt was anger toward those around me. It wasn't me who had the problem, I fumed. It was everybody else. I refused to acknowledge the part I had played in my own self-destruction, and I didn't want to take responsibility and accept that I still needed help.

Instead of trying to see where my family was coming from, I decided to sit and play the blame game. I thought about all the mistakes my loved ones had made, and I created excuses about why I turned out the way I did. However, about twenty minutes into the pity party, a switch flipped. I realized that I was the problem.

A wave of relief washed over me and I felt lighter than I had in years. Whether this realization stemmed from the fear of losing my family or from the deep understanding that I still needed time to heal, I'll never know. But I am thankful that I was able to accept my own responsibility for the negative turn my life had taken. I decided then and there to enter extended care.

Life had new meaning when I learned to let go of the past, correct the present, and plan appropriately for the future. The alcohol and drugs were symptoms of a more severe problem, and I was holding on to anger and remorse that prevented me from growing as a human being. Once I honestly looked deep into my soul, I started the healing process and allowed myself to envision a more successful future. The feelings of hope, change, and redemption were overwhelming in the best way possible.

Today, I have been sober for over seven years. At thirty-three years of age, I went back to college and earned my bachelor's degree. I'm now pursuing my master's in school counseling. The same year I continued my education, I married an amazing woman who is truly my soul mate. My relationship with my family is stronger than ever. Every morning I wake up with no regrets and a strong desire for self-improvement. As I continue to experience greater success in my life, I remind myself that it all started with an hour of self-reflection—one incredible hour that gave me the wisdom to seek a new beginning and a future that perpetually promises a better day.

CONTAGIOUS REVELATIONS

You're stuck in the corner with no place to go. You think about how you ended up in such disadvantaged circumstances and start blaming other people. But, often, there's no reason to blame others. Sometimes you have to hold yourself accountable for your actions. Once you understand and accept your faults, you'll be able to reverse your circumstances and pursue a course of action that you can be happy about.

SECOND CHANCES

LEJUNUE BUGGIE-DENT

Second chances don't come often in life.

My story is not unlike other people's. My family was dysfunctional. I was raised in a household with a heroin-addicted stepfather and a mother who worked as an LPN in a drug and alcohol unit. This combination was interesting and ironic. When they got together, he was fresh from the Vietnam War. She wasn't initially aware of his addiction, but she eventually found out.

From those experiences with my stepfather, I grew to despise anyone affiliated with drugs or the lifestyle. By the mid-1980s, my brother and older cousins fell victim to the crack epidemic, but I became more of an advocate against the use of drugs. I vowed, "That will never be me." It seemed as if everyone I loved was mesmerized by the white substance in that little glass vial. I felt responsible for my younger siblings and became the caregiver who made sure they wouldn't have to witness loved ones doing *their thing* as I had.

I kept busy by participating in as many extracurricular activities as possible. There was one youth council group called "The 5 W's" that kept me grounded and focused on the straight and narrow path, providing the support I needed so that I would not succumb to the pressures around me. I was determined not to be another statistic: young, black, pregnant, drug-addicted. It worked. I made it through high school and some college without so much as smoking a joint.

By the late 1980s, my stepfather was able to get clean, but the wreckage of his past left him with HIV, contracted from sharing needles with a buddy. My two little sisters escaped the madness and mayhem that came along with his addiction and I was grateful that the ugliness I witnessed didn't wreak havoc in their lives.

In hindsight, I realize that I too had an addictive personality. My addictions were "normal," though, like shopping, eating, and—did I say shopping? Even with all the knowledge and prevention I had in my life, I eventually fell victim to the grotesqueness that is drug addiction. It wasn't until my late twenties that my life spiraled out of control. You see, I wasn't chasing the drug to get high; I was chasing it to stay normal.

I started using because I was completely in love with a boy, and I was trying to be his savior. He got me high before I could get him sober. Unfortunately for him, he is still caught in the grip of his addiction. I, on the other hand, was given a second chance at life.

It wasn't easy. Like most addicts and alcoholics, I was in complete denial that I had a problem. I became my stepfather, and the sisters I had shielded from his addiction now watched me turn into a total lunatic and recluse. Losing the ability to function as a normal human being, I morphed into the type of person who merely took up space in the otherwise advancing world.

Rock bottom for me came in March 2004. I was released from jail after serving three months, only to return exactly one week later. It was humiliating. Upon my return to my temporary home after my week's vacation, I entered a drug dorm where I was able to make meetings and get counseling.

Most of the staff asked how I got there; I did not fit the stereotypical makeup of most women in jail. In reality I was no different than the other women: addiction is addiction, and anyone can fall at any time if they are not cognizant of what is happening.

I had to take a long look at where my addiction had taken me and where I wanted to be. Speakers came into the dorm to share their experience, strengths, and hopes. One particular woman's story made me believe that I could make my way back to a better life. I thirsted to be in her presence so I could learn as much as I could about staying off drugs one day at a time. I begged the staff to get me into a program. I was scared because it meant a huge change; however, change was what I needed in order to save myself.

Another few months passed and I was accepted into a strict halfway house. After arriving at the "Hall," I met my counselor. We hit it off okay, but I was completely standoffish because of my own trust issues.

As time went on, I was able to open up. I didn't want to revert to what I was. I was incapable of making rational life decisions. As much as I thought I knew and as smart as I thought I was, I didn't know a damn thing about myself—or life. The reality is that life will show up on its own terms. I could let it chew me up and spit me out or I could listen to someone who had a vast amount of knowledge about things I had no clue about. As much as I disliked taking suggestions, the suggestions worked: I made a meeting a day for ninety days, I got a sponsor, and I raised my hand at meetings.

Second chances are blessings; they provide you with a chance to mend broken fences and become the person you were meant to be.

CONTAGIOUS COMEBACK

There is a saying that sticks with me: "You may have done what the devil says you did, but you are not who the devil says you are." Even if you've made mistakes in the past, you can still be the person you have always wanted to be; you just have to believe and trust in a power greater than yourself. For me that Higher Power is God and I thank Him every day for His grace and mercy, because He didn't have to give me a second chance. Has there been a time in your life when you were given a second chance? How did you feel, and who did you feel grateful to? Maybe you felt grateful to a Higher Power, maybe you felt grateful to a friend or family member, or maybe you felt grateful toward yourself. Regardless of who you thanked for your second chance, you always have yourself to thank for making the most of it and making better decisions the second time around.

HELP FROM A CAB DRIVER

ESTER NICHOLSON

The alcoholic/addict will absolutely be unable to stop with the unaided will.

—*Bill Wilson*

The Twelve Steps of Recovery saved my life. What I didn't realize was that the monster would come back.

When the pangs of my addiction came creeping in again, I hopped in a taxi, shaking, driven to feed the monster raging in my body. Flooded with paranoia, I scrunched low in my seat and feverishly instructed the driver to take me to Dunsmere and Redondo. Ducking down in the back of the cab, I hoped that one of my AA buddies wouldn't see me and know that I had failed again.

After driving a few blocks, the driver stopped the cab and shut off the engine. What the hell are you doing? I thought. "Step on it, I need to get to the hood, man." As I angrily wondered what the holdup was, the driver turned around and looked at me. I saw his knowing eyes, as if the face of God was staring right at me.

After a beat, he said to me: "Young lady, don't do it. You're better than this. Don't kill yourself. God loves you. I love you." To this day, I feel like it was divine intervention that he knew what I was up to. I had never met this driver before.

For a moment, I was dumbfounded; the driver's words had

struck me like lightning. In that instant, I knew if I kept on that road, if I insisted that the driver mind his own business and keep driving, the only thing I would have to wonder about was when and how my life would end. As I let the driver's words sink in, I realized that my desire for freedom from my addiction was stronger than the demons inside of me. I gave in to his words.

The monster of addiction screamed in my head and tried to convince me that one more hit wouldn't hurt. But this time, I was listening to the right voice, the voice of God. With tears in his eyes, the driver turned the taxi around and drove me home. I felt undeserving yet thankful that grace had come to me in the form of a taxi driver, and to this day I proudly reflect on the moment when I humbly heeded his warning and made the choice to grab the life-saving branch he extended.

In the first step of recovery, we're told that we must admit we are powerless over our addictions. Those addictions can be the usual ones that come to mind when people hear the word *addict*. But they can also involve things that we don't typically call addictions, such as worry and fear. Sometimes addicts believe in a lifelong illusion that they're not worthy of anything good. That was certainly my experience for many years.

Many people like myself have constantly struggled to overcome this powerlessness and to find wholeness, and time after time, they have failed. However, I have come to learn that when we fail, it is because we are demonstrating a misguided reliance on a God outside of ourselves, a God who we don't believe to be available or friendly, and a God who deems us to be unworthy. But we keep begging and hoping that one day there will be mercy and a reprieve from the torment and pain of addiction. Believe it or not, this struggle is an important and necessary starting point in our spiritual journey.

The way to enlarge our spiritual life is to put God back

within our own heart. That's exactly what I did on that day in the taxi, and for anyone struggling with addiction or a sense of powerlessness, that is what you should do, too. It's from this conscious union that you are restored to wholeness. You can reclaim authority, dominion, and mastery over your life. Once you arrive at this place, you are on the road to true healing and transformation.

CONTAGIOUS HEALING

Do not allow powerlessness to rule your life and your decisions. Rather, admit to it and then understand that you can move past it. Continue on the road to health and healing.

A FIRST STEP IN THE RIGHT DIRECTION

GAY CARTIER

The Australian National Council on Problem Gambling reports that about one percent of the population, or two million people, fall under the category of compulsive gamblers, while another four to six million are considered problem gamblers. Males often start gambling in their teens, and females usually start between their twenties and forties. The problem with these statistics is that they only refer to people who are hooked on gambling. These figures do not take into account how gambling impacts the family and friends of those addicted.

Robert's Story

Robert grew up in a dysfunctional family. At sixteen, his parents finalized a messy divorce, which left him feeling stranded, resentful, and helpless. Alcohol and gambling fueled Robert's rebellion, which gave him the illusion of the control he craved.

He loved making bets, the chase of the cards, the bright lights, the music, and the rituals. He especially loved the euphoria that accompanied a winning streak. When he married and had children, Robert finally moved on from his earlier years of gambling and drinking. But with the unexpected death of his mother, Robert's desire to escape reality through gambling surfaced again.

Soon Robert's addiction stripped away his sense of responsibility to his wife and children. As he fed his addiction, he increasingly became distant from his family, friends, and work associates. Appalled over Robert's inability to stop gambling, his wife filed for divorce. Robert found himself living in a derelict hotel. He was poor and broken, and his future looked bleak.

Having bottomed out, Robert decided to seek treatment. He is now fully committed to the recovery process. Although the physical and psychological transformations that occur during rehabilitation are difficult, Robert has made the process his priority. To restore the life he led before addiction crippled him, the program calls for the reparation of personal relationships and also asks that he find a job and work with professionals to implement relapse-prevention strategies.

There comes a time in the gambler's life when seeking help becomes his or her primary goal. The road to recovery isn't an easy path, and it starts with abstinence. For most gamblers this is a difficult undertaking due to the strength of their cravings. But as with any journey, a first step, even if it is small, is required.

CONTAGIOUS SELF-HELP

Admitting that you have an addiction is the first step of the journey of recovery. With the right support and professional help, you can live the life you have always wanted and be your true self.

ARE YOU IN LOVE, OR LOVE ADDICTED?

JED DIAMOND

Love and addiction—it seems strange to see these two words used together. However, I've treated people with addictions for more than forty years, and I've found that love addiction is just as potent as drug addiction. In my experience, everybody wants to feel wanted and craves connection. Therefore, when people are under the impression that they have found that connection and have fallen in love, it isn't always clear whether it's true love or they are just addicted to the idea of being in love. Here are some comparisons that will help you recognize the difference between true, healthy love, and love addiction:

1. Healthy love develops after we feel secure. Addictive love creates affection in spite of the fact that we feel frightened and insecure.
2. Healthy love comes from feeling full; we overflow with love. Addictive love always tries to fill an inner void.
3. Healthy love begins with self-love. Addictive love always seeks love "out there" from that "special someone."
4. Healthy love grows slowly, like a tree. Addictive love grows fast, as if by magic.
5. Healthy love thrives on time alone as well as time with our partner. Addictive love is frightened of being alone.
6. Healthy love is unique. There is no "ideal lover" that we seek. Addictive love is stereotyped. There is always a certain type that attracts us.

7. Healthy love is based on a deep understanding of our significant other and ourselves. Addictive love is based on hiding from ourselves and falling in love with an ideal image, not a person.
8. Healthy love encourages us to be ourselves and to be honest with who we are, including our faults. Addictive love encourages secrets; we want to look good and put on an attractive mask.
9. Healthy love creates a deeper sense of ourselves the longer we are together. Addictive love creates a loss of self the longer we are together.
10. Healthy love gets easier as time goes on. Addictive love requires more effort as time goes on.
11. Healthy love makes us satisfied with what we have. Addictive love causes us to always look for more or better.
12. Healthy love encourages us to expand our interests in the world. Addictive love encourages our outside interests to contract.
13. Healthy love is based on the belief that we want to be together. Addictive love is based on the belief that we have to be together.
14. Healthy love teaches that we can only make ourselves happy. Addictive love expects the other person to make us happy and demands that we try to make them happy.

Addiction expert Dr. Stanton Peele said: "Many of us are addicts, only we don't know it. We turn to each other out of the same needs that drive some people to drink and others to heroin. And this kind of addiction is just as self-destructive as—and a lot more common than—those other kinds." I couldn't agree with this assessment more. If you think you're in love, consider whether this love comes from a healthy, secure place, or whether it might come from a needy, desperate place. Everybody deserves to find a healthy, loving relationship, and only you can decide whether or not you will settle for love addiction, or whether you will strive to find a true, honest, healthy connection.

CONTAGIOUS LOVE

Addictions can take root anywhere. Recognize the healthy signs of love so that you can feel comfortable in your relationships and continue to grow as a person.

CONTAGIOUS GIFT

Life is a miracle. As human beings, we are able to consciously ask for things, and the greatest miracle of all is that we often receive the things we ask for. Therefore, in truly challenging times when you don't know the answer, just know that you're alive, you're human, and you're a conscious being. Lovingly ask for a miracle.

RECOVERY

DEBORAH LITTLEJOHN

Once, there was an innocent time when I felt secure and was surrounded by loving people. I was raised with good morals and values and had respect for the world around me. I never thought that one day a disease would surface and I would find myself in insane and dangerous situations. Once this thing called addiction took control, all bets were off.

After running away to escape an abusive relationship of several years, I became homeless and this invasive disease became my new best friend. It impaired my every thought, brought countless negative consequences, and attacked me like a carnivorous animal, wanting to devour my very soul. Security and love became extinct.

My life was consumed by addictive behavior: heavy drinking, cocaine, and dope, stealing, jail, and psych wards. The worst was still around the corner. One night, after following a man behind an elementary school to get drugs, I was choked into unconsciousness. I awoke on the ground with him on top of and inside me, saying he would kill me if I screamed. Instead of calling the cops, I continued down this path of destruction.

After many years of this disease progressing and ravaging my senses, I lost all control of my life. It seemed as if there was no hope in sight. I wondered why this was happening to me and whether I would be cured before it killed me. "There is no cure!" Who said that? "No one is going to save you. Come die with me." WHO SAID THAT? Now I was hearing voices.

The voices were my fears—which kept me constantly wondering whether I would overdose with every hit and every drink, whether anyone would find me in time to save me, or whether they would even care that I was dying. In time, I stopped wondering whether this disease would kill me and instead wondered whether it would be swift, slow, or painful.

I knew people who tried to get clean, who would talk about drug treatment programs and twelve-step meetings. I said, "Yeah right. Y'all was in jail and that's how you gained that weight." It was never long before they were hanging out back on the corners with me. I saw no foolproof evidence of recovery.

One night, after walking in the middle of the street screaming and crying, with cars zooming by, I was admitted to a psych ward. I was so tired; I just wanted to kill myself. What I didn't know was that this whole time, God was fighting for my life. He needed me to be still so I could hear His soft voice telling me, "Don't give up, I gotcha. Follow me and you will have peace."

When I woke up, a very nice lady started asking me questions. I felt a sudden relief from all the pain and despair I had suffered. In that instant, it all just seemed to float away. I agreed to go to a sober house and start this thing called recovery.

I am still sober 2,555 days later. Seven years. I have not touched a drink or a drug since.

As a child, my mother and grandmother taught me to pray. I had always felt a loving and caring presence in my life, until addiction left me spiritually voided. I couldn't see or touch this presence, but I still believed.

Despite all the nastiness and hatred with which addiction plagued me, God saved me time and time again from the worst people, the worst places, and the worst things, while allowing me to learn many valuable lessons.

Recovery has put me back in touch with God. I do not let a day go by without getting down on my knees, saying a prayer, blessing all things, and being thankful for the ups and downs of those trials and tribulations. It is a part of my recovery. I wouldn't change anything that I went through to get to this serene state of being.

Recently, I prayed through my fear of being unable to get a job because of my arrest record. After four months of advocating for myself, I received clearance from the Department of Health to get my certification as a Home Health Aid. I have been an HHA for almost three years now. My mom is extremely proud of me, and I am proud of her for not giving up on me.

CONTAGIOUS RECOVERY

When you feel like there is no light at the end of the tunnel, walk a little further.

YES, I BELIEVE

JERRY KELLY
Some people don't believe in a power greater than themselves. As for me, I believe.

A few years ago, a person near and dear to me was living in my home with his wife, their three kids, and their Saint Bernard. Mind you, my house is not large, and I already shared this abode with other dear ones and a puppy. But I welcomed them because the dad had a problem. He was a full-blown alcoholic and was awaiting a court decision on his third DUI.

After getting into an accident, he blew a .36 on the sobriety test, which is four times the legal limit in New York. It looked like he was going to have to do time. Before he went to jail, he wanted to redo his bathroom, kitchen, and the main floor of his house. My house had a second floor with a kitchen and bath, so they had their own living area while their house was being repaired.

They lived with us for six months. During that time his anxiety increased and so did his drinking, which created tension and caused arguments with his wife and kids. I spent many days and nights counseling the kids and listening to his wife's complaints, and his complaints about them. Yelling became normal. Many times the kids wanted to escape to spend time in my part of the house. Their part was a war zone; mine was a place for peace talks.

About five months into our communal living, I went to India on a spiritual retreat. It was a beautiful trip full of bliss and spiritual charging. During my trip abroad, my guests' house was finished and they went home. I came home with a greater connection to my higher power and a true feeling of love for everyone.

The tensions in their family were still growing, and I now conducted my counseling via text or phone. As the dad's court date got closer, the stress became unbearable for the oldest child, who texted me her pains. She was extremely distraught, texting me from under her blankets so she could get her counseling without her father knowing.

One Sunday morning, less than a week before his court date, I woke up feeling lousy. The reason wasn't a mystery: their pain was contagious. I didn't know what to do. I loved these people.

I was inspired to grab a pen and paper and, with the childlike belief of a five-year-old, I wrote to Santa. "Dear Higher Power, please help this man. He has a problem but he's a good man. Please help his family."

The very next morning, the dad came to my house and asked me, "Jerry, how do I detox?" That Friday, he went to court. He was given only five years of probation and mandatory counseling. The following day, he signed himself into an alcohol rehabilitation center. It's been four years and he hasn't had a drink since. Although they still have their challenges, they are working through them as a family and not as enemies.

Miracles do happen. Yes, I believe.

MY NEW GUIDING ANGEL

LARRY GLENZ

Holding a grievance against someone is like drinking poison and hoping the other guy dies.
—Nelson Mandela

I have had three years to try to make some sense of my son's death. Kevin died at age twenty-seven from an overdose of heroin after seven years of addiction, recovery, and relapse. He was an all-American boy with everything to live for, but he could not resist his strong craving for opiates. His daughter, Olivia, was only three months old when he passed away. Kevin had a large family who loved him and many good friends. He was strikingly handsome, athletic, and personable. An outstanding student-athlete in high school, he earned a Division I scholarship to the University of Massachusetts, where he earned honors as a lacrosse player and graduated with a BA in social work. He was very lovable and he had a great support group.

How could we have let this happen? What did we fail to do that could have saved him? We had seven years to turn his life around and we couldn't do it. What am I supposed to learn from this?

My answers to these questions reflect my faithful study of two spiritual paths: *A Course in Miracles* and Al-Anon. From the time I first understood that Kevin was addicted to the prescription painkiller OxyContin, I turned to my Higher Power for strength. I was guided by Spirit to love him without judgment or condemnation. I asked for divine guidance to help me and received the answer: Treat him only with love, for he is a perfect child of God.

I found that directions from my Higher Power were very difficult to follow. I often used my anger and frustration to shame him and to make him feel guilty for what he was doing to himself and others. Although he attended many rehab sessions, he often went against his will. He relapsed every time and was deceitful to me, and I was scared. Still, Spirit reminded me to love him anyway.

Love him anyway? I would scream inside my own head. He's stealing, he's lying, he's committing crimes against strangers and those he loves the most to get the money to get high. How can I just love him anyway? I am his father. I have to fix this. And I asked for the Holy Spirit's help.

For several years, I attended parent meetings in a local drug recovery center where Kevin was a reluctant outpatient. As a result, I gained great respect for the people in the field of drug rehabilitation and recovery. They told me that it was my job to stop him with anything and everything at my disposal. I was told that Kevin was playing a dangerous game and that the results would be jail, insanity, or death if he did not stop. They said that drug use always progresses and the results are often fatal. I had to stop him.

I believed what the drug recovery counselors said and respected everything they advised me to do. I admire their integrity to this day. What they said would happen did indeed happen.

What they didn't tell me was that I was powerless to cure his illness of addiction. I learned this from Al-Anon, the spiritual path for the families of addicts that is based on the Twelve Steps of Alcoholics Anonymous. Al-Anon teaches the three

C's: I didn't *cause* it; I can't *control* it; I can't *cure* it. When I turned to my Higher Power, I was repeatedly encouraged to just love him anyway.

Spirit never told me that Kevin would overcome his illness. I was assured, however, that I would not be left comfortless. I didn't understand what that meant at the time, but I do now.

With the help of my Higher Power, I have been able to feel only love coming from Kevin, and so did many others who loved both him and our family. Kevin suffered as an addict. During his times of recovery, he would describe the agony of the cravings that drove him to use and the emotional guilt that he felt from it. The Kevin that remains in my heart and mind no longer suffers.

I have accepted that Kevin was meant to go through life as he did and live for only twenty-seven years. I have been taught by *A Course in Miracles* that the only part of Kevin's story that matters is the strong love we feel. Only the love is real.

On earth, Kevin loved people and received much love, though he was no angel. Now, however, he is an angel who guides me. Spirit and Kevin's guidance seem the same. When it's Kevin's voice, however, it contains his witty sarcasm, just to get my full attention.

The sadness of Kevin's passing also somehow seemed to heal our family—a family that had become bitter and chaotic when we were trying to "fix" him. We blamed each other at times for how we treated and handled his addiction. It was a turbulent time.

That bitterness has disappeared, and those who loved Kevin no longer want to hold any grievances. Somehow, we decided to forgive each other for not being able to "save" him and just appreciate the love we all shared with him. It was love for Kevin that caused this miracle: this change in our thinking.

These days I feel stronger than ever with Kevin in my heart

and mind. My connection to Spirit has only grown. Kevin's love allows me to be happy and to experience the love of others.

Thank you for that miracle, Holy Spirit. And thank you, Kevin, for all this love.

CONTAGIOUS FORGIVING

Forgiveness is the key to happiness. Whenever we are experiencing the negative emotions associated with fear and guilt, we can be certain there is someone or something we have not forgiven.

LOVE AWAY CIGARETTES

NANCY KOENIG

I was hopelessly addicted to smoking cigarettes for fifteen years. I attempted to quit scores of times, using every product and method I could find, but to no avail. I loved to smoke, and yet I despised myself for doing so.

Like many who have attempted to break off a toxic relationship with cigarettes, I tried to stop on significant dates, figuring the secret to smoking cessation was when and how I quit. However, I didn't love myself enough on Valentine's Day, free myself on Independence Day, or give myself the gift of greater health on my birthday. Smoking ten times more than usual on New Year's Eve did not disgust me enough to leave my carcinogenic friends behind in the passing year.

Nicotine replacement products served as deterrents, but using the exact chemical I was trying to distance myself from never worked for long. When I began to learn healthier ways to handle anger and stress and incorporate them into my life, I was able to amass a few smoke-free days here and there, but triggers often got the best of me. I quit several times a month and was in perpetual nicotine withdrawal—torturous for myself and for anyone who had to contend with me.

If the fundamental reasons one smokes are not addressed, relapse is inevitable. This dawned on me one night when I could not fall asleep after smoking. My heart was pounding and my throat was on fire. When I smoked all the time, I rarely noticed the effects, but the smoke-free stretches were great illuminators of the consequences; my body had become far more sensitive.

I beat myself up for the decision to smoke until I hurt as much emotionally as I did physically. I was about to light up, to lessen my discomfort, when it occurred to me what a vicious cycle this was. Smoking was a physical manifestation of the emotional abuse I served myself on a regular basis. It was an expression of self-punishment, but what I needed to learn was how to be accepting, gentle, and patient with myself.

Instead of lighting up, I began silently repeating the words "I love you" over and over. I didn't necessarily believe them, but there was power in this affirmation of self-love regardless.

I didn't smoke that morning, or for the next several months. Each time I was tempted, I stopped to ask myself what was going on within me that was propelling me to smoke. What did I need to let go of, accept, or forgive myself for? If someone or something else appeared to trigger the craving, I reminded myself that smoking didn't say, "Screw you!" as I thought it did as a rebellious teenager; it only said, "Screw me!" I couldn't control anyone else, only myself.

On rare occasions, I still chose to smoke one cigarette, socially. Since I did so with awareness rather than compulsion, I was able to stop. In addition, because I chose to stop judging myself for smoking, I eventually lost all desire to light up. The urge simply vanished.

When we try to force ourselves to stop an addictive behavior without addressing what is prompting us to engage in it in the first place, we waste a lot of energy in the fight. From an energetic standpoint, what we push against only pushes back stronger. Classifying ourselves as smokers struggling to quit only serves to deplete confidence in our ability to stop with each failed attempt. Smoking is a behavior, not an identity, and we must get to know what drives us to addiction. I have found that when cravings for smoking or other addictive behaviors arise, self-love is the safest path. Place your hand over your heart and take several slow deep breaths while silently affirming, "I love you," even if it feels untrue.

Today, I coach clients through smoking cessation, and I teach that in the face of powerful triggers, there is no better support than oxygen, an omnipresent ally. Deep breathing relaxes us and returns us to the present moment, where all addictive actions are a matter of choice.

CONTAGIOUS SELF-LOVE

We might experience addiction at some point in our lives. Some addictions can be trivial, while others can seriously harm you. It will be hard to quit the latter, but you need to remember who is being harmed by the addiction and you also need to know why. Once you spot the cause, you can change the effect.

THE GIFT OF CLARITY

JERRY KELLY

I wasn't even driving when I got my second DUI. I was parked with my motor running, waiting for a friend to come out from behind the factories in Copiague, Long Island. The factories were where you went at night to get smoked, toked, or stroked, if you know what I mean, and I was waiting for my friend to finish one of the three so that we could leave.

I was parked on the wrong side of street, which easily caught the attention of the Suffolk County Police. There was no time to hide the empty beer bottles as the officers approached my twenty-year-old pickup truck. One officer immediately asked the fateful question: "Sir, have you been drinking?"

"I only had one of those; the other twenty on the floor there are my friend's," I lied. "He'll be back in a minute." Of course, I knew I'd be out of luck and he wouldn't come back until the police officers left. They didn't leave. They wanted to see me touch my nose, say the alphabet, walk a straight line, and assume the position. I had gotten good at it, this drunkard's "Macarena," but I just hadn't gotten great. So off I went for a brief overnight stay at the county-owned hotel.

A day of reckoning, a lawyer, and a few court dates later, I was given three years' probation and court-mandated counseling. Of course, if you screw up on probation, you have to do real time. No problem, I thought. I'm not an alcoholic or addict. I'm just a guy who likes to have fun. I realized, of course, just how wrong this thinking was.

Thirty-three days later, I was at a christening for my friend Charlie's daughter. I vaguely remembered Charlie's wedding two years earlier. Yeah, that had been a blast: an eight ball of cocaine for my nose and fifteen beers before the first dance. I remember tearing open my shirt during that first song and dancing while fondling my fabulous five-foot-eleven, 340-pound frame on the dance floor. I don't remember much after that. I found Charlie's wedding card and the gift I had meant to give him in my jacket pocket the next day. Needless to say, people didn't have many positive memories of me when I arrived at this christening two years later.

Why is that old lady looking at me like that? I wondered.

Another friend chuckled and said, "You're not drinking? I guess they're selling ski gear in hell now."

"Good to see you've matured a little bit," another lady remarked.

Later that night, I was furious. How dare those people say such things about me? I'll show them! I thought.

However, my fury was interrupted by a sudden, shocking realization—a painful gift of clarity. This clarity came in the form of a voice in my head reminding me: "You did show them. Now, show them something different. You showed them an alcoholic; now show them someone in recovery." At that moment, I realized painfully how much time I had wasted, and saw how I had been selling myself short. However, I was ready and willing to make a change in my life. That night, I made a phone call to a friend from a twelve-step organization, and said those magic words: "Hey, man, I think I need some help." I fully realized that it was time for me to make a positive change.

It's amazing how fast God answers when you surrender. He really doesn't want us to be in pain, and that's why he sends the "angels of clarity." He just dresses them up to look like people we might know, but in reality, they are his words and his actions. Clarity arrived in the face of a cop, an angry old lady, and a sarcastic friend. It did not appear as an angel in white, whispering in my ear, but as different people slapping me in the face to wake me up.

I now know that the path I was traveling on would have killed me, left me incarcerated, left me institutionalized, or all three. Thankfully, clarity showed up, right on time. Although clarity still has to guide me from time to time, and though this guidance sometimes comes in the form of painful realizations or decisions, I'm grateful for her.

When I called my friend and asked for help, we talked for what seemed like hours. Next came twelve-step meetings, books, writing, crying, and cleaning up the past. Most important, a new journey began.

It's been twenty-two years since that night in Copiague, and occasionally I still get lost. However, ultimately, clarity always shows up and if I listen, life is great. When I don't, she speaks a little more assertively.

CONTAGIOUS REFLECTION

Look back on your life, especially the trying times, and reflect on the way people perceived you. Think about what you learned or what you should learn. Then, in a moment of peace, thank clarity for showing up. Make sure you listen to her message. Listen. She's speaking to you now, and she can help put your life on the road to wellness and happiness.

Press On Regardless

By Rhoda Beiser

When we feel we can no longer stoke the fire,
Should we continue to press on further,
Or should we give in to our wavering desire
And lapse into the depths of swirling disorder?

If you press on regardless, you will succeed.
No matter what your wishes or aims may be,
If you do not try at least to proceed,
You will never know the real feeling of glee.

Follow your feelings and do what you crave,
Let nothing deter you or make you recede,
Continue to press on and always be brave,
For the day will come when you will be pleased.

CHAPTER EIGHT

FIND YOURSELF IN SERVICE TO OTHERS

Contributions don't always have to be financial;
your time and talent can also serve others well.

Maybe you've won or earned a good amount of money, and you're in the spotlight; so now what? We often hear about successful people like people who have won the lottery, who claim that money or fame has ruined their lives. But that outcome can easily be avoided with optimism, gratitude, and philanthropy. Maybe you're not in the spotlight but you have the time and inclination to give back. In either scenario, helping others is one of the most rewarding things you can do—for yourself, your community, and even for mankind.

In terms of alumni giving, my alma mater, Fairfield University in Connecticut, believes that there are several ways alumni can give back to the school when writing a check is just not enough. They consider philanthropy to be a contribution of time, talent, and treasure. I like this expression because I believe that rolling up your sleeves and assisting someone in need is just as important as writing a check, if not more important. This applies to all forms of altruism. In my case, I share book royalties with my alma mater, along with other charities and nonprofits. I have also recruited interns around the globe for the past twenty-five years across a variety of business projects, and I continue to do so today.

This chapter focuses on how people have given back and what they have gained and learned in the process. "Paying it forward" with our time, talent, and treasure in order to help others allows us to gain and share wisdom. It is tantamount to our purpose in life.

David

Just imagine how your happiness would change if you accomplished goals that had a positive impact on others. You would be recognized by others and also be rewarded by your own sense of achievement.

—J. Todd Rhoad, Atlanta, Georgia

Showing the world your struggles by being bitter, resentful, and unhappy does not set a good example for others to grow in love and kindness. Instead, show the people around you that you are a magnet, not for destruction, but for peace and kindness.

—Daya Devi-Doolin, Orange City, Florida

MY SHINING S.C.A.R.S.

KRYSTIAN LEONARD

Turn your scars into stars.

—*Robert Schueller*

It's common for people to experience some type of accident in childhood that leaves a physical scar. In my experience, I have found that there is a sad misconception that if you have a noticeable scar, you must be damaged or broken. If you have a visible scar or flaw, many people think you are scary: you're an outcast, a monstrous character unworthy of social acceptance.

As a child I learned about beauty from movies and fairy tales about princesses. They had flawless skin and sparkling eyes, and I wanted to be beautiful like them. However, instead of having flawless skin, I had my first experience with stitches, resulting in a scar, at age four. It was above my lip, so I wouldn't smile for pictures and was embarrassed going to preschool. Then, when I was six, I had my first surgical procedure to remove a lipoma in my thigh. My lipoma was a benign fatty pocket that was growing at a faster rate than I was, and removing it left me with a nine-inch scar.

When the bandages came off, I was horrified; the scar was so ugly and it hurt terribly. In an effort to improve my appearance I underwent a revision surgery that left a smaller scar, but it was at the expense of reopening a wound that I was hoping to forget. I soon realized the pain of vanity was not worth the price. I decided then and there to accept my scar for what it was, and to choose not to pursue another revision attempt.

Because of my scar I was taunted, pushed down stairs, and called names. People treated me like an outcast, and my experience turned my physical wounds into a mountain of self-defeating insecurities. Nobody else thought I was worthy or beautiful, and I started to believe them.

However, when I was in fifth grade, I took my first step in learning to accept myself—scars included. A beauty pageant winner, Miss West Virginia, appeared at my school and shared "5 Steps to an Improved You." Her special message of self-empowerment and healthy self-image gave me the courage I so desperately longed for. When we graduated from elementary school that year and were asked what we wanted to be when we grew up, I bravely answered, "When I grow up, I want to be Miss West Virginia." She represented more than beauty to me. She represented the power of believing in yourself, even when others don't.

My peers snickered at the notion that I could be anything remotely close to a beauty queen. I ignored their put-downs. When I turned fourteen, I decided to go after my dream. With a seventeen dollar sale dress and a tiny bag of what I considered essentials, I entered my first beauty pageant. I quickly realized that I was in no way a front-runner, but I decided to learn everything I could from the experience, and I ended the day feeling as victorious as if I had walked away with the title. I had overcome my insecurities and stood before strangers, asking to be judged not only on outward beauty, but on the beauty I had within. For me, that was a true victory.

The judges saw me for me, not my scars. It was then that I knew I could overcome my feeling of brokenness and achieve my dreams: I entered the Miss America Scholarship Organization. For my platform, I chose to share my personal experience with visible scars and show what it meant to overcome the social stigmas and preconceived notions of what was beautiful.

Within the year I wrote and published my first children's book, *Shining Scars*, which is about the little star Eugene and his shining scar. I also reached out to children and teens staying at Children's Miracle Network Hospitals. Many of the children I have visited live with scars far greater than my own. Their ability to overcome each day is a reminder of what I strive to create through my organization, Shining S.C.A.R.S., a nonprofit that serves as an outreach for helping others with visible scars. No matter the circumstance, our scars remind us that we are strong, and that we have within ourselves the strength and ability to overcome obstacles and make our dreams come true.

By sharing my story, I work to break down my mountain of insecurities formed from certain painful memories. Anyone can climb a mountain, but for me the true victory will be the day the mountain is removed, giving me an endless view of the horizon. In the meantime, I may not always carry the title of a beauty queen, but I will always wear an invisible crown of strength, character, and self-acceptance, proving that I have risen above the stigmas of my physical scars.

JERRY SEGAL:
UNBOWED AND UNBEATEN

RICHARD J. ANTHONY, SR.
Meet Jerry Segal. Jerry is a husband, father, and grandfather. He is also a prominent Philadelphia attorney, an influential civic leader, a generous philanthropist, an avid golfer, and an indomitable quadriplegic.

Jerry's story began in 1988 when he underwent surgery for chronic back pain. However, the surgery did not go as planned, and instead of the promised relief from pain, he was paralyzed from the neck down. Although most people would feel defeated after the sudden shock of near total disability, it did not break Jerry's spirit, and he resolved not to be beaten. He set a goal to play golf again despite his condition, and vowed to establish a golf tournament to benefit the patients of the Magee Rehabilitation Hospital in Philadelphia, the place he credits with helping him reclaim his life and legal career.

True to his word, the first Jerry Segal Golf Classic took place in October 1990 after he had regained partial use of his upper body and was able to stand. Defying the predictions of experts and the laws of gravity, he stood, unassisted, on the first tee.

"I lost my balance and fell the first two swings," Jerry recalls. "But on the third try, I hit the ball over sixty-five yards straight down the fairway. That's when I knew I'd be playing golf again."

Jerry now uses crutches, braces, a walker, and a wheelchair in order to live a fast-paced life, which I discovered when I met him in his downtown office overlooking the Ben Franklin Parkway. This broad parkway stretches from City Hall to the steps of the city's art museum, the same steps that, fittingly, Rocky Balboa bounded up in his cinematic climb to the championship. Jerry's office was filled with photos, awards, and memorabilia that achievers accumulate over a lifetime of service, along with photos of his wife and family.

When I met with Jerry, he was overseeing the details of his September Golf Classic event, for which he had a goal of raising $600,000. The first Jerry Segal Classic raised $56,000; to date, the Classic has donated more than $11 million to the Magee Rehabilitation Hospital.

In addition to Jerry's charitable endeavors, he also enjoys swimming because it takes less energy to move his arms and legs. He especially likes to swim with his grandchildren, who are his greatest loves. On one occasion, his granddaughter Lily was helping him out of the pool. As they approached the steps to exit the pool, Lily said, "I've got you, Pop Pop. Lean on me." Jerry wasn't sure if Lily could take his weight, but she prompted each step, reassuring Jerry that she had a firm hold on him and that he was safe in her care.

As they started toward a chair, Jerry's legs gave out and he fell toward the hard surface. Immediately, his fall was broken by his son-in-law, Steve, who was standing nearby, watching his daughter compensate for Jerry's weakness.

"That's okay, Pop Pop," Lily said. "You did great! Tomorrow we'll take a few more steps."

Jerry had always been able to draw strength from an internal reservoir of grit and faith. This time, Jerry's source of strength was an eight-year-old who believed her Pop Pop could do better on another day with just a bit more effort.

"And she was right," Jerry told me, pointing to his head and chest. "If you have a positive attitude and a strong heart, there is no mountain that can't be climbed. I hope it's a lesson Lily will always remember."

CONTAGIOUS STRENGTH

Physical disabilities can break your spirit and limit your activities—or you can face them head-on. Even in the most hopeless situations, remain optimistic and know that only you can determine if your mental and spiritual abilities will be broken. Set goals and work to achieve them, despite the obstacles in your path.

CONTAGIOUS BEAUTY

Don't let your scars hold you back. You are more than your physical appearance. What matters the most is the passion that you have for life, and what you do to help others.

GOODWILL HAS NO PRICE

ROGER CANNON

In December 1970, I was managing a wholesale Christmas tree lot in downtown LA, close to where bustling trains would arrive daily from all over the country. These trains delivered tens of thousands of Christmas trees to consumers in southern California.

My chicken-wired lot with its trailer, cash register, and assortment of tools for cutting trees, nailing stands, securing trees on vehicles, and the like were normal for the trade. We got regular "drops" from the nearby trains most mornings. This was the time to get the setup done as quickly as possible, because once customers came in and it got busy, there was no time to stand new trees without taking a financial hit from making people wait. I would sell throughout the afternoon and deep into the night to people who owned small lots and wanted discounts for buying more than two or three trees. Many locals knew they'd find a really good tree fresh off the trains.

Once evening I was approached by a young man who introduced himself as Ray Robinson, Jr. I asked if he was related to Sugar Ray Robinson, the great world champion boxer. He said, "Yes, I'm his son, and I'm representing our Sugar Ray Foundation. We've used some of my dad's earnings to fund a place for inner-city kids to come and feel safe, and to learn to be good young men and women. We're interested in having Christmas trees for our clubhouses this year for the first time. I wanted to see if we could strike a bargain."

I told him to come back tomorrow around noon, because our on-lot selection was slim at that moment. Early the next morning, we got a good shipment, which included some Wisconsin white pines. I set aside a half dozen and marked them "sold."

Ray Jr. showed up right on time and was ready to negotiate. I showed him the white pines. He indicated he'd need six trees, but he didn't think he could afford them. I said, "These are for you. These are the ones you want. They're yours, Ray." He stammered, "Yeah, but how much are they?"

My parents' words came ringing back in that moment when I told him, "This is my goodwill gesture, Ray, and goodwill doesn't have a price, because it's not for sale. We know what good your organization does for the community. It's time for us to give back a little bit." He was floored. He must have said "thank you" a dozen times before departing.

Two weeks and two thousand trees later, it was Christmas Eve, nearing dusk. I had just put the last four trees outside the gate for any passersby to take, and was locking the gate for the last time that season. A shiny black limo swung around the corner and pulled up close to where I was. The back door opened and a man wearing an elegant tailored suit got out.

He asked, "You Roger?"

I nodded.

"Roger, I'm Sugar Ray Robinson. My son told me what you did for us, for the kids at our foundation. You have no idea how much happiness came from those trees. We'll never forget your kindness and what you said about goodwill not having a price. So now it's my turn. I've got something for you."

Ray reached back into the limo and pulled out an 8x10 photo of himself in a boxing stance. He signed it, "Best wishes, Rog. Sugar Ray Robinson." He told me he didn't like to sign things because of all the exploitation that went with memorabilia, but he made an exception in my case. He said, "Hang on to this. It'll be worth something to you someday."

He gave me a big hug, we shook hands, and we went our separate ways. Ray was right. Every time I look at the photo—really look at the photo—I smile inside.

CONTAGIOUS CHARITY

A charitable donation might not seem significant to you, but it can mean the world to others.

CONTAGIOUS REFLECTION

If you had to give an elevator speech at the end of your life, what would you talk about? What would be most important, what would you feel the most proud of, what would you want to be remembered by? As you decide, think about the positive things you have already done in your life, and then take it a step further and consider the ways that you can make a difference and help others in the future. Live a life of purpose and service, so that when you reach the end of your journey here on earth, you will know you had a positive impact on other people.

THE ELEVATOR SPEECH

JOEL HELLER

Have you ever had to prepare an elevator speech? This is the speech you would give to someone if you only had a few minutes in an elevator to pitch your idea or promote your product. I've had to give a number of them in my career, and sometimes they were effective and other times they failed miserably. However, I was recently thinking about elevator speeches in a different context. When we die and move into the great unknown, what if we have to present an elevator speech about our lives? What would we consider most important to include in our short recap, and what would our elevator speech say about how we lived?

Why am I, a forty-something-year-old fellow in pretty good health, thinking about mortality and life's accomplishments? I am thinking about these things because my uncle is in his nineties and he's living through some serious health issues. I've taken some time to visit him in the rehabilitation facility he stays in, and I try to send cards of encouragement to let him know he is in my thoughts and prayers. He means a lot to me, and thinking about his eventual death has made me realize how fortunate I am to know such a caring and giving person. My uncle is a remarkable man who has always lived a good life, and it has made me think, when my time comes, will I have left a meaningful mark on the world?

My uncle holds a special place in our family history. He was the best man at my parents' wedding, and as a deacon, he officiated over the wedding services for my marriage, my brother's marriage, and my sister's marriage. He has spent tireless hours working with his church to run charity and clothing drives and food kitchens for the less fortunate in the community. He never spoke about his work, about his time in the Army during WWII, or about meeting the pope or a mayor. Instead, he always spoke about his next service project and about the ways he planned on giving to the community. He could have retired and traveled the world, but he decided that a life of selflessly serving his community was what was truly important. I hope that at the end of my days I will have accomplished and given to my community in a similar selfless manner.

As I imagine my uncle's elevator speech would do, I would like my elevator speech to focus on the important things. Instead of being about job titles, it would be about the impact I left on those I met. At the end of our lives, it's not about the size of our bank account or our material things, but what we did to help each other on the road of life. It's about how we raise our kids, how we help those less fortunate than us, and what we do to make the world a better place. In the end, the things that really matter are the things we do to lift each other up.

CONTAGIOUS GIVING

If you are in the position to help someone, don't hesitate to do so. There are many ways you can reach out and lend a hand, and you don't always need to give money to make a difference.

THE VALUE IN SHARED
GOOD FORTUNE

ALAN A. MALIZIA
What does one do when they have "made it"? There are many different ways for people to reach a high level of success and thereby "make it"; one way of making it is financially. Regardless of the way some people reach their financial success, whether it be through hard work or luck, they are in a better position because they have the means to make a difference. There is an inherent value in giving, which affects both the receiver and the giver. However, one does not necessarily need money and financial success to give, and one's fortune need not be monetary in nature. A person's fortune can arise in the form of a gift or talent that, when shared, can affect people in a meaningful way.

When I was stricken with polio at the age of four, I had difficulty with functioning and self-sufficiency, and part of my recovery was accomplished at the Easter Seals Rehabilitation Center in my hometown. Although the state funded the physical therapists and services provided by the center, my mother wanted to give something back, and she shared her gratitude for my improving condition through her talent as a seamstress. Each year my mom participated in the center's fundraising events, where she would sew Christmas aprons using materials she provided at her own expense. The center's staff enthusiastically and gratefully received the items she donated. Her charitable donation not only brought joy to the patrons who purchased the aprons for the center's cause, but also to the patients who reaped the benefits from the care that the apron's proceeds partially financed. If even one patient's burden was lightened through therapy paid for as a result of my mom's charitable act, then it was worth the effort.

I was reminded again of how life-changing a loving, charitable heart can be as I neared high school graduation, long after I had progressed beyond my need for the center's therapeutic services. My parents and I were summoned to the center's Occupational Therapy department, where the department director informed us that no matter where I wished to attend college, all expenses would be paid. We were elated, assuming the scholarship was being provided by the center. However, we were informed that an anonymous donor had offered to finance my college education years ago when I was a young boy receiving therapy. I would never know my benefactor's identity, but I gave my best effort toward completing a degree in mathematics, as well as embarking on a successful profession as a teacher and coach. This, I believed, was the best way to honor my donor's most generous and charitable gesture.

The unknown donor lent me a helping hand and an opportunity: two things that many of us need from time to time. In my case, my donor's helping hand allowed me to get an education and stand on my own two feet, something I could not do at age four. An act of charity, just like my mother's aprons and the stranger's donation to my college education, is an act of love. When we have the means and the opportunity to give, we should do so and share love with those who need our help the most.

THE MAGIC OF MENTORING

NAVID NAZEMIAN

When a man named Jack Welch was GE's chairman, he became an expert on how digitization could contribute to GE's success. Back then he was already a seasoned retiree, so how could he have known so much about the new age of digitization? Because he received mentoring from an Internet-savvy twenty-five-year-old who knew a lot about computers. Although Jack already had years of professional experience under his belt, and though his mentor was only half his age at the time, he was still able to learn many valuable things from him.

So what is mentoring? According to *Webster's New International Dictionary*, "To mentor is to teach or give advice or guidance to someone, such as a less experienced person or a child." Mentoring typically focuses on the long-term professional and personal growth of the individual. It is about joint exploration and providing guidance regarding career and personal progression and preparation.

The benefits of having a mentor could be enormous. For example, a mentor's personal experiences can serve as a constant source of encouragement for mentees and can accelerate a mentee's learning. Mentees are able to use a mentor as a sounding board for concerns and thoughts, as well as a networking source. Lastly, mentees can gain fresh perspectives on an idea or project.

Personally speaking, I've been lucky to have quite a few mentors throughout my career. My most notable mentor was a senior manager for one of my previous employers. He was a man I looked up to, so when both he and I moved on and changed employers, I decided to ask if he would mentor me. I must say that I was a little bit daunted when I wrote him a note about a year ago asking if he would enter into a formal mentoring relationship. However, he agreed, and we are now able to speak freely and openly about a variety of topics. I value what he has taught me.

Although I found a mentor in one of my past colleagues, some people mistakenly assume that both parties must be employed by the same organization to benefit from a mentoring relationship. As a seasoned human resources professional, I can tell you that is not true. You can find a credible mentor in a number of places, such as in professional organizations, at conferences or seminars, or through alumni or faculty from undergraduate or graduate colleges. You can also enter a mentoring relationship with a person in a job you aspire to get one day, with a previous supervisor, or with a trusted friend.

Any person who is equipped with a set of professional skills or a bank of knowledge about a subject can be a mentor. Therefore, don't focus too much on age, title, or other labels when choosing a mentor. Rather, choose someone who inspires you, who can teach you, and who has the patience to help you. A relationship like this could be very beneficial.

WHY THE TOP ISN'T LONELY

KIMBERLEE M. HOOPER
When I was in high school, I was locally famous for my track and field performances. During the district championships, a teammate of mine came up to me and said, "Doesn't winning ever get boring?" His question was dripping with sarcasm and anger, and though I had no response, I could not get it out of my mind.

I mulled over his question for quite some time and came to the realization that he was speaking from a place of greed and negativity, a place I was unfamiliar with and had not encountered from a teammate or competitor in the past. True, I did achieve the spotlight many times for my efforts on the track, and I did win many medals and MVP awards. However, I truly appreciated every moment I spent on the track, every handshake I exchanged with a competitor, and every congratulatory high five I got from a coach or an official. I understood that none of my success would have been possible without the cooperation and support of the people around me.

Achieving fame or reaching the spotlight, whether it is within your company, your school, or the world, is something to keep in perspective. It is important to remember that your fame may not have been possible without the actions of other people. If people did not vote for you, you would not be named MVP. If people did not willingly sacrifice their time and effort training you, your talent never may have emerged. Acknowledging and expressing gratitude to those people who made it possible for you to be who you are is the most genuine way to accept your fame.

It is easy to be consumed by success and by the thrill of being in the spotlight. But always remember to ask yourself, How did I get here? Although you achieved success through hard work, long practices, and dedication, it is important to feel grateful to those who helped you along the way. Realize that your success does not mean you are above anyone, even if they were only a small part of your rise to the top. Seize the opportunity of success to recognize and appreciate others for all the things they did that helped you get where you are. Be proud but humble, excited but gracious, and supportive of all efforts, big and small, made by others who admire and support your journey.

CONTAGIOUS MENTORSHIP

We all need some guidance in our lives. Mentors allows us to learn and grow with someone who has been there and done that. Find someone to confide in and welcome what this person has to teach you.

THE LIGHTBULB WENT OFF

JC SULLIVAN

For many people, eye-opening things happen at the most unexpected moments. For me, one of these moments occurred when I was on vacation in Zanzibar, the Spice Island off the coast of Tanzania. I had just left an Internet café after answering work emails, and I was looking for some much-needed relaxation.

I was at the beach to catch the spectacular sunset, and though I was yearning for some alone time, a little boy plopped himself down beside me. As the boy spoke to me, I stayed lost in thought and only half-answered his questions. Then I heard him say, "I'd rather be a lamppost in America than a little boy in my country." After that statement, he had my full attention.

I was shocked. I managed to spit out, "Why?" The young boy said I'd never understand because I was white and a foreigner. He explained that in his country, you go to jail for life if you kill a white person. So dark-skinned people kill and steal from other dark-skinned people, to very little punishment. He explained that he thought America was different: the women sleep around and everyone is rich; life is easy. Then he asked me to adopt him, and my heart cracked in pain. I had no idea how to respond.

"Please just talk to me. Tell me what America is like," he implored. "You're the first American I've ever met. Tourists stay in expensive hotels where I can't go in. Why are you here on the beach and not in the bar like the rest of them?" When

I explained that I was there because I wanted to see the sunset, he asked if we didn't have sunsets in California. I couldn't bring myself to tell him that I worked right by the beach back home.

As we both stared at the gorgeous sunset, this little boy told me he was eight and would love to see his ninth birthday. He then asserted that he'd never be able to visit America. I told him he didn't know that, and that he might be able to one day. "Lady, I have an ID from Tanzania. I can visit Kenya. That's it. Kenya. No one else wants us. As for Americans, you spend money and go home. Everyone wants you."

"Well, it was my dream to visit Africa and go on a safari," I said. He looked at me funny; he went on safaris every year for school. "Tourists from all over the world work and save to visit Tanzania," I continued. "It took me a long time, but I did it. You can do it, too. You'll figure out a way." I handed him a notepad and told him to write down his dreams. In his country, a piece of paper was hard to come by; he held it as if it were a passport to another world, thanking me. As his friends called him, he shook my hand like a little diplomat, waved goodbye, and vanished.

That little boy changed my way of thinking. It is easy to take things for granted, but in our short conversation, he made me realize how lucky I am, and how thankful I should be for my lifestyle. Sometimes all you need is a small reminder to put things in perspective.

CONTAGIOUS PERSPECTIVE

It can be easy to lose sight of all the ways you are lucky, so it's important remember your blessings from time to time. No matter where you live, and regardless of what has happened in your life, remember that there are people throughout the world who are dealing with their own struggles. Be thankful for where you are and what you have.

CONTAGIOUS ACKNOWLEDGMENT

If you find success or fame in your life, it is important to remember the people who helped you on your journey. Without their support and dedication to you and your endeavors, you may never have found that success or fame.

A LIFE LESSON FROM TONGA

STEVE UIBLE

I was entering the Peace Corps as an idealistic college graduate in the late 1960s, and I wanted to make the world a better place. Because of my farming background, I was assigned a position in the agriculture department in a country I had never even heard of. My acceptance came by telegram—no emails in those days—for an assignment in the Kingdom of Tonga, which I assumed was in Africa. A trip to the library straightened me out. I discovered that Tonga is actually in the middle of the South Pacific, near Fiji and Samoa.

No matter which field we volunteers worked in, we were expected to promote population control, which was considered the most pressing problem in the world. There was a cover on *Time* magazine that depicted a bomb with a lit fuse and the heading "Population Time Bomb." As a side note, the world population at that time was only about three billion people. As of early 2015, we are already at 7.3 billion people, but that is a story for another day.

So, besides my work in agriculture, I made every effort to promote family planning and birth control. I felt good doing this: I would not only be helping the world, but also helping the families I was living and working with. That was especially important, because many of the families had six to ten children and were quite poor. Believe it or not, my next-door neighbor, Hafoka, had twenty-four children, all with the same wife. This prompted me to take every opportunity to talk about how much better it would be to have only two children, just like back home in America.

Fortunately, or unfortunately, I was having much greater success in agricultural education than I was in family planning, for reasons I did not fully understand. First of all, family planning was not considered a polite topic to talk about in public; sex was to stay in the bedroom. However, there were other challenges as well. Churches have a strong influence in Tonga and affect almost everything in daily life. Children are considered gifts from God, so limiting them by trying to keep the population down goes against a belief and trust in God. I was getting nowhere on this important topic and did not know how I could make my point.

After a few months of this frustration, I was ready to go back to my agricultural projects and leave the family planning to the church. It was around this time that I befriended a wise old Tongan man named Ini who gave me the answer I was looking for. What Ini taught me has shaped my understanding of people ever since that memorable day. Here is what he told me:

"Steve, we are a poor country here in Tonga and things are different than where you come from. You have noticed, I am sure, that we have several generations living in the same house. We don't send our parents to nursing homes like you do. The children take care of their parents for as long as they are with us. If we do what you suggest and have only two children, it could be very bad for us. You see, some children do not survive into adulthood and die young, even as infants. Some children are blinded by the big city lights and go to Australia or America to make more money than they can here in Tonga, and some just don't turn out to be good citizens. So if we have more children, say six to ten, we know there will be at least one child who will take care of us when we get old."

I was taken aback by his words. I never thought about it that way, but it made perfect sense to me. The Tongan people have no retirement pensions, no Social Security, and no Medicare, because their children take the place of all those programs. If we expect the people of Tonga to have smaller families, we must see that they have security in their old age first.

My lesson here—and it was a big one for a young American who thought he had all the answers—was never to assume you know it all. Make sure you know the facts and understand the situation as it really is—only then can you hope to make wise decisions that are based on reality.

CONTAGIOUS LIFE LESSON

Before jumping to conclusions, be sure you know the whole story.

HOMELAND CAMBODIA

NATALIE WEINRAUCH
An hour's flight away, and yet worlds apart. That sums up Cambodia for anyone living here in ultramodern Singapore. A wide gap, which can be filled by a lot of work, love, and optimism, stands between knowing that a community needs help and delivering that help.

It is impossible to grow up in Cambodia without some awareness of the desperation many people still face. From our earliest years at school, we hear of the country's misfortunes both past and present. Four million people, more than Singapore's native-born population, live on less than one dollar per day. Twenty-seven percent of Cambodians ended their education in fifth grade, and just five percent went beyond middle school. The "backwardness" of Cambodia is abundantly obvious when you visit. However, there is also a sense of energy, optimism, and, especially among the young, a readiness to pursue a better future.

There is a place in rural Cambodia, exactly at the Killing Fields of the 1970s, where this dichotomy of depression and hope merge. It's a local organization called Homeland, in Batambang. It manages a children's shelter. Kids arrive via two heartbreaking paths. Homeland provides residence, food, protection, and basic training to girls who manage to escape situations where their parents sold them for labor or trafficking. Homeland also runs a drop-off center. This facility actively collects abandoned street children and gives them a safe, friendly environment where they are fed and sheltered.

Homeland does what it can with limited resources. It has funds to send its residents to a local public school and feed its residents three meals per day. The training reflects Homeland's eye toward the future while providing a sustainable path. Amazingly, Homeland remains an oasis of pride and happiness. Severely scarred children begin to have fun and gradually gain a sense of safety, stability, and community. Homeland is a family. The teens become the older brothers and sisters for the little ones. The love missing in their former lives is somehow replaced; the children cling to the staff, but also to one another. You see laughter and hand holding, not the crying and pain as when they first arrived. If you visit, the children attach themselves to you with a warmth and longing, making it impossible not to return.

For me, it is a labor of love to be part of a group of students at the Singapore American School who are dedicated to raising awareness and funds for Homeland. This is critical now because of the global economic crisis. As their needs grow, we want to spread the message more widely of Homeland's good and essential work. Helping these Cambodian children is crucial proof of our own optimistic future. Mahatma Gandhi said it best: "We find ourselves in service to others." I am living proof of that.

CONTAGIOUS ALTRUISM

No matter how busy you are, roll up your sleeves and lend a hand. You will not only be helping others in need, you will quickly gain an appreciation for your own life and the blessings you have.

EMPATHY

A poem by Karen Lyons Kalmenson

Empathy is a precious word
Often uttered
But rarely heard.
Man needs to learn
That the greatest joy of all
Is to share oneself
And feel ten feet tall!

CHAPTER NINE

STAY INSPIRED

Inspiration is fuel for the heart and the mind.

When our cars are low on energy, we need to fill up with gas, diesel, or electricity. When we get hungry, we need to fill our stomachs with food and drink. What do we do when our brains are starving?

From a scientific viewpoint, the brain gets most of its energy from the oxygen-dependent metabolism of glucose (i.e., blood sugar) along with fatty acids and amino acids. Based on today's science, many believe that the brain is simply a physical housing for the mind. Yet the mind has different energy needs. Those needs include imagery, imagination, emotions, reasoning, decision making, and other mental stimuli. As humans, we have the benefit of being able to choose those stimuli.

In addition to exercise and hobbies, I stimulate my mind by taking in real stories from real people around the globe and sharing those stories with others in order to help them find their silver linings. I enjoy the positive and I make it the catalyst that gets me out of bed every morning. Sure, I follow the news and take in all the current events—good or bad. After all, reality is an important part of life, like optimism. But I also make sure that I don't let bad news consume me or become my focus. I don't let it convince me that all of the world is bad and falling apart—because it isn't. On the contrary, the world is craving inspiration and positivity, and I feel blessed to be a part of this **Contagious Optimism** movement.

Staying inspired for one person may mean something as simple as enjoying music or practicing the culinary arts. For another, it may mean rock-climbing or skiing expert slopes. Whatever your passion, don't let excuses stop you from enjoying it. As far back as we can know, men and women have endured tough times and overcome obstacles, while, at the same time, usually finding the bright side of life and living it accordingly. People are not stimulated by temporary issues or worries, but by the beauty of natural resources, the miracle of life, and the power of the mind.

What stimulates you? Enjoy the stories in this chapter and ponder that question. I am certain you already have the answer in you.

David

> *I see our later years as an opportunity to do things we never had the time to do before. It is a time for people to keep living life to the fullest, but on their own terms.*
> —Peter Nicholls, Adelaide, Australia

> *Hiking is more than a hobby to me. It has helped me celebrate and develop a strong spiritual connection with nature and the universe. Just as I did, you may find some clues about your dormant passion by thinking about what you enjoyed as a child.*
> —David Martin, Reno, Nevada

FINDING STRENGTH

LANCE STRANAHAN

When searching for an example of someone who truly exemplifies the meaning of the word optimism, I look to my father, Frank Stranahan.

Those who are aware of his early life would probably agree that initially, he had every reason to be optimistic. His father was the cofounder and president of Champion Spark Plug Company, so my dad was born into a wealthy family. At an early age, he found his passion in the game of golf and became known as the best amateur golfer of his era. In addition, he was very handsome and had developed an excellent physique from vigorous weight training. He believed weightlifting would make him a longer hitter and he was the first person ever to combine strength training with golf. The results of this earned him the nicknames "Muscles" and "The Toledo Strongman."

By the time my dad was in his mid-thirties, he had married the woman of his dreams and become a father to three sons. He retired from the golf tour and went back to school. He earned a master's degree in finance from the University of Pennsylvania's Wharton School and began to embark on a business career.

Shortly after, he encountered his first real tragedy.

My brother, my dad's oldest son, Frank Jr., was diagnosed with bone cancer and had to have his leg amputated. Unfortunately, he died from the disease months later at the age of eleven. Less than ten years later, my mother got pancreatic cancer and died at the age of forty-six. If losing his beloved wife wasn't devastating enough, my other brother, James, died of a pill and alcohol overdose eight months later.

What I remember about this period was that my father always remained positive and upbeat. I never witnessed him sinking into depression or anger. He had taken up long-distance running a few years before, and he would get up every day at 3:00 a.m. to run at least fifteen miles. He never deviated from his diet and weight training regimen. He eventually completed more than one hundred marathons.

I didn't find out until many years later that during this same time, my father had tremendous business setbacks as well. He was a major shareholder in several large corporations when the "Black Monday" stock market crash occurred in 1987. Unbeknown to me at the time, he ended up millions of dollars in debt. However, never once did I see him succumb to despair. He continued his Spartan regimen and only spoke in inspiring and positive terms. He used to carry around a notebook filled with his favorite quotes, and he would lecture me on the importance of setting goals and never being negative.

My dad continued to play golf with me each afternoon, and he did his best to coach me in the game. Then, as he approached his late sixties, he became interested in bodybuilding competitions and began to compete in them. He loved going to the gym every day and he formed a wonderful camaraderie with the guys there. They would yell, "Come on, Frank, push it! Do one more!" My father was in great shape, and many of the gym members were inspired by the sight of a sixty-eight-year-old man training with such high intensity. He ended up winning several titles, including more than sixty national bodybuilding championships. He continued to compete until his late seventies.

I noticed when my father was around eighty-one that his memory began to diminish. He had been treated for a blood clot in his leg, which may have been a complication from a previous automobile accident, and it's possible the blood clot had affected his brain. It saddened me greatly to see someone who had devoted so much time and effort toward his health become unable to care for himself. Remarkably, even this setback didn't discourage my dad; he continued to work out enthusiastically until a week before he passed away. I would have his caregiver drive him to my gym and I would help him work out with the weights, or we would go to the driving range and hit balls together. He always greeted me with a huge smile, and according to the people who took care of him, he was never down or depressed.

I will never forget my father's amazing attitude and constant optimism. I can only hope that his inspiration will keep me optimistic throughout whatever challenges life may throw at me.

CONTAGIOUS STRENGTH

When you think of someone who exemplifies the word optimism, who do you think of? What have they done to show that they can defy odds, overcome difficulties, and remain upbeat through challenges? There may be multiple people in your life who serve as examples of optimism and perseverance, and they can teach you and others important lessons about how to live a happy, determined life. When you're going through a hard time, think of the optimism shown by these people, and remember: your struggles feed your strength. Even after experiencing tragedy, difficulty, or disappointment, try to be optimistic, and try to find strength by doing the things you love.

THE GURU APPEARS

BHARATH GOPALAN

In India, we say, "The guru appears when you are prepared." The Sanskrit word *guru* literally means "remover of darkness." *Gu* denotes the darkness and *ru* means who or what removes darkness. But *guru* does not necessarily mean a person in the physical sense.

Have you ever wondered about certain coincidences or the way things sometimes surprisingly fall into place? You might have bumped into a person whom you were dying to meet for some time, or a piece of information you wanted very badly may have popped up out of nowhere. We often brush these moments aside as casual coincidences, without really acknowledging the power of our mind in making them happen.

But the fact is, more focused minds reap greater rewards. For example, consider serendipity or accidental discoveries. These occurrences and discoveries are not accidents at all; they are just ways in which nature rewards focused minds with unexpected results. It is the attentive mind that sees the gravitation in the apple fall or the buoyancy in the bathtub. After all, Beethoven was mostly deaf, and he composed his symphonies not simply by listening to the music, but by focusing his mind and listening to the silence within.

The world abounds with plenty of everything; how it appears to us depends on our attitude. What are opportunities for an optimist may be problems for a pessimist; and what are challenges for the courageous may be nerve-racking for the jittery.

There is an old story that demonstrates how our mind and attitude has the power to bring certain things into our lives. A stranger visiting a village asked a wise old man sitting by the road, "How are the people in this village?"

The old man replied, "How were they in the village you come from?"

"They were all cunning, greedy, and jealous over there."

The old man said, "They are no different here."

Later, another passerby came by and asked the old man the same question about the people in the village. The old man asked his opinion about the people in his previous village.

When the passerby said, "They were caring, loving, and happy people," the old man gave the same reply: "They are no different here."

Just as in the story, the way the world appears to us and how we perceive the things that come into our lives depends on our attitude. If we see things as negative, then they will be negative. When your mind is alert, things do start happening and conspire within you to produce the results you want. Simply focus your mind and prepare yourself, and the guru will appear.

CONTAGIOUS MINDFULNESS

Take up one idea that you haven't paid enough attention to; it could be writing an article or solving a problem. As you go to sleep at night, stay with that thought until you completely sink into it. You will wake with your solution or article the next morning.

REVELATION AT 18,500 FEET

BECKY WOODBRIDGE

I was so tired of crying. That's all I had done for the better part of six months in the aftermath of my divorce. However, the only thing the tears did was mask a deep, troubling truth that, sooner or later, I had to face: I was lost. And I was scared. After eighteen years of marriage, I didn't know who I was.

My ex-husband had found his identity as a pilot, and I had helped him get his career off the ground. We met when I was fifteen and still in high school; three years later, we married. Being so young, I didn't yet have the confidence to stand by my convictions or express my inner voice, so I played the role of the dutiful wife and supported my husband.

By the time he earned his pilot's license, I had worked three different jobs to pay for his college and flight school. I spent much of our marriage swept along in his orbit, while my own identity was barely a blip on anyone's radar. What was worse was that I wasn't doing anything about it.

When we finally separated, the pain was unbearable. Not only had I lost my friend and lover, but I had lost my connection to the world around me. If I wasn't the wife of the pilot, who was I? I didn't know, and so I cried. However, crying wasn't helping. I slowly came to the realization that in order to find myself I might have to lose myself on a journey that had nothing to do with my ex-husband—and everything to do with me. Still, I needed a jump-start, something that would sever the cord that was tying me to post-divorce angst, and this meant stepping out of my comfort zone and tackling new challenges.

The first thing I did was skydive, and at the time, it felt like the best way to find some confidence. It worked. The thrill I felt doing something with that kind of fear factor motivated me to keep pushing myself. So I trained for and ran the Walt Disney World Marathon in Orlando, and from there, I learned how to snowboard on a trip to Wyoming. On that same vacation, I climbed on a mechanical bull, which was set up near the slopes, and it took less than ten seconds for the metal beast to toss me onto a patch of packed-down snow. I suffered two broken ribs, but it didn't matter; I'd crossed yet another adventure off my bucket list.

And so it went. Every chance I had, I took a trip with family, friends, or groups—you name the destination, and I was game to visit. But for all the excitement and accumulated frequent flier miles, something was still missing. I wasn't yet entirely comfortable in my own skin, and I needed to rid myself of some baggage. To accomplish that, I'd first have to travel 8,000 miles from home and into the shadow of the world's highest mountain.

While at a party for the 2000 Super Bowl, I overheard a gentleman named Frank talking about an upcoming adventure to climb Kala Patthar, a landmark in the Nepalese Himalayas. My ears perked up. I had recently read a story about Mt. Everest, and an adventure to Kala Patthar was a chance to see the mountain in all its regal splendor. Kala Patthar's peak, recorded at 18,500 feet in elevation, provides jaw-dropping views of Everest; it is challenging yet accessible for people without significant mountaineering experience. I wanted to go in the worst way, and I shamelessly begged Frank to take me with him.

On March 15, we all boarded a plane for Kathmandu, the capital of Nepal. Our expedition included a team of sherpas, who served as guides, and I was the only female in our group. Although I was determined to be as tough as the men during our fourteen days on the mountain, it wasn't easy. There was the physical strain of day-long climbs in thin air, dealing with extreme cold, and overcoming the drowsiness incurred by taking Diamox, which prevents altitude sickness. I also suffered from a mild altitude-related headache that stayed with me for the duration of trip. With each passing day, the climb grew more and more challenging, and at one point, I was breathing so hard for so long that I pulled the stomach muscles around my rib cage.

Tents, meanwhile, did little to protect us from the elements. It was so cold at night that we slept in full gear, including ski jackets, gloves, hats, complete face covers, and a heavy-duty sleeping bag, but even that didn't give us a respite from the Arctic-like chill. If that wasn't enough, I was battling my own vanity. I had no makeup, no hairbrush, no shower, and only two sets of clothing for the duration of the trip. Since I was on a mountain populated by men, not having a mirror for two weeks was killing me.

The day of our summit, we awoke at 3:00 a.m. to begin the slow climb to the peak, and on this particular day, I emerged from my tent in a panic. I couldn't find my goggles, an essential item, given the elements. One of the hikers was kind enough to loan me his spare pair, but they were the ugliest glasses I had ever seen. Here I was, 1,000 feet from the summit of Kala Patthar, and I was distressed because I had to wear unattractive goggles.

However, a few hours later, standing almost 19,000 feet above sea level and reveling in the splendor of the Himalayas, the silliness of my vanity hit me so hard. No one cared what I looked like, how bad my clothes smelled, or how ugly my borrowed glasses were. The baggage I had brought to the top of Kala Patthar was all mine. And it was time to let it go.

I was no longer the wife of a pilot. I was my own person; someone who had the confidence and the courage to step out from behind the shadows, overcome adversity, take risks, and live life on her own terms. I knew my strengths and my weaknesses. I knew where I had been and where I was going. And I was okay with all of it.

I may have found my identity at a high altitude, but, in that moment, I actually felt more grounded than ever.

CONTAGIOUS IDENTITY

Identity can be lost, but it can be found again. Don't completely remove yourself from society; that only means you'll lose yourself more. Instead, immerse yourself in something new and exciting, and get reacquainted with who you really are.

LIFE ON WHEELS

JORDAN LOWE

When I was seventeen, a month away from my high school graduation, I was in a motor vehicle accident.

My boyfriend and I were driving back from a dirt track race that ended late. It was 1:30 a.m. We both fell asleep and I woke up when the truck rolled off the road and crashed. I knew something was wrong immediately but I was more focused on my boyfriend and how he was doing. He got out of the vehicle and called the cops, and stood by me until the paramedics arrived. The tests and X-rays made it official: I suffered a spinal cord injury. The doctors diagnosed me as a quadriplegic and told me I would be in a wheelchair for the rest of my life.

I decided I wasn't going to let my condition get the best of me. I was going to move on with my life. I knew too many people who just gave up after something like this, and I wasn't going to do the same. My mom was diagnosed with postpartum depression after I was born. Instead of getting help for her problem, she turned to drugs and alcohol. But I have always been a strong-willed and stubborn woman, so when I was dealt this hand I decided I was going to play it to the best of my ability.

I went through three months of intensive inpatient therapy and I continue to go back when I need it. During those three months I learned how to get dressed, and how to move from place to place, and other important day-to-day activities. It was extremely difficult relearning how to do simple tasks, but

I stuck it out. Being in rehab and listening to everyone's stories made me a better person. It gave me a different outlook on life and on my situation. I realized all the things I had taken for granted and saw that I had a second chance to appreciate my life. I finished my senior year in the hospital and, to my surprise, the doctor let me go to graduation. When I got out of the hospital I reenrolled at Fairmont State University in the psychology department.

Since my accident I have overcome so many obstacles. Many people doubted my ability to live a normal life. When I started school my sister would come home and tell me that people believed I would never make it in college. They said I was going to live off disability the rest of my life and I wouldn't make anything of myself. They were wrong.

In the summer I ride a four-wheeler almost daily. I am a country girl, so hunting is a must. I also like to fish and to swim—well, float—in the river. This past summer my friend Jennifer and I decided to try horseback riding. Though we don't have it perfected yet, I still got to ride. It was incredible. I am also in the process of getting my driver's license. I can drive with hand controls that work with the gas and the brake. The rest of the vehicle works the same as a regular vehicle.

In September 2013, I entered the Ms. Wheelchair USA pageant. I was named Ms. Wheelchair West Virginia and I represented my state in the national pageant in July 2014 where I placed second runner-up for the crown. As a participant I had to come up with a platform I felt strongly about. I chose educating and promoting awareness about people with disabilities and the type of support they may need. I chose this platform because I know people who have experienced no support and have traveled down the wrong path time and time again.

Nowadays, I spend my time going around to different events and hospitals talking about my platform and sharing my story.

One thing I always tell people is that the only true handicap you can have is yourself. You can do anything as long as you set your mind to it.

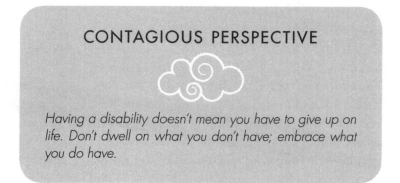

CONTAGIOUS PERSPECTIVE

Having a disability doesn't mean you have to give up on life. Don't dwell on what you don't have; embrace what you do have.

THE POWER OF SPORTS

SALVATORE TRIFILIO

I was born and bred a New York Yankees fan. I may not be from the Bronx, and I may not own season tickets, but I have always and will always bleed pinstripes. Long story short, if you're a fan of any Boston franchise, chances are we won't get along.

I'll be up front with you. If you've met me before and told me that you're from Boston, or even if you've told me you like Boston, I would have filled you in immediately about how much I detest the place and—by association—you.

But, hey, can you blame me for disliking Boston? We're talking about the city that sold Babe Ruth, whom I consider to be the greatest baseball player of all time, to allegedly fund a Broadway play. I guess it's not so bad, since Ruth went on to play for the Yankees. I also watched Red Sox player Pedro Martinez throw a defenseless Don Zimmer, the seventy-two-year-old Yankees bench coach, to the ground during a bench-clearing brawl.

However, though I spent so much time rooting against Boston, Monday, April 15, 2013, forever changed the way I see the city. On that Monday, when two bombs exploded on Boylston Street near the finish of the Boston Marathon, I was shocked, but the bombings did not hit home for me as quickly as I expected they might. Everything seemed so distant and surreal. I feared for those affected and I hoped that all their families would recover; however, at the time, it felt like an emotional link was missing.

It was strange that the bombings didn't immediately affect me, especially since I could imagine what the spectators at the marathon were going through, and I know all too well how terrifying it is when a loved one is so close to something so tragic. I grew up only thirty minutes from New York City, and my sister attended NYU, just blocks away from the World Trade Center. I feared for her and the people of my own city during the September 11, 2001 terrorist attacks, but for some reason, the news of the Boston bombings did not immediately affect me the same way.

Then, on Thursday, April 18, as I sat in my living room drinking my morning cup of coffee, it hit me. I was watching *SportsCenter* when a clip of the Boston Bruins vs. Buffalo Sabers game came on. My immediate reaction was distaste for the Bruins and all Boston sports—but then it happened.

As the National Anthem played before the drop of the first puck, the singer was interrupted by the entirety of the stadium singing the anthem in unison. A cold shiver ran up my spine, and I was covered in goose bumps. My heart raced as tears began to well up in my eyes. It was incredibly powerful to see all the fans in the stadium come together and show their pride and support in the face of the Boston attacks.

I began to think about that first game the Yankees played after the attacks on September 11, 2001, and how an entire nation was with my beloved Bronx Bombers that night. That night there were no Yankees fans and there were no Red Sox fans; there were only Americans.

After watching the clip of the National Anthem before the start of the Bruins game, I couldn't help but find myself rooting for the B's to win at home. Was I really having a change of heart? I'm not ashamed to say that I was. Sports can do amazing things. They can divide people and make them fight with their best friends. But more importantly, sports can heal and bring bitter rivals together. I will forever respect Boston after seeing that amazing display of human spirit after the city was shaken by tragedy. I can only speak for myself, but I think every Yankee fan will agree: with Boston, "united we stand."

CONTAGIOUS UNITY

You might dislike another team from another town because of loyalty to your own team. However, beneath these rivalries, and behind the fans rallying against each other, there is a common humanity. People understand that in times of need, sports have the ability to unify and ignite the kindred human spirit.

A SURPRISE PEARL OF
WISDOM

MARIAN HEATH AXLEY
In 1954, the basketball coliseum was the only place large
enough to seat the University of Kentucky's College of Arts
and Sciences freshman class for their first indoctrination. The
class ranks overflowed with Korean War veterans who had
opted to get an education with the GI Bill, and the university
personnel would be severely strained to accommodate the huge
increase in student numbers. A university dignitary on the po-
dium gave a welcoming speech and then an admonishment to
the newbies. "Look to your right, look to your left. One of you
will not be here next year."

However, I had no plans of failing out or dropping out. To
my right was a mature, beefy guy. To my left was a scrawny
fellow. It ain't gonna be me, I said to myself. I am gonna be
here next year.

I had made my way to college after receiving a religious
education from a small group of teaching nuns in Kentucky.
In high school, we had concentrated on thorough work habits
and a no-nonsense dedication to learning. Although I didn't
know what college would be like, I was happy to be there, and
knew that with hard work and dedication, I would do well.

As I sat through my first university indoctrination, I was
imagining what college would be like when all of a sudden
the administrator interrupted my thoughts. "We are going to
call out the majors in alphabetical order for the Arts and Science school," He said. "When we call out your major, walk

to the entrance where a guide will meet you."

Major? I was caught off guard because I had never thought about a major; I just knew that I was going to be the first member of my family to go to college. I didn't know what I wanted to study during my four years in college, so I decided then and there that I would simply leave the coliseum after they called out the first major.

"Agriculture!" the administrator said into the microphone. I stood up and then immediately sat back down. I was familiar with tobacco fields and cornfields but knew that I had nothing in common with that line of work.

"Art," the administrator said next. I hesitated a moment. I had never taken an art class; I just knew I could draw a little better than some of my friends. Several people near me rose and began to file out. I can do this, I thought, and followed the group.

And I did do it. Although I came to realize that my casual method of choosing a vocation not only showed naïveté and probably stupidity, I graduated from college four years later with a degree. Fast-forward sixty years. I not only have a bachelor's degree in fine art from the University of Kentucky, but also a master's degree in art from Florida Atlantic University. I am a retired high school art teacher from the Palm Beach County school system.

During the past ten years I have become a nationally accredited professional watercolorist. I am now exhibiting pieces internationally, and I have received numerous professional awards for my paintings. I was named a Signature Member of several state and national watercolor organizations and feel privileged to use their initials after my name.

There are some pearls of wisdom in this story. Yes, it is important to have a hard work ethic because if you are committed and you work hard, you can do anything you set your mind to. But the most important thing to remember is that hard work and dedication are more important than talent. I had almost zero artistic talent when I decided to make art my life work, but I remained dedicated, and I worked my hardest, and that is how I found my success.

I always told my high school art students that a lack of talent wasn't an excuse in my classes. "I can teach you to draw. I can teach you to paint," I would say. "Otherwise why am I standing in front of this class?" I wanted to convey to my students that if they remained interested and motivated, they could succeed. Therefore, even if you don't think you're good at something, work hard, remain focused, and approach the challenge head-on, and you can not only improve, but also excel.

CONTAGIOUS FUTURE

It is impossible to imagine where life can take you. Take each day one step at a time and never be afraid of the possibilities.

CONTAGIOUS CHOICE

Remember how powerful you and your choices are. The path you take does matter and how you react to things does make a difference.

WHAT DOES YOUR "HAPPY FORK" LOOK LIKE?

AMY SPENCER

One morning I pulled up Google Maps in the car to help me figure out the best route to my breakfast meeting in Burbank. One option was a direct path with heavy traffic. Another was a longer, roundabout route with very little traffic. But either way, I would arrive at the same time; two choices, same result. Well, sort of the same result, because each path would make me feel different along the way.

See, the shorter route had awful traffic—but with the right podcast playing, I might not even notice the slow go. The longer route would take me through streets I'd never seen—but would require my concentration for all the twists and turns so I wouldn't get lost. It was a small choice, but one that would set my whole day in motion. So I pulled out my imaginary "Happy Fork" and asked it: Which route will make me happier? Since I was early and up for the adventure, I chose the roundabout route. And I enjoyed every second of that drive.

That's how life works; we make choices every single day. And as positive psychologist and *Learned Optimism* author Dr. Martin Seligman discovered, choice is one of the most important elements in our optimism. We *need* to feel that we have a stake in what happens to us, and that our choices matter.

In the 1960s, Seligman, along with fellow psychologist Steven Maier, conducted a groundbreaking study that taught them about "learned helplessness." They gave subjects small electric shocks and allowed some of them to stop the shocks if they wished, while the others had no such control. The shocks were very mild, similar to what happens when you walk on carpet and touch a piece of metal. What happened next was astounding: When they put both sets of subjects in rooms with low partitions and gave them more small shocks, the subjects who had previously been able to stop the shocks simply jumped over the partition and out of the box. But the subjects who had been essentially *trained* to feel helpless? They didn't try to escape. It's almost as if they were thinking, No matter what I do, it won't help, so why bother?

This speaks volumes about our vital need for a sense of control over our destiny. Luckily, humans have control. We *always* have a choice. In fact, we make choices every day. We choose what time to wake up, which shoes to wear, whether or not we go through the yellow light, what we say in the meeting, how we treat our partners, what TV channel to watch, and what time we go to bed. Even when it feels like we're backed into a corner and don't have a choice in a certain situation, we still do—because we can choose how to feel about it.

So here's an idea for you: Build your own imaginary Happy Fork. Design it to your liking, and get a solid picture of it. Then, every time you reach a fork in your life road, see your choice as an opportunity. Hold up that Happy Fork in your mind, and ask yourself: "Which path will feed my true happiness?"

For instance, a few times a day, you have a simple choice about the food you eat. Which meal will make you feel like you can conquer the world? For me, one day last week, it was steamed vegetables. But a few days later, at a restaurant known for its burgers, I ordered one with cheese and rosemary bacon—because I'd been building up giddy anticipation for my burger splurge all week. Only you know which meal will feed your happiness.

If you're arguing with a partner, you have a choice in how you address your needs. Maybe it's taking their hand and apologizing in an open, caring way. Or maybe it's standing up for yourself and speaking your mind for the first time in a long time. Again, only you know which approach will feed your happiness.

And then there's the biggest fork of all: how you see, react, and feel about what happens to you. When my friend Stephen was diagnosed with Stage IV colon cancer, he didn't have a choice about his diagnosis, but he did have a choice in how he handled it.

"The future is uncertain, for me, and for everyone," he wrote on his blog, *Fear of Beauty*. "As the saying goes, no one gets out of here alive. The key for me has been to learn to relax, so that I can keep my wits about me."

Stephen chose to see his situation positively and as an opportunity for change. So he chose a new diet, new healers, a new meditation routine, a new temporary home in a peaceful place in Arizona, and most importantly, a new attitude. His latest blood tests, just a few months after his initial diagnosis, showed him cancer-free.

Put yourself in that position of confidence. We are not those helpless subjects in Seligman's study. We have exits in life, often from many angles, and the road ahead is full of options. So picture your blissful future, hold up your Happy Fork, and choose the path that takes you there.

IT'S NOT ABOUT THE GIRAFFE

SHARON DUNBAR

I am often told that I have a gift of patience. I think this patience evolved from the two years I spent in Maine working with a seventy-eight-year-old man who was suffering from dementia. When I first started working with him, his dementia was just beginning, and he was doing some erratic, nonsensical things. This patient had a multimillion-dollar trust, and in the throes of his deteriorating condition, he fired his personal assistant after two years for no apparent reason.

My job was to teach this man computer skills and to help him learn how to use Rosetta Stone, a foreign language CD set that measures voice skills as one tries to learn new languages. He enjoyed using this program because of his life of wealth and travel; it must have made him feel like he was his old self. No matter what type of therapy we were doing, I always tried to think outside the box.

During one of his first weeks back from a pacemaker surgery, he saw a giraffe on television and ordered me to get him one. He didn't realize how irrational that request was. Instead of dismissing his idea, I entertained it. I didn't say, "No, this is Maine—it's below twenty degrees outside," as some caregivers would. I simply replied, "A giraffe would be so cool for you to have. You could feed it from your bedroom window!" We discussed how we would transport it, where it would sleep, and even walking it around the courtyard of his community so that it could visit with other residents. I didn't want to discourage him, even though I couldn't actually fulfill his request.

My staff thought I was crazy, but they understood how to take care of a client with dementia. The secret is to keep them feeling calm, loved, and positive; my reaction to his request for a giraffe kept his mind at peace. It wasn't so much about getting the giraffe as it was about making him feel respected. He was encouraged by my gesture, and I provided him with some excitement. Although the giraffe never came, I made my client feel valued and cared about as a person. He began showing more focus and amazing improvement in therapy for his Alzheimer's.

Although he didn't get the giraffe, he did get his wish to take his last breath in his own home. He died at eighty years old in a place where he felt safe and loved. This client changed my life. I learned a lot from working with him. I know how crucial it is to show people that they are respected, and that when someone asks for a giraffe, it's not always about the giraffe.

CONTAGIOUS VALUE

Everyone around us has value. Rich or poor, black or white, sick or healthy—it does not matter. When you show others that you respect their value, you are adding meaning to their life and meaning to your own.

Stay Inspired

A poem by Karen Lyons Kalmenson

Stay inspired
with open heart
and eager mind,
for you will see beauty
in everything you find.
The world will indeed
be a happier place,
as you navigate the
hills and valleys
with a smile
upon your
face.

CHAPTER TEN

HAVE AN ATTITUDE OF GRATITUDE

Count your blessings. If you don't, you will never be satisfied when they're staring you in the face.

Appreciate the mistakes and the obstacles, for they are the sources of wisdom that ensure your success on life's journey.

Sometimes it's hard to have gratitude. We get caught up in our own richly rewarded lives and feel burdened with agendas and commitments, or we feel down about losses that we may be enduring. Ironically, there are people in third-world countries who would be shocked with our lack of appreciation for the things we do have, such as clean water, food, shelter, and clothing.

For some people, gratitude seems impossible; they wonder how they can be thankful when things go wrong in their lives. Appreciation doesn't happen easily when the chips are down, but the strength and character we build by hitting life's curveballs is something we should be thankful for. Unfortunately, it's difficult to see that when we are at the bottom, but it becomes very clear as we persevere.

For others, gratitude seems unnecessary, and they think, I am so caught up in my life; I have no time for... Many people achieve wealth and high levels of success. The routine of events and obligations and the consistent grind to maintain elite status seem to distract many from gratitude.

I always try to have the attitude that being down about something serves me no good. It doesn't change the situation—sometimes, the anger and bitterness only make things worse. I remember a day when I was under pressure trying to meet business obligations and keep up with a stressful travel schedule. At the same time, the financial markets were crashing and my car had a major breakdown. Just as I thought things couldn't get worse, a close relative suddenly passed away. That day felt like a perfect example of the domino effect. I realized that no matter what obligations and agendas stood before me, or what was happening to my investments, those were trivial matters. Illness and death put it all in perspective.

"You should be thankful for what you have. There is always someone worse off than you." We hear those words all the time, and they are easy to say for people who don't have bills, debts, and obligations hanging over them. But it always impresses me to hear that statement from people who are just getting by. Time and time again, I observe people with very little appreciating what they have, while many people with an abundance of wealth and "things" always seem to be complaining. I have found that when you stop, look at the sun, moon, water, or any other natural object of beauty, you realize that wealth is fleeting, while nature is constant.

Whatever can go wrong will go wrong if you always think the grass is greener on the other side. I try to avoid that at all costs. Regardless of how your day is going, remind yourself that your own grass is green, and keep appreciating what you have on your side of the fence. You will find that consistent optimism and confidence will ultimately bring better results to your life. As I said in volume one of this series, "You have nothing to lose by being positive versus the stress you will definitely gain by being negative."

This chapter focuses on the need for all people, rich or poor, to be grateful. You can express gratitude toward each other, toward the universe, toward a higher being—it doesn't matter; just simply have gratitude.

David

We can all find fault with almost anything, if we look for it. Start focusing on the overall experience instead of little inconveniences. Positive thinking and being thankful can change your life and outlook. Concentrate on talking in the present and future with the words "I can," "I have," "I will," instead of "I did" or "I was." Being lucky is really about dwelling on the best things you have.

—Joan Meyers, Greenwich, Connecticut

Long ago, people wrote letters to each other because they had no choice. No telegraph service, no telephones, and no Internet. Letters were meant for love, news, regrets, apologies, and announcements of all types. Today people write letters only by choice. And what a powerful choice that is! A real letter is your truth put to paper in the most loving and compassionate way possible. Although romance is a wonderful reason to run for the pen and paper, so is the desire to make amends or express gratitude!

—Janet Gallin, San Francisco, California

UNEXPECTED GIFTS

PAUL LIPTON

Gifts come in different types of wrappers. Some come with bright, shiny bows and happy faces embellished on them. Other gifts come in brown paper bags or the most unfriendly-looking wrapping paper. Some gifts can change your life for better or for worse, but that may depend on how you respond to these gifts.

My gift came over twenty-five years ago in the form of the most excruciating pain that had ever hit me. It dropped me to my knees. Panic, pain, and fear overrode all other sensations. Pain and panic can either cripple you or make you reevaluate your life—which is what happened to me. Time becomes more relevant and precious than ever before at moments when a choice must be made. Should you be the victim or hero of your own life story? Do you curl up into a fetal position or reach for the stars? Do you remain a victim of your circumstances or decide to rewrite your story and take the heroic path?

For me the suffocating pain was on the right side of my face. I was diagnosed with trigeminal neuralgia, also known as tic douloureux. Some even refer to it as the suicide disease because those afflicted with it often consider this ultimate choice.

I decided to do something about my problems. After over fourteen years of pain and mind-numbing medication, I sought out a specialist and had surgery in 2003 to basically resheathe the fifth cranial nerve. A hole was drilled into the back of my skull and this amazing team of doctors and nurses did their magic.

That surgery was a crossroads in my life, and I realized that it was a moment of rebirth and resurrection. A moment of salvation. Like me, everybody eventually reaches some crossroads in their life where they need to reevaluate how they are living. These are moments when people are able to find their voice, discover their calling, and embrace their purpose; they embrace the gift.

I went back to my job as a trial attorney, but I kept thinking that I had been granted a gift, and I needed to reevaluate my path in life. As each day went by, I felt like I had to let go of one journey and begin a new one. A third chapter needed to be written. My wife of forty-five years, Margie, and I decided to step back from our successful professional careers. We sold our home in Miami and moved to Colorado to be closer to our kids and grandkids. We wanted to seek personal fulfillment that came from experimenting outside of our limitations, so we ventured into the unknown.

Some believe that entering the unknown is just for the young, but any ageless seeker can do the same. There is always the possibility of a next chapter—a different story line. We decided that our jobs did not define us. We would define ourselves. We let go of fixed income and the certainty of what each day would bring. The drive to work. The office routine. The lunch break. The traffic home. We had to believe that making it through the day was not the same as experiencing a full life.

Instead of thinking about my life in years, I decided to reframe it into days. Ten years turned into almost 3,650 days—or just about 500 Saturday nights. Once this shift took place the day itself took on a whole new meaning. It became much more important and a life adventure in and of itself.

After moving to Colorado we settled into this new phase of

our lives and we asked how we could live a life that matters. I finished penning *Hour of the Wolf: An Experiment in Ageless Living*, which I had always wanted to write. I wanted to tell the story of the adventures and misadventures that made up our lives, and I wanted our kids to see that age should be taken off the table when it comes to risk.

There is no time expiration on seeking a higher meaning to each moment. Since no one gets out of life alive, each day should be an adventure. Once gone, it is gone forever. So let's accept that truth and wake up to a new day every day.

CONTAGIOUS GIFTS

We must be open to the possibility that a gift may come in a form that we would normally reject. That gift can possibly open the door to a new you.

AN ORDINARY LIFE

WILLIAM SWEET

Sometimes reading a book can lead you through an unanticipated chain of thoughts. This happened to me while reading *The Gift of Travel*, a collection of short stories written by professional writers. Most of the stories take place in little-known areas of foreign countries. The writers describe tales of harrowing experiences, eating strange food, and living under difficult conditions. They sought out these conditions, intentionally looking for adventure and intrigue.

After reading this book, I was impressed by what these people dared to experience—but, in contrast, it made my life look pretty dull. What had I missed? While I have visited other countries, the conditions were comfortable and safe, and I was with other travelers. After thinking about this, I decided to create a list of some unique things that occurred in my life. Though I had no way of knowing if these world travelers had done something similar, I felt it would help me appreciate my own story.

I was born four years after my parents adopted a baby girl. I had a brother who died from encephalitis before I was born; he was only nine years old. I was a very longed-for child. When I was three years old, my picture was on the front page of the *Detroit News*, taken at the city zoo with a man who was the millionth passenger to ride the zoo's little train. We were the youngest and oldest passengers that day. When I was seven, I went on my first airplane ride in an open-cockpit biplane. I was wearing a leather helmet and goggles, and I was sitting on my father's lap. When I was nine, I was seriously ill with viral pneumonia and was in the hospital for ten days. Sulfa drugs saved my life. When I came home, my mother's hair had turned white; her fears were based on the memory of my brother. I learned how to milk cows and slop pigs on my uncle's farm when I was ten. I was the leader of a Boy Scout drum and bugle corps on the fourth of July when we marched down the main street in Ypsilanti, Michigan.

I played clarinet in the junior high orchestra, and I competed with other schools in regional oratory contests and won some awards. I was elected president of the student council during both my junior and senior years of high school. I played four years of varsity football and was elected captain of the football team in my senior year. Back then, I played both offense and defense. I was called the "Mighty Mite" because of my size. I also preached a sermon from the pulpit at St. Luke's Episcopal Church when I was a teenager.

I sang in a college fraternity glee club competition at the University of Michigan. We took first place. On a road trip with three of my high school buddies, we spent the night on a sandy beach on Cape Cod, Massachusetts. In the morning when we woke up, the rising tide was two feet from our sleeping bags. What did Midwesterners know about tides? I flew on an American Airlines jet aircraft when it set a commercial flight-time record from Los Angeles to Washington, DC. I touched the stones at Stonehenge, England, and kissed the Blarney Stone in Ireland.

My life has been filled with joy and sorrow. I married my childhood sweetheart in 1951 and had three children. In 1960, my thirty-year-old wife was diagnosed with breast cancer. She lived courageously for four more years. I held her hand when she died. I met my daughter's third-grade teacher at a school conference, fell in love, and married her three months later. Our children adore her and our life has overflowed with love and happiness ever since. We now have three grandchildren who worship the ground she walks on.

In addition to my travels, I have many hobbies to keep me busy. I retired at age fifty-nine as the Fleet Systems Department Associate Head. I am not a licensed pilot, but friends have given me some "stick time" in their airplanes. I flew a Piper Seneca over Lake Michigan near Chicago for thirty minutes. I coauthored a textbook on systems engineering, which is still selling well; a second edition has recently been published. I have won best-in-show two years in a row in a local photography contest.

The most important thing I've accomplished is taking care of my healthy family, whom I love deeply and find great pleasure in being with. I will be eighty-three in March 2013. After reading through these events in my life, I realize that none of them, individually, is particularly unique or noteworthy. However, taken together, they tell a story. Upon reflection, I realize my ordinary life was maybe not so ordinary after all.

CONTAGIOUS EXPERIENCE

Even when life seems humdrum or mundane, it is important to make the best of the little things, and realize that all the small things put together are what constitute a beautiful life worth living.

LIFE'S PLEASURES AND A SMILE

ARNOLD SARROW

As a man in my eighties, I am healthy and vital both physically and mentally. At my age, I view life as an exposed manuscript lying unprotected in the breeze. The breeze blows gently yet unceasingly to reveal the next page, and the next. However, these pages are a metaphor for age and life, and I am prepared for the day when a stronger wind will blow the remaining pages, and I will come to find that there are no pages left.

It seems like a millennium ago, in another life, that I was standing at my mother's kitchen stove while she cooked. I would eat almost as fast as she churned out her amazing recipes. I am now much older, I've shrunk, and I've gained a bigger waistline, but my posture is still better than that of most people my age. I can still play great tennis, and I'm a better-than-average dancer. I can't complain.

Every so often in the obituaries I read the stories of many people who were much younger than myself when they passed away. They make me more thankful for the beautiful sky, the puffy white clouds, and the sunset's magnificent colors. My mirror shows my age but does not reflect the advantages that come along with living a long life: my family, my friends, and the license to do pretty much as I please. I care less about what other people think and care more about what I think, and about the opinions of my family.

In the last decade I've noticed a decided difference in myself. I concern myself less with future projects, and I focus much more on past and current pleasures that still bring a smile to my face. Although, logically, I have more reason to be tolerant, I am not; I'm more selective in whom I call my friends. Conversely, I cherish the things and the people who provide me with understanding, happiness, warmth, love, and joy. For myself and for others who are lucky enough to live a long, fulfilling life, these are the things that give comfort after our long journey.

CONTAGIOUS LIVING

Age is only a number. We must focus on all the beautiful, positive things in our life, cherish the time we have been given, and make the most of every day.

CONTAGIOUS GRATITUDE

Keeping up with the pace of the world around us is not nearly as important as keeping in touch with what matters most to us. Take a moment each day to allow yourself to know and feel the ways that you are blessed.

THE NOISE

KERRY FLYNN MOEYKENS

It's hard to see the forest for the trees.

—John Heywood

In today's world, we get caught up in so many trivial things that we are unable to see the big picture. As a society, we have become wrapped up in the minutia of work—the "gottas," the "have-tos," and the daily demands of life. It is increasingly difficult to see what we have and appreciate it for what it's worth. We are caught up in "the noise" and forget what life is about.

However, in this fast-paced world, it's more important than ever to take a moment, step back, and appreciate the ways in which you are blessed. I've had to be reminded to do this myself, and each time it is humbling. I remember one night in particular when I was overwhelmed and stressed, and "the noise" of life had drowned out my senses to the point where it was virtually all I was able to hear. I heard the phone, the television, and the dryer. My mind was consumed with thoughts of the pile of bills on the table, the miles of emails I needed to answer, and my own inner voice reminding me of all things I "needed" to do before my day was done.

Instead of taking a step back and calming down, I let myself get worked up and I started ranting at my teenager. But as I unleashed my worries and annoyances on him, he said, "Aw, does someone need a hug?" He was being a wiseacre, I know, but he was right! He gave me a big bear hug, and it made me stop and breathe, probably for the first time since my feet hit the floor that morning. In that moment, my son brought me back down to earth and reminded me of what was important in the bigger picture.

For many people, a hug from a loved one doesn't always do the trick, and it is hard to keep in mind all the ways they are blessed. More often than not, it takes a natural disaster or personal catastrophe for people to realize they are lucky. People need reminders, as when news agencies broadcast stories about people who have lost all their worldly possessions due to fire, flood, tornado, or some other calamity. They focus on victims who profess how grateful they are to be alive, and how the pile of rubble they now stand upon means nothing. In such instances, "the noise" dies away and we recognize what we truly value and hold dear.

If you're like most people I know, you don't have a Mercedes parked in your driveway or a summer home in the Hamptons. You may feel overwhelmed with the demands of life, and it can be hard to feel grateful for all the things you *do* have. However, it is important to celebrate all the reasons you are fortunate in your life.

FINDING THE GOOD IN THE BAD

BECKY WOODBRIDGE

A good fortune may forebode a bad luck, which may in turn disguise a good fortune.

— Chinese Proverb

There was a certain irony to shutting the lights off inside my office for the last time in December 2007. After all, it was a three-week stretch without power—following Hurricane Wilma in October 2005—that marked the beginning of the end for my fledgling real estate business.

The damage wrought by Wilma stymied real estate sales for months. My phones stopped ringing and never really picked up again. Real estate values plummeted, and the economy took a turn for the worse—as did my income. I went from expanding my business to wondering how I was going to stay afloat.

My parents were a tremendous financial help during these times, but their generosity wasn't nearly enough to stave off the inevitable. My combined office and personal expenses were in excess of $40,000 per month. The money going out—to employees, for marketing, supplies, and equipment—remained high, while the money coming in slowed to a trickle. I started taking out loans just to pay the monthly bills, and I eventually reached a point where I realized I could keep borrowing, or I could stop putting myself in debt and shut my business down.

After downsizing the business for a brief period, I finally

decided to close the door and turn off the lights for the last time. It was one of the worst days of my life. However, looking back on it, I also can say it was one of the best days of my life. In the weeks following the decision, it felt like an enormous weight had been lifted off my shoulders. My indecisiveness had been nothing short of crippling; taking this step, however dramatic, allowed me to draw a much-needed deep breath and refocus. But the cloud didn't lift overnight. I bogged myself down with concerns—some legitimate, like how I was going to repay my debt, and some admittedly petty. I worried about what people would think of me, and how I would explain my failed business.

After initially stewing over these non-issues, I began to ask myself more profound questions. What is important in my life? What do I have to be grateful for? As it turned out, plenty. I had my health, my friends, my dog, and an unbelievably supportive family. When times got tough, my parents were right there for me, and their words of encouragement and inspiration kept me from tumbling into an emotional abyss. My mother must have told me about every successful person who had ever failed before finally achieving greatness—including Walt Disney. Those stories, and the intent behind them, meant the world to me.

Although it was difficult to see all my hard work go down the drain, especially knowing that some of my choices contributed to the downfall, I knew I couldn't change what had happened. Today, I can reflect on all the lessons learned and forgive myself for what I couldn't control. I can look back with pride and gratitude for the overwhelming support that I had. I built my business with strong relationships and a community of people; when life became challenging, they were the uplifting part of my day.

Pulling the plug on my business may have closed one door,

but it opened another—one that continues to pay dividends to this day. It set me on a path of personal growth for which I'm eternally grateful. I choose to see the positive side of the business, despite its closing, and I choose to remain thankful for the lessons learned.

CONTAGIOUS LESSON

We can't change the facts, but we can change our interpretation and assessment of the facts. We can see the lessons from a perspective of what worked and what didn't work during our life's ups and downs, instead of what was right or wrong.

CONTAGIOUS VIEWPOINT

It's the little things that matter. Once you realize all the good that you have in life, it will be easier to handle the challenges that come your way.

MIND THE GAP! GRATITUDE—ACCOUNTABILITY—PERSISTENCE

SUSAN ROSS

The simplest success mantras can be the most powerful. "Mind the GAP" is a mantra that I came up with to let more positivity into my life, and it is a simple, memorable, and effective success strategy that anyone can practice daily.

G stands for gratitude. Gratitude is being thankful for all that you have in your life, and it is a practiced mindset that leaves no room for negativity or doubt. You simply cannot feel grateful and grumpy at the same time. Try being grateful for where you are now, especially when not everything is perfect. Practice dwelling in your "grateful head," and ask yourself, What is working for me right now? Trust that gratitude will beget more gratitude because you are "vibing" it out into the universe, and like an energy magnet, you will attract what you are.

A stands for accountability. To be accountable means to take responsibility for your life and your actions. Simply put, it means actually doing what you say you intend to do. If you'd like to become more accountable in your own life, then start by defining your goals based on your purpose and passion, and either write them down or tell someone about them. By holding yourself accountable to both yourself and others, you will be more likely to follow through. Next, identify what you need to do, anticipate the obstacles you might encounter and how you might overcome them, and create a timeline with benchmarks for completing each step. The more accountability you create, the more success you will enjoy.

P stands for persistence. Persistence is the drive to push past procrastination and your own setbacks, and to keep striving to be better. Living your dream takes passion, purpose, practice, and persistence. So find your individual passion and define your purpose, and then set your mind to achieving your dreams. Some people respond well to rigid daily disciplines and routines on their way to their goal. I create personal daily rituals that allow me to persist and to keep moving forward. Hold on to a successful, peaceful, productive vision of yourself, own it as if it had already happened, then go out, be persistent, and create it!

The life we truly, deeply desire is ours if we are inspired and passionate, and if we remember to "Mind the GAP."

CONTAGIOUS ACTION

Always faithfully pursue your dreams with gratitude, accountability, and persistence, and you can achieve any goal.

ALLOWING YOUR BLESSINGS TO OVERFLOW

DR. COLLEEN GEORGES

I spent several years of my life thinking about what I didn't have and how great life would be once I finally had all those things. I would think, Once I complete my degree, then I'll feel accomplished, or Once I get married, then I'll feel settled. I believed that my life was at a standstill; I didn't have the things I needed to be happy, but I would—someday. Interestingly, I also did a lot of worrying during that period. I worried so much about so many things that I began to have panic attacks. After two years of increasingly more frequent panic attacks, I recognized that I needed to change.

Through serious introspection, I discovered two critical things. First, I realized how much time I was missing while I was waiting for the future. I was allowing wonderful moments and daily blessings to pass by, and I was missing out on time with those I loved. I forgot to be thankful for all the beautiful things I already had.

Second, I recognized that I was so focused on being in control that I didn't allow myself to have any faith. I believed that my worry could somehow control my future and make things work out the way I wanted them to. Instead, worrying did the opposite: it signified a lack of faith that things would actually work out well for me. This lack of faith was correlated to a pessimistic view of my future possibilities.

I was finally able to realize that worrying is not control. But choosing to live in the present, having faith in your future, and having gratitude for what you already have—that is control. I have so many blessings—it seems as if my blessings double every day. I now realize that my blessings have always been there, but it just took me some time to become aware of them. The amazing thing about gratitude is that if you nurture it, it will continue to grow.

When I started working on my gratitude I began sitting quietly before I went to sleep and recalling all the good things that occurred that day. At first, it took some thought, but it got easier to find things to be thankful for. Initially, I gave thanks for the big things such as a job promotion. Today, I find myself giving thanks for just about everything—a person who lets me make a left turn when I'm driving, someone who holds the door for me, or a nice conversation with a stranger in the supermarket checkout. At the end of the day, I realize that what seem like little things are actually big things. I always remind myself to be grateful for a roof over my head, my health, a wonderful family, a career I love, and the many possibilities I have for the future.

The more good I allow myself to see in life, the better I am able to handle the challenges I encounter. While positivity breeds more positivity, all people face stresses and difficulties, and I'm no different. However, I am able to more quickly, and I readily see the silver lining behind the clouds, which helps me remain calm in challenging times. Sometimes I can hardly believe that I was ever a pessimistic worrier. Now that I have allowed true gratitude to enter my life, panic attacks have become a ghost of my past.

LIVE LIFE OUT LOUD

INEZ BRACY

Viewing life with positivity, optimism, and gratitude is a choice. Some people choose to simply put their toe in the water and let fear hold them back, while some dive in headfirst, and choose to live life out loud. In my own life, I have continued to find that being an eternal optimist, taking chances, and always looking for the silver lining allows me to live fully. Several recent experiences have helped me realize even more clearly that the fullness or emptiness of my life is totally determined by my perception.

How do we focus on all of the good in life when we see so much suffering and disappointment? We do so by realizing that though things seem negative, everything only seems as we perceive it. For example, my individual perception of the world allows me to see abundance instead of what's lacking even when my checking account is overdrawn. You might wonder how that can be. I am like this simply because I choose to be grateful for what I have, rather than being held back by what is missing. When you accept the curveballs that life throws at you, you open up the channels to release struggle and resistant energy. This is the energy that paralyzes us and keeps us stuck.

I have always tried to let go of this resistant energy and be positive, despite the fact that I have suffered with severe motion sickness all my life; if something moved and I was on it, I felt sick. Even with this handicap I dreamed of skydiving.

I'd often go out to an area near the jump zone and watch as the skydivers descended with their colorful parachutes. They looked so free, as if the world was theirs, and they made me imagine myself experiencing the freedom of jumping.

Although I held on to this dream, I had no idea what it would take to actually jump. Then one day, a friend who skydives asked if I'd like to jump with him. I thought, How awesome is that! When I explained my condition to him, he suggested we just go for it and see what happened. The day of the jump, I wasn't as nervous as I thought I'd be, and I will always remember the moment we stepped out of the plane at 13,500 feet. I was surprised at the amount of noise and then, when he opened the parachute, the silence. I could see for miles, and the beauty of the sun and clouds was breathtaking.

Miraculously, I didn't feel sick. Perhaps the excitement of being wholly focused on the jump surpassed the feeling of motion sickness. The feeling of freedom and joy of jumping from a plane stays with me. To this day, I'm glad I went for it.

Looking past your own setbacks and seeing life with light and positivity is your magic wand. Be grateful for your life. Don't allow it to pass you by and don't allow fears to hold you back. Instead, focus on your dreams, your ideas, and the things you desire in your life. If you put all your energy into these positive thoughts, good things will automatically come your way.

CONTAGIOUS CHOICE

Think about some of your goals and dreams in life. Is there something that you have always desired to do, but failed to accomplish due to fear, procrastination, or insecurity? Perhaps you've always wanted to take an art class, but you never signed up because you are afraid you won't be good enough. Perhaps you've always wanted to run a marathon, but you never started training because you don't think you're athletic enough. Whatever it is that you imagine you'd enjoy, go for it. Forget the fear of failure and take a risk. You'll never know what you can accomplish if you don't try new things, and your passions and talents may remain hidden if you don't give them an outlet through which to shine. Don't allow yourself to be defeated or held back. Instead, redirect your thinking, take chances, and turn your stumbling blocks into stepping stones.

CONTAGIOUS EXPRESSION

If someone or some organization meant a lot to you, feel free to let them know. You will feel good sharing it, and they will feel good hearing it.

LIFE IS WHAT HAPPENS WHEN YOU'RE BUSY MAKING PLANS

EILEEN KELLER

All my life, the only thing I ever wanted to be was a mom. I thought it was destiny, and I believed that I would meet the right guy, fall in love, and have a family. Although I did eventually become a mom, I never anticipated that I would be a single mom. My journey as a single mother began when I was thirty-eight. At the time, I was in a relationship with a great guy, but he wasn't the right guy, and though he wanted to get married and suggested we have children, I knew it wasn't right. I was almost forty years old, and depression started to take over as the fear of running out of time crept in. In my heart I knew I had my whole life to find love, but logically, I knew I only had a few more years to have a baby. I wanted the full motherhood experience: pregnancy, maternity clothes, the baby kicking inside me, and delivery. I discussed my plans with my family, doctors, and friends. Then I met with a fertility specialist and decided to have a baby through intrauterine insemination.

After months of searching, I decided on a donor and was blessed to get pregnant on the second try of my fertility treatment. Although it never occurred to me that I could store vials to have another baby someday, I was certain that I would only have one child on my own; if I were to meet someone later and have a family, it would be icing on the cake! When my son, Ryan, was born, I was so content. He was perfect, and my dream to have a baby had come true.

When Ryan was about two years old, I still had not met Mr. Right, but I was involved with Mr. OK-for-Now. Around this time, I figured it was time to make a second dream come true, and that was to move back to Connecticut, which I thought would open new opportunities for life and love. I took a new position with my company, put my house on the market, and looked at houses. Then, life stepped in to kick my plans to the curb.

One day, I had a strange feeling, one that I had only experienced when I was pregnant with Ryan. I tried to ignore it, but the feeling persisted, so I bought a pregnancy test. When I tested positive, I was shocked—I couldn't think of anything worse than being pregnant at that time. I went back to the store and bought four more tests—all with the same result. Unlike the time I found out I was pregnant with Ryan, which left me feeling happy and complete, this pregnancy left me feeling frantic. I didn't want a future with Mr. OK-for-Now; I wanted to move on and start a new chapter. He was perfectly happy to have no part in the child's life. He wanted me to move back East with both of my children and tell everyone that I had used another donor. At first, that's what I intended to do, but moving no longer felt like a dream—it made me feel like I was running away.

God knew what I needed better than I did, because He seemed to step in. In addition to having a toddler to care for, I was experiencing a difficult pregnancy and was sick all the time. My mom was my savior, taking care of my son and me, and her help made me wonder how exactly I thought I could just move away and do everything on my own. In addition, my house wasn't getting any offers, and I finally realized that moving back to Connecticut, away from the only support system I had, was probably not a good idea. I took my house off the market, and shortly after that the office that I had planned to work for in Connecticut closed. If I had moved, I would not only have been on my own with two children, I would have been unemployed.

After I decided not to move, God stepped in again to help me find a new kind of strength and courage that I didn't know I had. Although I didn't want a life with my baby's father because I knew he was not right for me, I also knew that he had a responsibility to my daughter. Therefore, we went to court, and he has chosen to have no part of her life other than to provide child support. Someday I will need to explain to my daughter that she does have a father, and that he supports her financially, but he cannot be in our life. His reasons will be his story to tell.

Now my beautiful daughter, Emily, is four years old and Ryan is six and a half. My journey as a mother has been the most difficult and most rewarding time of my life. Although I probably wouldn't have chosen this exact path, I know how blessed I am for God's wisdom. My children teach me something new every day and even when things are hard, the littlest moments make it all worth it. I learned not only how to be a mom, but also how to be a stronger, happier, and better me.

CONTAGIOUS TRIALS

Life's path is not narrow and straight; there are twists and turns that you'll have to endure in order to get to your destination. But once you achieve your goal, you'll look back and realize that it was all worth it.

GRÁCIAS

HAROLD PAYNE
Although I make my living as a singer and a songwriter, I graduated from college with a degree in Spanish. Sometimes I write or sing in this beautiful language, though I'm a bit rusty when I speak it.

I credit my ability to speak Spanish to my first Spanish teacher, Mrs. Tarot. As a first-year high school student I felt overwhelmed by the new environment, and I was a bit anxious. I did not have a lot of self-confidence. Until the day destiny brought me to her class, I had never studied a foreign language. Other students had told me that Mrs. Tarot was a strict and difficult teacher, but she helped me discover an affinity for Spanish. In each class, this "strict and difficult" teacher inspired me with her enthusiastic and sincere desire to teach those who really wanted to learn.

With her direction and enthusiasm I gained confidence not only in her class, but in all my classes. From that first moment, I discovered I had a love for languages, which came with the knowledge that if one studies and listens, one can learn almost any subject. I remember clearly one day when she brought a friend from Mexico to our class to speak with us. She told him to speak with me because I was her best student. It was a proud moment, and I realized that I could, in fact, be a good student.

I know that it's not easy to be a strict teacher and that this might not have made her popular with some students. However, those who wanted to learn discovered not only the knowledge of the language, but also the lifelong good habits that she taught us along the way. Her enthusiasm and dedication remain with me. Like a rare wine that improves with time, my gratitude for her contribution to my life also continues to mature.

Thanks to her, I took every Spanish offering in high school, and I graduated with a university degree in Spanish. Although I am a songwriter and singer in English and a musician, I have used Spanish a lot. The things she taught me I will always carry with me. From time to time, I sing a song in Spanish.

One day, I thought that I should thank Mrs. Tarot in some way. I decided that it would be even better than announcing her name to an audience when I sing a *canción* to thank her directly. I've always held teachers in high regard and felt this was a good opportunity to honor one who had inspired me. So I called my old high school, and fortunately someone helped me find her. I wrote a letter in Spanish and, just to be sure, I had my native Spanish-speaking neighbor look it over for me. After all, I didn't want it returned with corrections in red ink, or have her think her teaching had been in vain.

In the letter I told her that I was sure it would be a surprise for her to receive news from one of her students from almost thirty-five years ago, but I felt that she left such an indelible impression on me. I expressed my gratitude for all she had given to her students who had the good fortune to receive her inspiration. I told her that we would always remember her.

She responded to my letter—and there were no red marks on my paper! She was grateful for my kind words and was happy to know that I was still using *el gran idioma de Cervantes*, or the great language of Cervantes, author of *Don Quixote*.

I think of her when I sing "Sabor a Mí." Muchísimas grácias, Señora Tarot!

I met Agape

By Jaki Murillo

I came in and was welcomed
with open arms,
led toward another light and
into another world.

They saw in me what I could not.
They stretched out their hands and
opened doors for me.
One shed tears for me;
she felt for my broken spirit
that was still healing.
She said she'll be there—
She said call her when I need her.

Another knew me by just looking at me
This little lady, she tugged at my soul,
even from across the room.
She has seen me as vulnerable
as I could ever be.
I was an open book to her;
she wrote about me and also opened
another door for me.

These beautiful beings have given
my mind and my heart
everything.

I am safe here;
I've never felt safer.
Until meeting everyone,
I had stayed away from new crowds.
But I always hungered to feel—
their different energies, vibes, and cultures.

Everyone was there for the
same thing: love and comfort,
spirituality and purpose,
openness and willingness,
and a connection with our one and only God.
We all want to lead, help, and welcome
those who want the same in life.

I want more of this beautiful, powerful
place that is full of amazing people—
more of the euphoria and the life
and the endless
possibilities at my feet.

Their kindness is out of this world 'cause
it's not of this world but of the most
high.

Because of them,
I have seen what's real.
It's here—opportunities
I asked for and thought I'd never get.

It's too good to be true,
yet how realer can this get?
This place called "Agape," meaning uncondi-
*   tional love,*
a spiritual place where everyone shares
their love, joy, passion, creativity, knowledge,
and so much more.

Now it's all up to me.
It was always up to me.
I want the whole world to feel
how Agape made me feel—
the gift of happiness.

I want to share this feeling.
This is better than any drug,
what I've found to be Agape's unconditional
*   love.*

ABOUT DAVID MEZZAPELLE

DAVID MEZZAPELLE believes that we all have the capacity to make optimism contagious just by sharing our life's adventures. He was inspired to write this book series based on his life's experiences, his own contagious optimism, and the encouragement of his Alma Mater, Fairfield University in Connecticut.

Mezzapelle was the founder and director of marketing for Goliath Technology, a data center infrastructure company that supported organizations worldwide, from 1990 to 2007. In addition, he orchestrated one of the most innovative internship programs ever created which has become a staple for organizations today. Prior to 1990, he was an intern for IBM while attending school at Fairfield.

Goliath Technology was sold in 2007. Today, Mezzapelle consults on various projects along with serving on several boards and philanthropic initiatives.

Throughout his life, he has encountered great peaks and valleys, all of which he is grateful for. He never lost sight along the way and has kept his glass "completely full." He has influenced many people with his outlook and the **Contagious Optimism** brand is his way of offering optimism to others.

Mezzapelle has been a guest on many radio and television programs and is a frequent contributor to various publications around the globe. He is also a speaker for TED and **Contagious Optimism LIVE!** and a cohost on the Universal Broadcasting *Contagious Optimism Show* in Hollywood, California. www.contagiousoptimism.com

ABOUT WILL GLENNON

WILL GLENNON, a native Californian, founded and ran the *Santa Barbara News and Review* in 1971, attended law school, and worked as a legal analyst and political consultant in Sacramento from 1983 to 1990. In 1992, he collected, edited, and published a collection of individuals' stories about giving and receiving kindness from strangers in the *New York Times* bestselling book *Random Acts of Kindness*. The overwhelming response to the book led him to establish a grassroots annual Random Acts of Kindness (RAK) celebration, which has grown to include 5,000 communities in thirty-five countries. Glennon's book has received recognition from well-known figures like Oprah Winfrey and the US Congress. The RAK movement has spread rapidly, with participation doubling every year. Featured on numerous television and radio programs as the national spokesperson for RAK, Glennon was invited to Japan in 1997 by the Japanese Small Kindness Movement and implemented the groundwork for a world kindness movement. Will Glennon and the RAK organization believe that practicing kindness affects human interactions and reminds each person that we are all intricately and beautifully connected, making a kinder world.

ABOUT JIM CATHCART, CSP, CPAE

JIM CATHCART is one of the world's most decorated professional speakers and authors. His sixteen books have been translated worldwide and his concept of "Relationship Selling" has become so popular that he was inducted into the Sales & Marketing Hall of Fame in December of 2012. His website and blog Cathcart.com and RelationshipSelling.com contain over 300 pages of free resources to help people grow their businesses and careers. A professional executive speech coach and leadership advisor, Jim sits on numerous boards and serves as a success mentor to many prominent individuals. He's the author of *The Acorn Principle* and fifteen other books. www.cathcart.com

MEET OUR COAUTHORS

DR. EMILE ALLEN is an accomplished surgeon. He built three successful private practices and was the chief of urology and vice chairman of surgery at Scripps Memorial Hospital, San Diego, California. Although he no longer wields a surgeon's scalpel, Emile now heals through his inspirational speaking and writing. His life story, vividly described in his book, *Eaten By The Tiger: Surrendering to an Empowered Life*, is captivating and entertaining audiences nationwide. www.emileallen.com

RICHARD J. ANTHONY, SR. is the founder and managing director of The Anthony Group, Inc., a management consulting firm specializing in business advisory services, human resource management, and performance improvement. He is also founder of The Entrepreneurs Network, a venue for aspiring and serial entrepreneurs and angel investors. His book, *Organizations, People and Effective Communication*, is available on Amazon. r.anthonysr1@verizon.net

MARIAN AXLEY moved to Florida in 1960 after graduating from college in Kentucky because her husband had been hired by an airplane engine manufacturer to do research on their engines. Today, Marian is retired, and spends her time lecturing, critiquing, and judging art shows.

JANET S. BALES is a musician. At an early age she traveled on tour with America's Youth in Concert and the Janesville Symphony Orchestra, and recorded in Carnegie Hall in 1976 with the BBC. Janet now serves as the director of Tychicus Ministries, Inc. www.tychicusministries.org

ANNE BENNETT-BREADY is a parent of a child with autism, and she wears the title of "supermom" with pride. She is fifty-one, but thinks that age is only a number. Hope and faith are two things that often get her through the day.

EDITH BERGMAN was born in Brooklyn but considers her hometown to be Fall River, Massachusetts, where she raised three children. Bergman joined the Life Learning Program at Nova South-eastern University in 1997 as a student and part-time instructor. She is a resident of Brookdale Senior Living. www.brookdaleliving.com

INEZ BRACY, MS, CNLP, CGC, is a lifestyle coach, speaker, award-winning author, and radio and TV personality who helps women reju-venate, reinvent, and redefine their life. She is also a frequent guest on the *Fox 4 Morning Blend* as its career coach, giving tips to help boom-ers successfully navigate the workplace. www.thebracygroup.com

ESTELLE BERK was born and raised in the Bronx. Estelle was a nur-turing mother and grandmother and a committed friend with a zest for life. Going forth with optimism during life's many challenges was how she chose to live every day. Estelle was a resident of Brookdale Senior Living until her passing in March 2014. www.brookdaleliving.com

TERI CATLIN has had music as her passion since she was a child. At the age of twelve, she began playing in the Flint Youth Symphony Orchestra. She studied for three years with the Wisconsin Symphony School of America and won a Silver Medal in the Worldwide Or-chestra Competition in Ottawa, Canada. Teri has taught herself to play many instruments professionally, including drums, rhythm/lead guitar, bass, djembe, doumbek, didgeridoo, and the wooden flute. www.tericatlin.com

CHRISTINA CALLAHAN received her bachelor's degree in English in 2012 from Fairfield University. She enjoys writing and going to the beach with her yellow lab, PJ. She resides in Fairfield, Connecticut, with her family. www.therusticmermaid.tumblr.com

ROGER CANNON writes as often as possible, still loves Wisconsin white pines, and lives happily in San Pedro, California.

MICHAEL CARLON is a qualitative research professional who en-gages consumers in highly personal conversations about the products they buy and the services they seek. www.vertigopartners.com

GAY CARTIER is a recovery coach, addiction counselor, master NLP practitioner, and the founder of Addiction Recovery Interna-tional in Sydney, Australia. Her services include providing telephone and online recovery coaching and addiction counseling within her trademark system called the New Life Recovery Program.

CLAUDETTE CHENEVERT is the founder of Coaching Steps LLC and is a certified master stepfamily foundation coach, specializing in stepfamily relationships and conflict resolution. She has a degree in psychology of communication and is a member of the International Coach Federation and the International Positive Psychology Association. www.stepmomcoach.com

THOMAS COLLINS is from Smithtown, New York. He is presently a biology major at SUNY Geneseo in upstate New York. He is enjoying his time in school and is looking forward to the future.

JENNIFER CUTLER LOPEZ was born and raised in Newfoundland, Canada, and resides in Virginia. She recently published her book, *American Scars: Stories on Display. American Scars* combines photography and uplifting biographical essays to reveal the stories of people and their physical scars. www.jennycutlerlopez.com

ERNEST FIELD was from Vienna, Austria. He is survived by his wife of sixty years, Kitty. Both Ernest and Kitty are Holocaust survivors with amazing stories and accounts of their lives leading up to, during, and after their concentration camp experiences. Kitty is a resident of Brookdale Senior Living. www.brookdaleliving.com

HAYLEY FOSTER is a married mother of three who says that nothing will teach you more about yourself than raising children. Her mission is to bring as much good into the world as possible. She has helped hundreds of clients find the perfect combination of who they are and what resonates best with their audiences. www.shorttalkexpert.com

ALLISON FRATTAROLI is a student at St. Luke's School in Darien, Connecticut. She is also an active ambassador for Kids Helping Kids in Stamford, Connecticut. www.kidshelpingkidsct.org

SALLY GATES is the mother of two children and the grandmother of three. She has been employed by HCR Manor Care in Florida since 1991 as a regional director and an administrator of a skilled nursing facility.

BARBARA GELSTON lives in Stamford, Connecticut, with her husband, Art, who graduated from Fairfield University in 1961. They have two children, Nancy and Tom, both of whom also graduated from Fairfield University. Barbara and Art both enjoy gardening, golfing, visiting their vacation home on the North Carolina Outer Banks, and spending time with friends and family.

DR. COLLEEN GEORGES has been serving as a counselor and coach for over 15 years, helping to guide individuals through self-discovery and personal and career goal achievement. Her publications include coauthorship of *Contagious Optimism: Uplifting Stories & Motivational Advice for Positive Forward Thinking* and *101 Great Ways to Enhance Your Career*, scholarly psychology journals, and *The Gallery of Best Resumes, 5th Edition*. www.colleengeorges.com

DR. DONALD E. GIBSON, PhD is the dean and professor of management at the Dolan School of Business at Fairfield University. He has published articles in *Organization Science, Journal of Management, Journal of Vocational Behavior, Academy of Management Perspectives,* and *Journal of Business Ethics,* and is the author of *Managing Anger in the Workplace*. Prior to entering academia, Donald worked in the entertainment industry in Los Angeles, managing postproduction and distribution for television shows and motion pictures at Lorimar Productions.

FRED GILL joined the Metro-North Railroad of New York in 1984. He has held several positions, including being responsible for the identification and development of potential employees. Fred is an active member of various civic and community organizations, and was recently appointed the chair of the Connecticut Business Advisory Council.

LARRY GLENZ is the author of *Forgiving Kevin: A Son's Addiction Becomes a Father's Greatest Teacher*. As a travel tour group leader, he supervised hundreds of teenagers to destinations in Europe, Australia, Asia, and Africa. Larry received his ordination as a reverend for his church, Pathways of Light, in 2008.

WILLIAM GOLDBERGER is a retired professional engineer and former vice president of research at a company that manufactures highly specialized industrial products. He is a named inventor on twenty-five US patents and has published technical papers and articles in the field of chemical and metallurgical processing.

MELODY GOODSPEED suffered health complications that caused her to lose her vision in 2003. Her fight to regain and resculpt her life has given her a new perspective on what is truly important in life, and she is grateful to God for all the gifts He has given, including a loving husband, family, friends, and a new career.

BHARATH GOPALAN steers the learning and development practices at Ramco Cements, a leading cement company in India. He also holds certifications in NLP, psychometric profiling, and quality management systems, and is deemed by the government of India as a national resource for conducting trainers' training courses. He recently authored the book *Break Your Boundaries*, a compendium of some of the best books on personal excellence.

JIM AND RACHEL HARPER lost both their spouses tragically in the 1950s. They eventually met through an amazing set of coincidences and serendipity. The Harpers are residents of Brookdale Senior Living. www.brookdaleliving.com

JOEL HELLER worked in the insurance industry for twenty-five years in various underwriting and management positions. He left the industry in 2010 to open a retail clothing, jewelry, and gift shop in Vermont. Joel has a bachelor's degree from Fairfield University and resides with his wife in New Hampshire.

CHRISTINE HENCHAR REED, MA, M.DIV graduated from Fairfield University, where she majored in politics and minored in religious studies. She was awarded the Harry S. Truman Scholarship for dedication to public service and academic excellence. She resides in Franklin, Tennessee, with her husband, Roland.

JOHN BRANTLEY HOOKS, IV is the founder and chief content officer of The WWRG Networks, a global network of high-profile women on five continents and in thirty-six countries. www.wealthywomensresource.blogspot.com

KIMBERLEE M. HOOPER, M.ED works in the field of higher education, where she directs the school relations office at Middlesex County College in Edison, New Jersey. With over ten years of experience in the field of education, she finds great joy in helping others achieve their educational goals.

EILEEN KELLER is a single mom of two children who lives in Chicago. Eileen works at AT&T as a senior technical team leader. She leads a team of project managers and is certified as a project management professional.

JERRY KELLY is a licensed massage therapist and canine caretaker in his hometown of Massapequa Park, New York. He has been on the self-transformation path for over twenty years, studying multiple religions and new thought technologies.

NANCY KOENIG is an author, speaker, certified life coach, and EFT Practitioner who motivates others to stretch beyond illusory limitations, follow their deepest passions, and reach their highest aspirations. Today, she leads women through weight loss, smoking cessation, and toward other goals while helping them dramatically improve the most important and often most neglected relationship of their lives: the one with self. www.namemynovel.com; www.nancykoenig.com

LIISA KYLE, PhD is the go-to coach for smart, creative people who want to overcome challenges, get organized, get things done, and get more out of life. She has coached individuals, facilitated groups, and delivered inventive workshops on four continents. She cofounded *The Da Vinci Dilemma*, an online community devoted to helping multitalented people. www.davincidilemma.com

KRYSTIAN LEONARD is a high school student who wrote her first children's book, *Shining Scars*, at age fifteen as a way to teach healing and promote character for children healing with visible scars. www.shiningscars.org

BARRY L. LINDSTROM has authored hundreds of nonfiction papers, user manuals, and presentations for those confused by complexity and wearied by the pace of change. Barry's first significant work of fiction is *Considering SomeplacElse*. www.soiwrotethisbook.com

PAUL R. LIPTON is author of *Hour of the Wolf: An Experiment in Ageless Living*. Paul is a frequent speaker on the topics of living a balanced life in a world that seems out of balance. He resides in Boulder, Colorado. www.theagelessexperiment.com

DEBORAH LITTLEJOHN has spent the past three years working as a certified home health care aide. She was a Girl Scout, cheerleader, and homecoming queen.

LEE LIVELY-GARCIA, CPM is the president of One Great Kid, Inc. Her philosophies on life come from many life trials she has experienced, including being jobless and nearly homeless, morbid obesity, and breast cancer. Lee feels it is important to learn from these challenges in order to grow stronger and empower ourselves to meet future challenges.

JORDAN LOWE suffered from a spinal cord injury when she was seventeen years old that left her in a wheelchair. She now travels as a motivational speaker; her goal is to show others that they can do anything regardless of their obstacles. She is currently the titleholder of Ms. Wheelchair West Virginia and also placed as second runner-up at the 2014 Ms. Wheelchair USA national pagent. Her mantra: "Never give up on your dream, no matter how hard the journey." jlowe793@yahoo.com

KAREN LYONS KALMENSON is a poet, blogger, and animal and human rights activist who has contributed her rhymes to many places and causes. In the process, she has made friends worldwide and touched many hearts. She finds a rhyme and a laugh almost everywhere she looks. fayely10@aol.com

CYNTHIA MAKRIS has been an opera singer for thirty years. Throughout her career, she has sung almost every leading role written for soprano. Critics have praised not only the beauty of her voice, but also the honesty, integrity, and depth of her portrayals. www.cynthiamakris.com

ALAN A. MALIZIA's professional experience includes corporate positions with companies such as Waldenbooks. After he shifted gears to teaching, his true passion, he became a renowned coach for girls' volleyball as well. Alan has written two books: *The Little Red Chair*, an autobiography that deals with his life experience with polio, and *A View from the Quiet Corner*, a selection of his poems and reflections. amalizia1@ct.metrocast.net

CHARLES MARKMAN started creating cartoons in grammar school. He worked as an apprentice cartoonist while going to night school. During his three-year Army stint, he was able to get his drawings into several Army publications. He began working in the commercial art field as a graphic designer. Charles never really retired; he is still drawing cartoons today. He is a resident of Brookdale Senior Living. www.brookdaleliving.com

DAVID R. MARTIN is a retired wealth manager and founder of Happy Day Adventures. He is also a comedian at venues in California and Nevada. www.happydayadventures.com

RICHARD MASTERSON is a serial entrepreneur who, at age twenty-five, became the first business-to-business advertiser on Prodigy Interactive Personal Service, a joint venture of IBM and Sears that was the forerunner of the World Wide Web. He was named *Inc.* magazine's "Entrepreneur of the Year" and went on to become the founder of US Interactive. After that company's successful IPO, Rich became a philanthropist and real estate developer. He was the first Entrepreneur in Residence at the University of Pennsylvania Wharton School of Business. www.mastersondevelopment.com

DIANE MAY, originally from Detroit, has lived in Florida for the past forty-five years. She has been a teacher and librarian, and has worked in special education. She also spent time in India, where she organized a library for children. Diane is a resident of Brookdale Senior Living. www.brookdaleliving.com

PATRICK MCKAY is a fitness consultant based in Jupiter, Florida. He helps people of all ages and fitness levels improve their quality of life and achieve long-term results through commonsense nutrition, challenging cardio routines, and constantly varied workouts. patmckay1@aol.com

SUZANNE MILLER is a graphic artist and media designer who lives in Collegeville, Pennsylvania. A recent widow and cancer survivor, she is finding her new life after cancer. smiller@in-tandem.net

KARIE LYNN MILLSPAUGH resides with her daughter in Las Vegas, where she recruits business coaches for global organizations. She also coaches others on personal development and finding their own source of happiness and well-being. www.kariemillspaugh.com

FRED MOORE served in the Navy during World War II as an interpreter in Normandy. After a bout with cancer, he ran a real estate management business. He also served on the board of directors of a local Florida AIDS support organization. Fred is a resident of Brookdale Senior Living. www.brookdaleliving.com

KERRY FLYNN MOEYKENS is a veteran teacher who lives in

Kentucky and works in the financial industry. She loves to spend time with her three children, work on light home renovation, and write.

MERRY NACHEMIN, LCSWR was born and raised in Brooklyn. Following thirty years as a social worker, with the last twenty as an administrator, she shifted gears and started her dream business as an image consultant and makeup artist.

ALISON NANCYE has made it her life's work to inspire others to go after what they want in life. As an author, speaker, and media spokesperson, she encourages people to take positive action in their lives. She is the author of several nonfiction self-development books and a novel, *Note to Self.* www.alisonnancye.com

NAVID NAZEMIAN is a global human resources professional who has worked for world-class organizations such as Adidas, General Electric, BAT, and Roche. He is author of several published articles on management and leadership and has coauthored two books, *Interimsmanagement* and *HR Service Management.* Navid lives in Basel, Switzerland. Twitter @NavidNazemian

ESTER NICHOLSON is an author, an Agape International–licensed spiritual therapist, a motivational speaker, and an inspirational recording artist who brings twenty-five years of sobriety and spiritual teachings to audiences around the globe. Ester hosts shows on Hay House Radio and Unity Online Radio, facilitates workshops, and gives keynote addresses. Her book, *Soul Recovery: 12 Keys to Healing Addiction*, is based on spiritual principles and a progressive Twelve-Step recovery process. www.esternicholson.com

HAROLD PAYNE is a multi-platinum songwriter whose soulful, uplifting songs and husky heartfelt vocals have graced stages around the world. He has written songs for such diverse artists as Rod Stewart, Patti LaBelle, Kelly Rowland, and Carlos Santana—literally from Peter, Paul, and Mary to Snoop Dogg. The album *Bravest Man in the Universe* by Rock and Roll Hall of Fame inductee Bobby Womack, cowritten by Payne, won the prestigious 2012 "Q" award in the UK for "Best Album of the Year." He also launched the *Power of Positive Music* series, which led him to performing with motivational speakers like Mark Victor Hansen—cofounder of *Chicken Soup for the Soul.* Today, Harold is a partner and the musical mastermind for the *Contagious Optimism LIVE* event series. www.haroldpaynemusic.com

MELINDA PETROFF lives in Bridgeport, West Virginia. She is Gavin Morris's great-aunt (from the story "Superheroes Do Exist" in chapter four). Melinda assists the Morris family with their social media and fundraising efforts for childhood cancer research.

BARBARA RADY KAZDAN is the founder and principal consultant at Achieving Change Together and the strategic development officer at Parents Alliance. Barbara created a literacy awareness campaign that became a national initiative, and she has chaired city, state, and national planning groups. As a certified JobsOver50 career coach, Barbara helps individuals shift into nonprofit careers. www.achievingchangetogether.com

SUSYN REEVE is the bestselling author of *The Inspired Life: Unleashing Your Mind's Capacity for Joy*. She has forty years of experience as an international leadership development coach, and she is a life mentor and interfaith minister. Susyn is the cohost of the popular weekly radio show *The On Purpose Show: Your Path to Fulfilling LifeWork*. www.susynreeve.com

VANEETHA RENDALL is a freelance writer working on a memoir about her childhood. She previously worked in the fields of marketing and finance for Gartner Group, Sara Lee, and Bank of Boston. She speaks frequently on the topic of overcoming adversity. www.danceintherain.com

After a decade of being a top producer, **SHANE J. REPMANN** returned to higher education in order to pursue a bachelor's degree in psychology and a master's degree and state certification in school counseling.

SUSAN ROSS's career spans twenty years in business education, new business launch, consulting, speaking, and team building. She has worked with more than 500 organizations. Susan launched a private business college, which achieved national accreditation and approval from the US Department of Education. After selling her college in 2005, Susan founded Blue Ocean Business Coaching and Masterminds. www.blueoceancoaching.com

JACQUELYN SAAD is president of Inter-Change Consulting Inc., a full-service human resources and organizational development consulting firm specializing in change and problem management. interchange@rogers.com

ARNOLD SARROW left college to enlist as a private after the Pearl Harbor bombing, and then became a fighter pilot. He flew 101 combat missions and sorties, and obtained several letters of achievement from France, Australia, and the Czech Republic. Since that time, Arnold has experienced many personal and professional achievements. Arnold is a resident of Brookdale Senior Living. www.brookdaleliving.com

ARTHUR SCALZO is a retired US Drug Enforcement Administration special agent who conducted investigations and paramilitary operations in countries such as the Philippines, Peru, and Bolivia. Arthur also served in Iraq as a civilian criminal investigator embedded with the US Army 4th Brigade. He identified and brought to justice terrorists involved in the manufacturing and placement of IEDs that were targeting US and coalition forces in Baghdad. He has also served in the US Secret Service, the U.S. Immigration and Naturalization Service, and the Suffolk County (New York) District Attorney's Insurance Crime Bureau.

IRA SCOTT is a certified master practitioner of neuro-linguistic programming, is certified in neo-Ericksonian hypnosis, and is a member of The American Board of Hypnotherapy. He is also certified in "Belief Craft—Knowledge Engineering and Sleight of Mouth" and is a certified practitioner of The Havening Techniques—a psychosensory therapy. www.leanintolife.com

LEE E. SHILO holds a nine-to-five job and has a passion for writing. He has published a variety of books and eBooks. Contributing to *Contagious Optimism* has been a pleasure for him. He lives on Vancouver Island in Victoria, British Columbia. www.shilocom.com

SOPHIE SKOVER is an author, a holistic life coach, and an inspirational speaker. She started her own company, LSS Harmony Life Coaching, to help others experience harmony in their lives. She works with clients, conducts workshops, and encourages us to grow into the most impressive version of ourselves. www.lssharmony.com

TINA SLOAN's career as an actress has spanned over forty years in TV and film. Tina is best known for her twenty-six-year role as nurse Lillian Raines on the acclaimed CBS daytime drama, *Guiding Light*. She has also appeared on other TV shows including *Law & Order* and *Third Watch* and has been featured on *60 Minutes, The Montel Williams Show*, and *The Young Turks*. In film, Tina has appeared in Woody Allen's *Celebrity* and the *Curse of the Jade Scorpion*, *The Brave One* with Jodi Foster, *Changing Lanes* with Ben Affleck, *The Guru* with Marisa Tomei, *People I Know* with Al Pacino, and *Black Swan* with Natalie Portman. www.changingshoes.com

COURTNEY SMITHEMAN is a long-term resident of Jupiter, Florida and runs a real estate brokerage. www.cranereedproperties.com

AMY SPENCER is the author of *The Happy Life Checklist: 654 Simple Ways to Find Your Bliss*; *Bright Side Up: 100 Ways to Be Happier Right Now*, which was recommended by *O, The Oprah Magazine*; and the "dating optimism" guide, *Meeting Your Half-Orange*. Amy is a journalist who has written for *Glamour, Redbook, Real Simple, New York Magazine*, and the *Huffington Post*. www.amyspencer.com

LANCE STRANAHAN is a real estate investor and commodity trader from West Palm Beach, Florida. He is also an independent filmmaker and actor.

JC SULLIVAN is addicted to backpacking the world. Having been to more than 120 countries, her goal is to see them all. Not financially rich, she barters, takes odd jobs, and sells an inspirational poem or story. backpackingpoet@yahoo.com

WILLIAM SWEET is a retired engineer living in St. Mary's County, Maryland. He is married and has three children and three grandchildren. Sweet was employed by Johns Hopkins University's applied physics laboratory for thirty-seven years.

SÓNIA TREJO is a certified life coach and master core energy coach. Her passion is to inspire others to achieve their greatest potential, turning their challenges into opportunities. Sónia resides in Pasadena, California. www.thealchemistcoach.com

SALVATORE TRIFILIO was raised in Waldwick, New Jersey, and is a graduate of Fairfield University. He is a reporter for the *Daily Voice* in Connecticut.

STEVE UIBLE served as a Peace Corps volunteer in the Kingdom of Tonga from 1967 to 1970. He is a consultant to the construction and farm equipment industry, and is the owner of Time Service Consulting, LLC. www.timeserviceconsulting.com

NORMAN WAIN worked at various radio shows as a DJ. He was on the air during Army service in Japan for the Far East Network. He went on to be a program director, advertising account executive, and salesman in Cleveland. Years later, he formed a company to buy and operate radio stations. He retired in 1994.

PETER WALLIMANN graduated from ETH Zurich with a degree in chemistry. Later, he conducted research at the Massachusetts Institute of Technology in Cambridge. His project, termed "SENSIGNS," is a unique fusion of art, nature, and poetry, with a focus on beauty as a universal key to higher understanding and deeper compassion. Peter works as a writer and sound therapist in Zurich, Switzerland. www.sensigns.ch

NATALIE WEINRAUCH is a student at the Singapore American School. Although she is American, she was born and raised in Singapore. This experience has presented her with many opportunities, including the ability to build relationships across nationalities, becoming fluent in Chinese, and traveling around Asia. Her main focus is spreading awareness of children's shelters in Cambodia.

MONSIGNOR ROBERT WEISS completed his seminary studies at Saint Bernard Seminary in Rochester, New York, and was ordained in Saint Christopher Church, North Chili, New York, in 1973. Coming to the Diocese of Bridgeport in 1976, he served as parochial vicar at Saint Andrew Parish in Bridgeport, Saint Leo Parish in Stamford, and Saint Jude Parish in Monroe, before becoming Pastor of Saint Joseph Parish in Shelton in 1990. Msgr. Weiss was also the spiritual director for Stamford Catholic High School, has been a member of the College of Consultors, and was Territorial Vicar of Vicariate V. In 1999 he was appointed Pastor of Saint Rose, where he now resides.

HENRY WISEMAN is the president of CDS Global Logistics, Inc. He has over thirty years of experience in international air and ocean transportation, customs brokerage, and supply chain logistics management. Prior to joining CDS, he was senior vice president of FedEx Trade Networks, North America.

BECKY WOODBRIDGE, founder of Becky Woodbridge & Company, is a professional speaker and executive coach. She trains and coaches individuals, teams, and organizations around the world to "unleash the extraordinary." www.beckywoodbridge.com

BARBARA WOODWORTH is a freelance writer who specializes in diversity and career-related nonfiction. Her 1,500 articles have appeared in more than fifty international, national, regional, and local publications.

REBECCA ZERBO lives in Boca Raton, Florida, with her family and attends Eagles Landing Middle School. Becca graduated from the Young Entrepreneurs Academy (YEA) in June and won the national title for the Saunders Scholars Bright Ideas Competition, where she earned a $30,000 scholarship to RIT. and University of Tampa. www.positivepocket.org

EMMANUEL OFOSU YEBOAH is an athlete and an activist for disabled rights. His story is told in the critically acclaimed documentary, *Emmanuel's Gift*, which was narrated by Oprah Winfrey. www.youtube.com/watch?v=BHUDh82sZYs

ACKNOWLEDGMENTS

I thank Fairfield University, not only for their involvement and efforts in copyediting this book, but also for the education and experience this wonderful school offered me years ago. I am an eternally grateful alumnus and a proponent of this fine university.

FAIRFIELD UNIVERSITY

- Tom Baden, editor in chief of the *Connecticut Post*, a Hearst Newspaper. Tom served as adjunct professor for the advanced publishing class that copyedited this book.
- Dr. James Simon, associate dean of the college of arts and sciences.
- Dr. Wook-Sung Yoo. Dr. Yoo served as chair and professor for the school of engineering that assisted in various aspects of the **Contagious Optimism** project.
- Student copyediting team:

Katie Acompora	Vincent Ferrer	Shauna Mitchell
Margaret Andrew	Katrina Finkernagel	Evan Murphy
Sarah Bennett	Alexandra Fylypovych	Drusilla Ollennu
Christina Callahan	Jamie Gallerani	Mabel Polanco
Danica Ceballos	Andrew Hoover	Thomas Shea
Shawna Clark	Kerilee Horan	Olivia Snoddy
Megan Clarke	Loan Le	Gabriella Tutino
Jessica Delahnut	Ryan LeClair	Sal Trifilio
Emma DiGiovine	Julie Labbadia	Gabriella Visconti
Luigi DiMeglio	Cate Martel	
Whitney Dorrington	Matt Mastrianni	
Jessica Estrada	Marty Misiaszek	

Learn more about Fairfield University at www.fairfield.edu.

SHARE YOUR STORIES

Thank you for reading *10 Habits of Truly Optimistic People*, volume II in the **Contagious Optimism** book series. We hope you have found it helpful and inspirational. We are proud of the hard work and effort that went into this project. Our team of authors, copyeditors, and contributors have given this project 110 percent.

We look forward to future volumes. Our goal is to continue delivering stories from around the globe that remind people that any cloud can have a silver lining, and that everyone can power their life with the positive.

Please tell a friend about *10 Habits of Truly Optimistic People*. Our books and eBooks are available in any bookstore or online at www.contagiousoptimism.com.

Should you have a story or reflection offering a lesson of hope and inspiration that you wish to share, please send it to us at submissions@lifecarrots.com. We will consider it for a future volume and would love to have you on board.

Stay positive and make it contagious!

David Mezzapelle and the **Contagious Optimism** team

Facebook: www.facebook.com/OfficialContagiousOptimism
Twitter: twitter.com/coliveus

TO OUR READERS

Viva Editions publishes books that inform, enlighten, and entertain. We do our best to bring you, the reader, quality books that celebrate life, inspire the mind, revive the spirit, and enhance lives all around. Our authors are practical visionaries: people who offer deep wisdom in a hopeful and helpful manner. Viva was launched with an attitude of growth and we want to spread our joy and offer our support and advice where we can to help you live the Viva way: vivaciously!

We're grateful for all our readers and want to keep bringing you books for inspired living. We invite you to write to us with your comments and suggestions, and what you'd like to see more of. You can also sign up for our online newsletter to learn about new titles, author events, and special offers.

Viva Editions
2246 Sixth St.
Berkeley, CA 94710
www.vivaeditions.com
(800) 780-2279
Follow us on Twitter @vivaeditions
Friend/fan us on Facebook